Flow Design for Embedded Systems

a radical new unified object-oriented methodology

by

Barry Kauler

R&D Books

Lawrence, Kansas 66046

Published by:
R&D Books/Miller Freeman
Suite 200
1601 West 23rd Street
Lawrence, Kansas 66046

ISBN: 0-87930-469-3

Distributed in the U.S. and Canada by:
Publishers Group West
P.O. Box 8843
Emeryville, CA 94662

Distributed in Europe by:
McGraw-Hill Publishing Company
Shoppenhangers Road
Maidenhead
Berkshire SL6 2QL
UNITED KINGDOM

Contents

iii

Introduction

The revolution has arrived.

There are those who design software-based digital electronic systems in an ad hoc fashion, some people who employ very basic aids, such as flowcharts, and those who go the whole way and use sophisticated Software Engineering methodologies.

These three broad groups of people can be further split into those who use the object-oriented concepts and those who don't.

The particular class of applications that we refer to as *embedded* is one in which many very basic tools and methodologies dominate, particularly in the smaller ROM-based systems, such as those involving the 8-bit and 16-bit microcontrollers.

Designers in this "bottom end" still work with assembly language, Forth, C, and Basic, and C++ is viewed as "pie in the sky". Also, most of these practitioners view the sophisticated Software Engineering methodologies, especially the object-oriented ones, as being out of their league.

In fact, one survey estimated only 30% of developers of embedded systems use any design method at all, and a mere 3% use object-oriented techniques (source: ICSE 18, Berlin, April 1996).

Larger embedded systems may involve C++ and object-oriented development techniques, yet the developers may or may not be following a systematic methodology.

Yet anybody who has worked on any non-trivial project knows that methodology is required — some kind of systematic approach to analysis, design, implementation, and maintenance of the project.

Apart from the size and type of projects you work on, there could be many other reasons that keep you away from using a modern methodology, not the least being that you may have read some books .... but, you don't understand them.

What is the point of sophisticated methodologies, if you find them too complex to use or if they *can't* be used with the simple tools you work with, such as assembly language?

Somebody once asked about a certain real-time development methodology, "is xxx good for complex projects?" He posted his question to a newsgroup, and someone responded, "yes, if you use xxx, your project will be complex".

Wherever you are coming from, whatever level of knowledge you have, check out the diagramming notation and design methodology expounded in this book: *GOOFEE.*

GOOFEE is applicable to the tiniest project, is incredibly easy to use, and is the *only* true unified methodology. It is a revolution.

Read ahead and catch this excitement for yourself.

Acknowledgements

I would like to thank Gary Bundell, University of Western Australia, for his constructive critique of many of the GOOFEE principles. Some of the ideas for GOOFEE came out of my PhD, titled *Generic I/O*, and I greatly appreciated the atmosphere of UWA; unlike some other places, it has a minimum of red tape, and I had total freedom to "do my own thing". The University's Department of Electrical and Electronic Engineering is particularly dynamic.

The ideas in GOOFEE derive from many sources, and although it is a synthesis that I believe is revolutionary, it belongs to the world. Please use, and further develop GOOFEE; all I would like is to be acknowledged as the original developer.

I also wrote *TERSE*, my Tiny Embedded Real-time Software Environment, as a public service, and people are free to use it and further develop it, as long as I am acknowledged.

I lecture in the Department of Computer and Communication Engineering, Edith Cowan University, Perth, Australia, and I am grateful for the environment condusive to research. Professor John Renner, at Edith Cowan, was particularly helpful with the provision of a seed-grant a couple of years ago, to investigate dataflow software; seminal ideas from that work contributed to the development of GOOFEE.

My GOOFEE Diagrammer CASE software was, and is, a monumental effort. I have written it as a private commercial project; however the decision was made to bundle it at no extra cost with the book, at least for the time being. It is not specific to GOOFEE and is a generic diagramming tool, so it can go in any direction.

I would like to thank Jon Erickson and Berney Williams at Miller Freeman Inc. for their vision, and everyone associated with GOOFEE Systems Pty Ltd.

Also, I wish to express appreciation to all members of my family, who have enormous patience.

1
Programming philosophies

Preamble

There are many languages, such as assembly, C, Basic, Pascal, Forth, Modula-2, C++, and there are many methodologies for designing code, such as the Structured techniques and the newer Object-Oriented techniques. You know that for any project, you need to have some kind of systematic approach to every analysis, design, and implementation phase, otherwise your code will be a mess.

Even if you are working on the tiniest project — say, a microcontroller for a washing machine — design methodology is required, but the requirements for methodology and documentation become more stringent as the project size grows. A distributed system in an aeroplane must be very rigorously designed, for example.

Many people are using ad hoc approaches to program design or methods that they know are inadequate. The object orientation paradigm has not filtered down to many people working on embedded applications, yet many people have become aware that there may be potential benefits.

This chapter looks at where you are now, and suggests how you can progress, from what you are already familiar with, toward an object-oriented (OO) methodology.

It is not necessary to be confused by OO terminology or concepts, nor is it even necessary to use an OO language to make use of OO concepts. OO conceptualisation can take place at the analysis and design phases, and any old procedural coding will suffice ... however, we are getting ahead of ourselves.

There is an approach to design that is "wholistic", that is totally unified and highly consistent. It leads you gently from whatever your current level of understanding is, to utilisation of advanced OO concepts, and it enables you to design and document extremely complex and sophisticated applications in an very systematic and integrated manner.

That's the sales pitch ... now, let's get on with it.

At this early stage, my GOOFEE notation, at least part of it, must be introduced. This notation is extremely simple, but do take the time to look at it before reading further, because it forms the building blocks for all later work.

GOOFEE: some notation

This book utilises a very simple graphical notation, called *GOOFEE*, that has very few elements. In fact, the basic building block is just one element, the *node*, that can have various types, which are the *Iterative-node*, the *Composite-node*, and the *Super-node*.

Figure 1: The GOOFEE node.

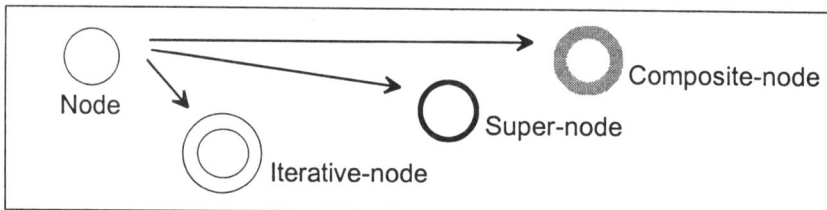

Figure 1 shows the types of nodes, and Figure 2 is the entire GOOFEE notation.

Figure 2: The entire GOOFEE notation.

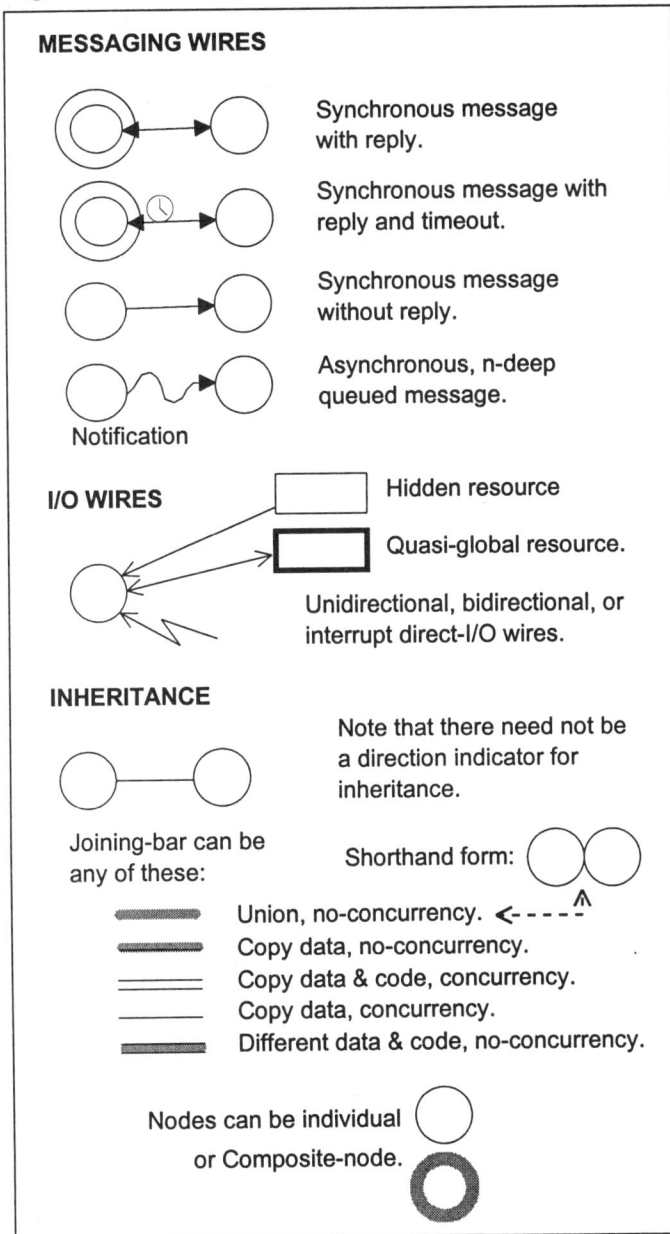

MESSAGING WIRES

Synchronous message with reply.

Synchronous message with reply and timeout.

Synchronous message without reply.

Asynchronous, n-deep queued message.

Notification

I/O WIRES

Hidden resource

Quasi-global resource.

Unidirectional, bidirectional, or interrupt direct-I/O wires.

INHERITANCE

Note that there need not be a direction indicator for inheritance.

Joining-bar can be any of these:

Shorthand form:

Union, no-concurrency.
Copy data, no-concurrency.
Copy data & code, concurrency.
Copy data, concurrency.
Different data & code, no-concurrency.

Nodes can be individual

or Composite-node.

Figure 2 is mostly placed here as a point of reference as you progress, so don't worry about understanding all of the notational elements just yet.

A node is some kind of module that has inputs and outputs. That's it. The basic node can be used to illustrate various types of design.

Sequential machines

A very basic approach to design is by diagrams that represent change of state or sequential progress. The *Finite State Machine* (FSM) is a good example of this. At the moment, we are not concerned about structure, hierarchy, or concurrency.

Figure 3: State machine.

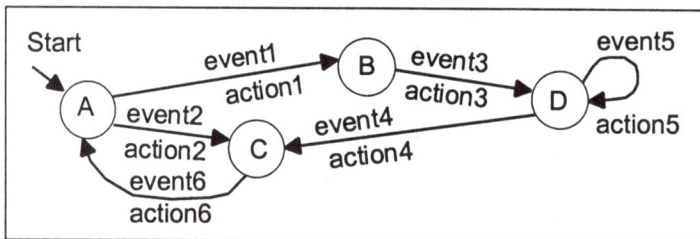

Figure 3 illustrates a State Machine. Say that execution starts in state A. An *event* is something that happens in the system, say a variable exceeding a certain value, or a temperature reaching a critical point. An *action* is some code in your program, that executes in reaction to the event, such as turning off the boiler.

The FSM technique of designing a program is ok, except that it has fundamental limitations. It is inherently sequential, meaning that the system is only in one state at the one time; however, that does not preclude the design from having multiple FSMs, allowing potential concurrency. In fact, there is an excellent notation developed that extends FSMs into concurrency, known as the *Statechart*, that we will have a look at.

There is something else wrong with the FSM; it is not *structured*. That is, it is what is known as GOTO programming, which results in very messy code as complexity rises.

The basic FSM is said to have no *hierarchy*, that is, have no concept of level, such as the procedures and functions we are familiar with in programming. However, it is easy to extend the basic idea by designating a node as a "super-node", which itself is an FSM; again, this is done in Statecharts.

The FSM is a nice tool for basic designs, but we need something more. In fact, many methodologies incorporate FSMs as part of the design procedure at the lower levels. As we progress, I will show that GOOFEE has no problem with representing FSMs, as in Figure 3, but can also represent every other higher level of design, *all with the same notation*.

Concurrency machines

The Statechart was developed by David Harel and extends the FSM into hierarchy and concurrency. The hierarchy aspect is simply that any node can be a super-node. A computer design tool based upon Statecharts, for Microsoft Windows, is Doron Drusinsky's *BetterState*: he designates a super-node by shading it, and double-clicking on it to view and edit the underlying Statechart.

An FSM is only in one state at any one time, so Dr Harel utilises multiple FSMs placed in a divided "enclosure", as shown in Figure 4. An exit from node A will enter the enclosure, and the Statechart diagrams on each side of the central divider will execute concurrently.

Concurrency introduces a need for communication and *synchronisation* between the *threads* of execution. Note that I use the word *threads* here, as it is a common term in concurrent programming, referring to two or more paths of concurrent or parallel execution.

Figure 4: FSM and Statechart.

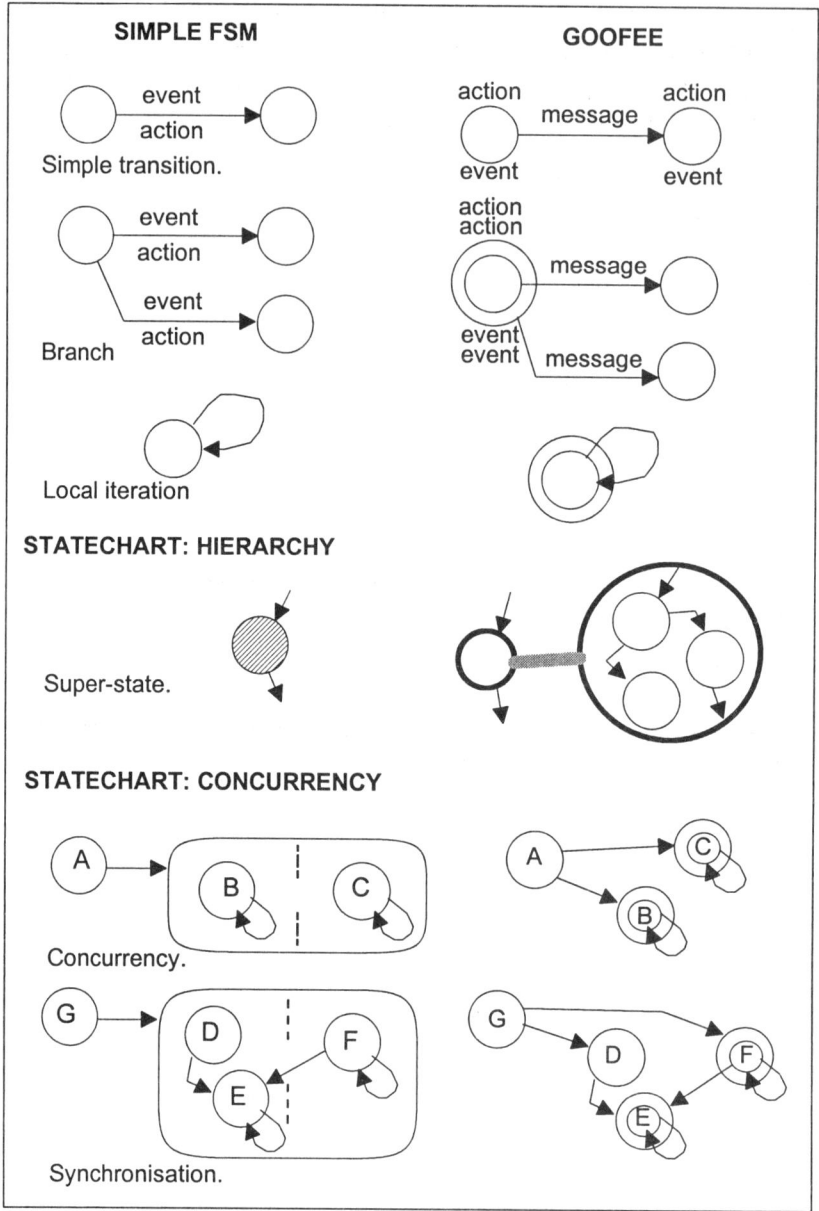

As Figure 4 shows, a node, represented by a little circle, can be a state and can be the building block for FSMs or Statecharts. However, when designing GOOFEE, I devised an extension to the basic node that I called the *Iterative-node*. This is a decision point, allowing execution to take different paths. This is part of an overall philosophy for GOOFEE, in that decision points are constrained to be at an Iterative-node.

In fact, you are already familar with this line of thinking in the form of the ancient *Flowchart*, shown in Figure 5.

Figure 5: Flowchart and Iterative-node comparison.

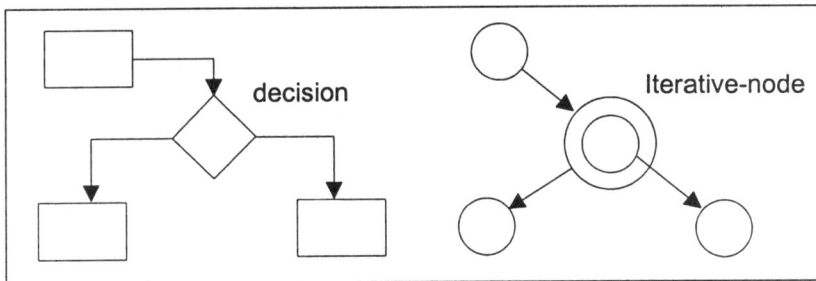

Figure 5 shows how the Iterative-node *can* perform the same function as the Flowchart decision diamond (although it is not recommended for structured designs, at least at higher levels of abstraction).

So far, I have not given a precise definition of the Iterative-node; in actuality, it is far more than just a decision point. Note in Figure 4 that I have used the Iterative-node for modeling the case of an FSM node looping back; that is, a specific event that causes it to stay in the same state. The reason for this will become clear later, when I explain how well-structured designs are made with the Iterative-node.

So far, we have seen that GOOFEE can model FSMs, Statecharts, and Flowcharts. It can also model *dataflow* diagrams, as illustrated in Figure 6.

The traditional synchronous dataflow model is based upon the idea that the lines, wires, or arcs, between nodes, carry data, and when all data has arrived at a node, it executes. This is synchronous in one sense at least, in respect to the synchronisation of execution of a node to arrival of all data, although, to be more correct, the node then becomes *eligible* to execute.

Ward and Mellor *(Structured Development for Real-Time Systems*, 1985, Yourdon Press) and others deemed this simple execution scheduling inadequate for real-time applications and introduced FSMs, or State Transition Diagrams, to control the sequencing. This required special control wires, shown as dashed lines, that could execute, prime, or turn off a dataflow node.

Figure 6: Dataflow with State Transition enhancement.

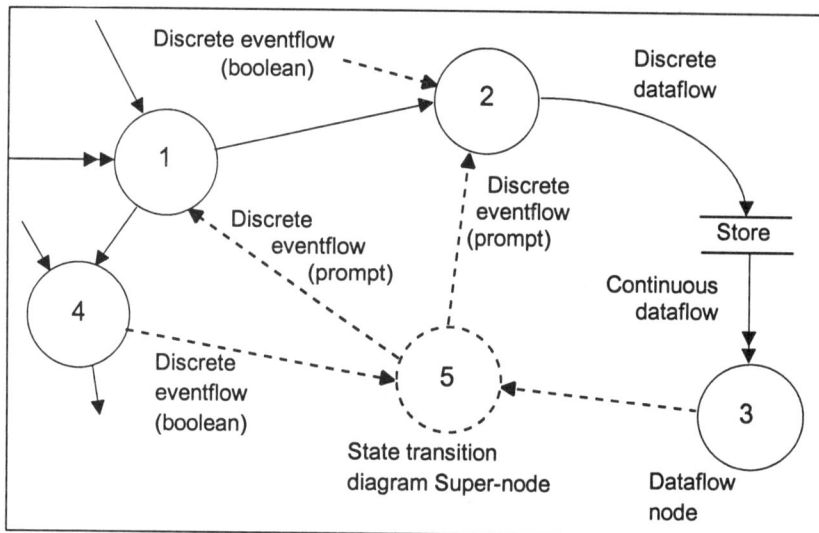

The double-headed arrow represents continuous data, and the single-headed arrow represents discrete data. The two parallel lines represent a data storage; the illustration shows that discrete data messages to the data store are made available as continuous data, i.e., continuously available to be read.

I personally find this division of dataflow and controlflow to be an unnecessary contrivance.

We won't go into further detail on the Ward/Mellor approach, nor its various derivatives. Nor will I map Figure 6 across to the equivalent GOOFEE diagram. Although GOOFEE can map to anything, there are fundamental conceptual differences, and I wish this chapter to be very focused.

Figure 7 illustrates synchronous dataflow. Assuming that execution starts from node A, when it exits it will post messages 1 and 2. Node B will fire next, and it will post messages 3 and 4. The situation then, is that both nodes C and D are eligible to fire, so in theory at least, the dataflow diagram is a natural for representing concurrency. Whether we can translate that to code that will execute concurrently is another matter.

Finally, node E can only execute when messages 5 and 6 have arrived.

Figure 7: Synchronous dataflow.

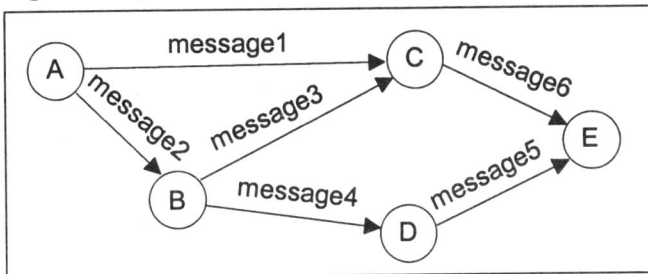

We see from Figure 7 that although the dataflow diagram is great for representing concurrency and synchronisation, it has the fundamental limitation of an (almost) fixed execution sequence. This sequencing limitation is what Ward and Mellor tackled by introducing the FSM and controlflow (eventflow) wires.

Figure 7 has a simplicity about it, and there is a way to retain that synchronous simplicity and still have a scheduling sequence that can change at runtime, dynamically, in response to real-time events. GOOFEE follows this path of thought, and uses the Iterative-node to implement what are referred to as *local iterations*, which provide a carefully controlled runtime variation on scheduling; this is described further in the next chapter.

Many researchers have tried to devise the perfect notation that represents everything in a simple, elegant, and consistent fashion. Statecharts come close, though I personally have a problem with the wires used to represent synchronisation between threads. Refer back to Figure 4, and look at the example of synchronisation from node F to node E. Node E will await the arrival of the synchronisation message, which will be when node F exits, so this wire is not a normal transition; it is more akin to synchronous dataflow, and I find this mixture disconcerting.

Another problem I have with Statecharts is that code reuse, as in procedures or objects, cannot be represented by the notation.

Structured programming

The basic idea here is that we avoid using GOTOs. Structured programming is what we endeavour to apply in any form of programming, whether it be assembly language or Ada, although some languages do provide better support for structure. The use of functions or procedures supports structure.

Note that there is a branch of Software Engineering called *Structured Design*, but this is not to be confused with structured programming. Structured Design is mostly associated with design techniques that are not object-oriented, which is somewhat of a negative definition. They target implementation in the non-OO languages, often referred to as *procedural* languages, such as C. The actual coding can be structured, but that is a different issue from the structured design methodologies.

There are various graphical notations that can model structured programming, but I have shown the example of Figure 8 using GOOFEE, because it is very elegant.

Figure 8: Structured program design.

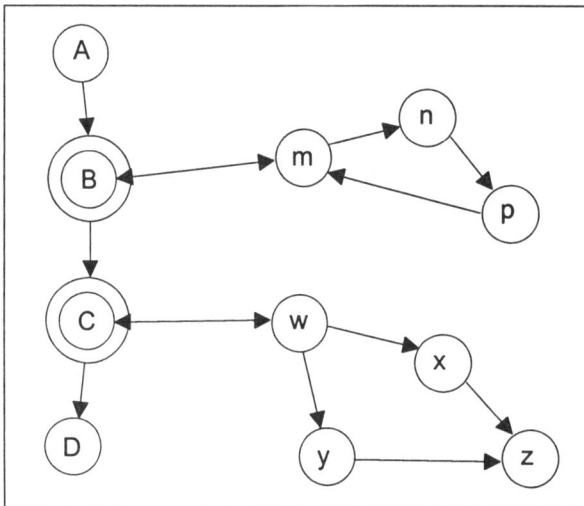

In the scenario of Figure 8, the "mainline" procedure is nodes A, B, C, and D, whereas two lower level procedures are nodes m/n/p and nodes w/x/y/z.

Notice here that the Iterative-node is more than a branching point, because there is a return from the procedures (or *functions*, if you want to be pedantic). This requires a more precise definition of the Iterative-node, which is given in the next chapter.

Figure 8 shows how the Iterative-node can be used as a juncture for representing a "lower level" diagram, or procedure, but what about the situation where a procedure is to be called from different places in the code?

The sharing of blocks of code, such as a subroutine or procedure, has always been a problem to represent in the various FSM extensions and the dataflow models.

After all, you can't just draw another wire going into node m (Figure 8) from somewhere else, as that implies two synchronous messages to node m. GOOFEE has a very nice solution, referred to as the *clone* technique.

Clones can be made of any procedure, one for each separate access.

Figure 9: Clones.

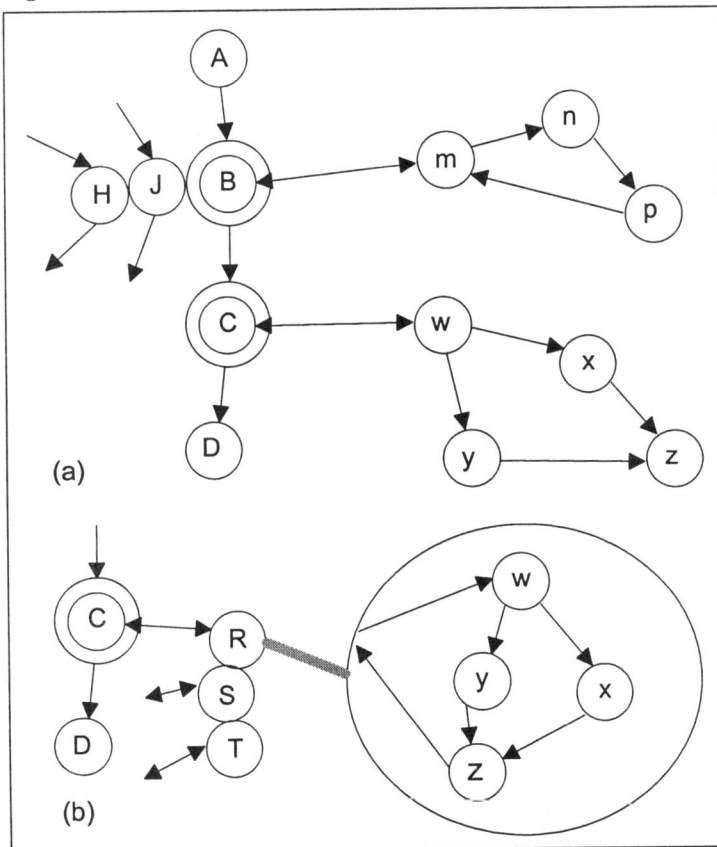

Figure 9(a) shows that node B can be cloned as nodes J and H, and the clones will be identical to node B, including the lower level procedure composed of nodes m/n/p.

You are new to this, and you will find it to be unique and probably very strange. However, it is an extremely consistent way to expand a program. Any node in the diagram can be cloned, and the exact nature of the clone, i.e., the exact relationship between a clone node and its "parent", can be specified by means of a *Joining-bar*. The Joining-bar is summarised back in Figure 2.

I hate to do this to you again, but the Joining-bar is also explained in the next chapter, and Chapter 4.

Clarification of the clone concept

Just to be sure that you have the basic idea of clones, consider them as separate nodes from the point of view of their terminals, i.e., the external view. The "clone" aspect refers to their internal construction, i.e., they inherit from the neighbour they are joined to. They could have the same code, same data, or copies of code, copies of data, or some combination of these four. They could also have a no-concurrency relationship with the joined-to neighbour.

So, if the input wire to node H (Figure 9(a)) has a message, node H becomes eligible to fire. When node H exits, it will produce a message out of node H as shown, not out of any other clone. From the execution sequencing and messaging perspective, consider them as completely separate nodes.

However, Figure 9(a) is not the way you would normally construct clones. The reason for this is that it is cloning an Iterative-node, the node that calls the "procedure", when in fact what we really want to clone is the procedure itself, not the decision point (or, maybe you do; it depends on the application).

Therefore, Figure 9(b) is a reconstruction, in which the procedure diagram is grouped into the Super-node (or it could be a Composite-node), R, that can be called from node C.

Node R can be cloned (S and T), thus making the procedure available to as many callers as required. You can clone *any* node, be it single, Iterative,

Super, or Composite, and with any inheritance relationship you like, as suits the application.

Object-oriented ...; they are the jargon words required these days, and if you are not willing at this stage to move in the OO direction, that's fine. GOOFEE will model anything and is the most powerful tool I know of for structured program design.

Object-oriented programming

The clone is also a fundamental GOOFEE building block for designing object-oriented programs.

Let's keep this section simple. I'm reminded of a seminar I went to some years ago, hosted by Borland when they launched C++ version 1.0. They explained that the three "cornerstones" of OOP are *polymorphism, inheritance,* and *encapsulation.*

A dataflow diagram does not, in the encapsulation sense at least, seem at first glance to be very object-oriented, as the data is so exposed.

An object can inherit code from its parent object (or objects). An object can consist of one or more functions (code) and data, and it is usual that those functions are the only way for another object to get at the data.

Figure 10: Traditional procedure-oriented object.

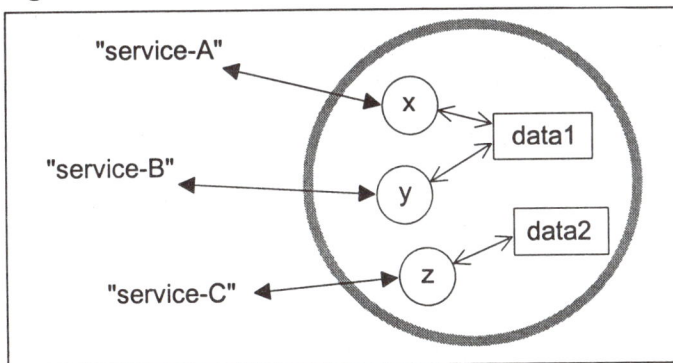

Figure 10 shows the traditional concept of an object, represented by the grey ellipse. If it is the template of an object, many languages, such as C++, refer to it as a *class*. It consists of procedures/functions, shown here as x/y/z, and hidden data, shown here as data1 and data2.

The normal situation is that data1 and data2 can only be accessed by routines within the object, not directly from outside, and this is the principle of data hiding, or encapsulation, so vital to OOP.

What is not well known, is that this model of OOP is only a subset of the more general dataflow object model, illustrated in Figure 11.

Figure 11: Dataflow object model.

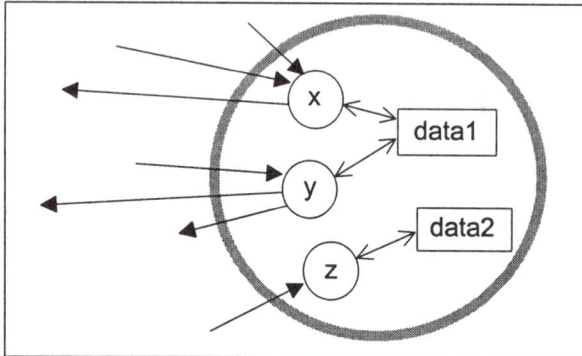

In this generalised model, the nodes x/y/z are dataflow nodes, and do not have a single specific caller. The various inputs to node x could come from various places, and the one or more outputs can go to various places.

If synchronous dataflow is imposed, it becomes a subset of this general model. The GOOFEE notation allows both asynchronous and synchronous wires, and therefore is able to represent the generic model of Figure 11, or any subset, including the procedural model of Figure 10.

The constraint of calling a service provided by an object, from one caller, and having execution return to the caller, as in Figure 10, is a subset of Figure 11.

The GOOFEE notation is used in both Figures, showing that GOOFEE can model either approach. The grey ellipse, being the class, is none other than the GOOFEE Composite-node.

This chapter is only an introduction, but, as I have stated earlier, the clone mechanism is the main building block for OO diagrams, and I would like to give you an indication of this. Just as I showed clones being used in structured programming, so too can they be applied to objects. If multiple instantiations of a class or object are to be in a program, each accessed from different places in the program, Figure 12 shows how simple this is to represent.

Figure 12: Multiple instances of objects.

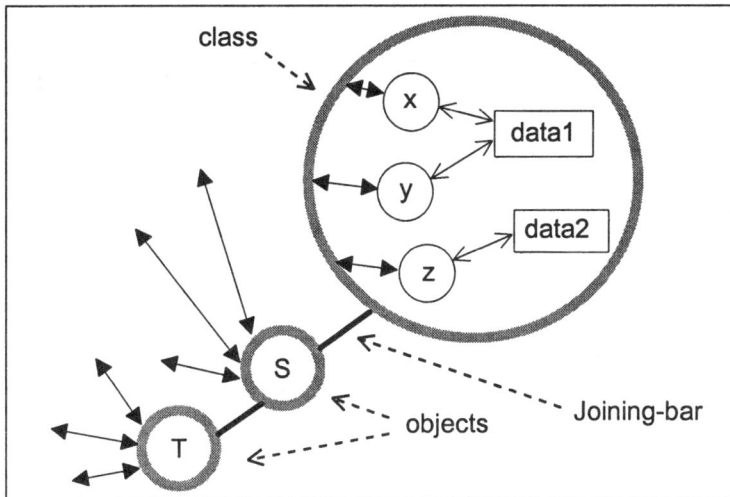

Figure 12 is an example of a class and the Joining-bar used to show objects (S and T). Of course, this implies static, compile-time allocation of objects. Dynamic behaviour is another story.

When is an object not an object?

In GOOFEE, an individual node is the basic building block, but even that is an object. If you take just node z from Figure 12, along with its hidden data, that on its own constitutes an object.

It is an object that provides just one "service" or, in the more generic sense, one transform of data.

Furthermore, taking node z and data2 on their own, data2 is still considered private to node z, regardless of how visible it is on the diagram.

Thus, GOOFEE is inherently object-oriented, right down to the nuts and bolts.

In conclusion

There is really not much difference between the structured programming of Figure 9 and the object-oriented programming of Figure 12, and the transition can be made effortlessly. Also, every programming paradigm introduced in this chapter can be represented by the same notation and intermixed as required: this is not a recipe for confusion, as you may think!

I know that a great many embedded system designers are not comfortable with OO methodology, and I do not want you to think that if you use GOOFEE, you *have* to go the OO route. No, I think that you will make the transition quite painlessly when you use GOOFEE in the structured way that you already know.

Building on your background in structured programming, or even if all you know is GOTO programming, you will understand the next chapter. It is extremely pragmatic: how to design an embedded system that does what you want it to. If you want simple rules, like steps A, B, C, study Chapter 2 carefully.

2

Structured programming

Preamble

As discussed in Chapter 1, GOOFEE can model structured designs that are non-object-oriented but can very easily make the transition to OO design.

Modeling the design with diagrams is one thing, translating to code another; dataflow is particularly difficult, due to the inherent concurrency and synchronisation. For this reason, I developed an operating system, tightly coded to run on the tiniest microcontrollers, that provides an underlying message-delivery and scheduling of nodes.

However, if you constrain GOOFEE to only model the procedure-based subset of the generic dataflow node, as described in Chapter 1, the translation to code becomes easier, maybe not requiring anything identifiable as an execution scheduler or operating system.

For hands-on work, you might like to take the constrained approach first, and progress to the use of the operating system (OS) later. I make reference to my OS through this chapter, and you can use your discretion how much of that aspect you want to study. The OS is called *TERSE* (Tiny Embedded Real-time Software Environment) and is conditionally public domain (see inside front title-page of this book).

If you have experience with some other RTOS, fine; you can map GOOFEE designs onto it.

Combining control and dataflow

There are many research papers and books on dataflow notations and design methodologies and many software tools.

"Synchronous" dataflow diagrams have an elegant simplicity about them, and naturally impose an order — a node fires when all of its messages have arrived, and not "too soon". Also, it is extremely easy to specify concurrency, even if it cannot be exactly achieved on a single-processor system.

Note that the current "8051" versions of TERSE do not use *time-slicing/preemption*, and rely upon *cooperative* scheduling, i.e., are node-sequential, in which yielding can take place between nodes. My x86 version does have time-slicing, between virtual machines. I only mention this here to let you know that "concurrency" is a very complex and emotive issue, with many conflicts and philosophies. I have tackled this in Chapter 3.

Commercial visual dataflow languages

A good example of the implementation of a "synchronous" dataflow model, with structured controlflow enhancements, is the commercial product *LabView*, which has become almost a de facto standard in the engineering and scientific instrumentation field. LabView is sold by a US company called National Instruments.   Another commercial implementation is *HP-VEE*, sold by Hewlett Packard. It is interesting to examine dataflow products that have made it out of the research and development phase and are succeeding in the real world. Of particular interest is the diverse manner in which these two products have solved the problem of imposing controlflow onto dataflow, in the same diagram.

A clarification though, is that these two products are full-cycle CASE tools for desktop PCs and workstations, not microcontrollers. By "full-cycle", I mean that they can be used as visual tools for all stages of designing a system, down to actual execution — in fact, LabView will generate an actual .EXE file, with help from an optional utility called Application Builder.

The "hello world" beginners program in LabView can be made into a .EXE, but it won't even fit onto a 1.44Mb disk!

What I am concerned with here are the *ideas* in these products, and their possible usefulness for microcontroller system development.

Figure 13: LabView local iterations.

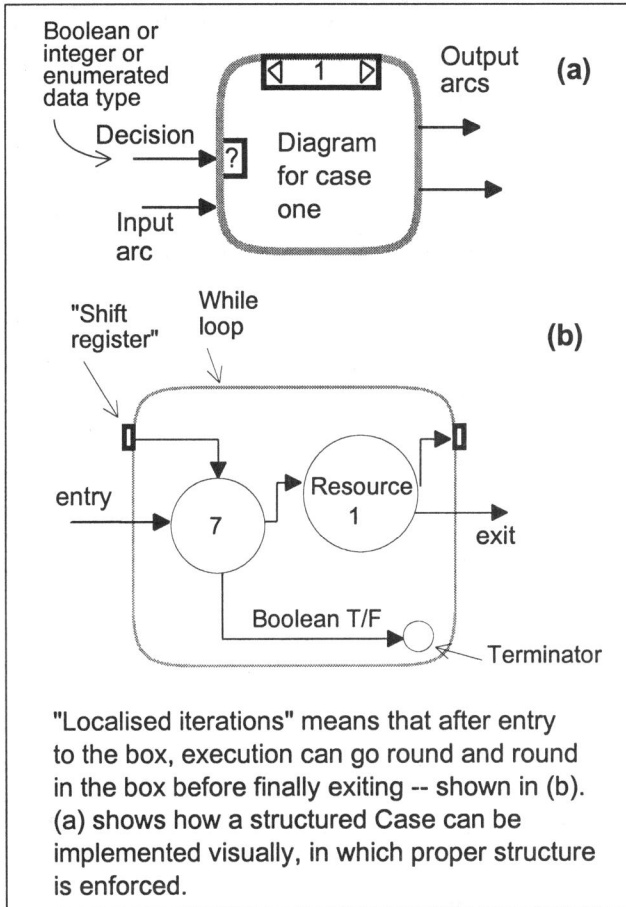

Boolean or integer or enumerated data type

Decision

Input arc

◁ 1 ▷

? Diagram for case one

Output arcs **(a)**

"Shift register"

While loop

(b)

entry

7

Resource 1

exit

Boolean T/F

Terminator

"Localised iterations" means that after entry to the box, execution can go round and round in the box before finally exiting -- shown in (b). (a) shows how a structured Case can be implemented visually, in which proper structure is enforced.

The familiar structured programming constructs, such as CASE, FOR, WHILE, etc., require enhancements to classical synchronous dataflow. The LabView approach is extremely effective for practical work, as it conserves screen "real estate" while being very readable — the localised iterations are achieved by enclosing them in "boxes" and by the provision of "shift registers" to feed output wires back into the input side of the box.

HP-VEE, on the otherhand, uses an open-ended IF—THEN structure.

Of course, real-time performance implies timing constraints, and putting nice structure into the design goes quite a long way toward designing a system that will definitely meet the timing requirements — but not all of the way. Microcontroller systems, in particular, are very concerned with I/O, and I wanted the design structure to not just have a strong structured discipline, and meet timing constraints, but to have a very strong orientation around I/O. That is, I/O is the focal point, and all usage of I/O (and resources in general) from various parts of the program should be clearly defined and visually represented.

Some criteria for real-time systems

GOOFEE diagrams also require a notation for representing localised iterations, but as the goal is embedded systems, I saw a need for a strong focus on the target hardware from the early design phases. I wanted the diagrammatic representation to clearly show the following (with relation to I/O):

- Spatial locality
- Mutual exclusion
- Handshaking
- Persistence of ownership

Basically, I am concerned with the problem of ad hoc access to resources, whether they be physical, such as some I/O interface, or RAM, or logical, such as a file or node.

"Spatial locality" means that all access to a resource is shown at one physical location on the flow diagram. Therefore, the LabView representation of local iterations cannot be used, and an open-ended approach (remotely akin to HP-VEE) is required.

That is, I have shown in Figure 13(b) a node that accesses Resource 1 — if any other node in the diagram accesses Resource 1, the relationship, i.e., all nodes that access Resource 1, may not be apparent simply due to the physical separation of the nodes on the diagram and in different levels of the diagram.

The last three points listed above, are closely linked. The issue here, is that the manner in which a resource is accessed must be clearly specified, with mechanisms to avoid resource contention and deadlock.

There are many other issues with design of the flow diagram, such as ensuring completion under all circumstances, of which deadlock is one aspect. I developed three basic "building blocks" for GOOFEE, that go a long way toward meeting the criteria so far discussed, as shown in Figure 14.

Figure 14: GOOFEE structures.

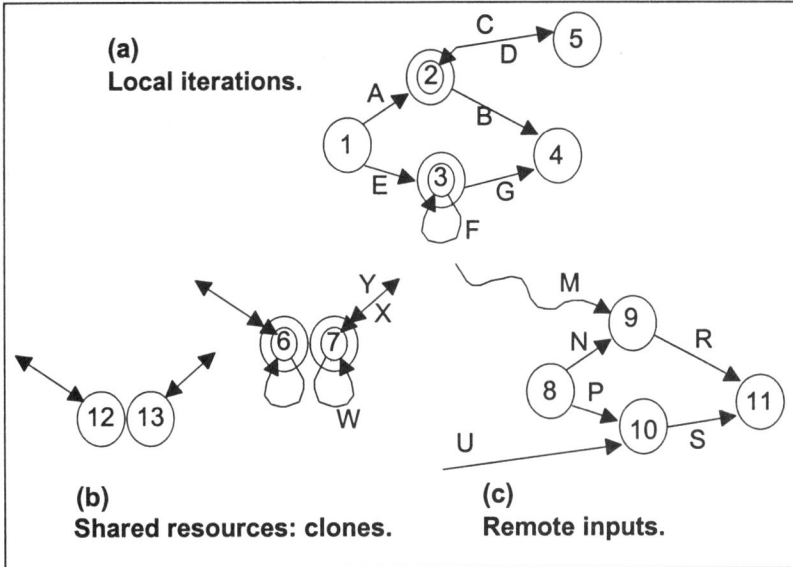

Local iterations

Nodes 2 and 3 in Figure 14(a) show how local iterations can be represented. The two rings indicate exclusive-OR on inputs, and exclusive-OR on outputs. Node 2 will fire when message A arrives, whereas at exit, node 2 will post either message B exclusive-OR message C. This allows a decision to be made by node 2. If exit is from the inner ring, posting message C, node 2 will only re-fire on arrival of inputs to the inner ring, being message D. The Iterative-node is unambiguously defined in Figure 15, using "!" to denote an output action and "?" to denote a conditional input.

I would like you to study Figure 15 carefully, because the Iterative-node and the clone are the most important of the GOOFEE building blocks. In fact, the principle of multiple rings can be extended to three or more rings, and the same rules apply. The two rings shown in Figure 15 form a quasi-Case-structure, with just two choices, whereas multiple rings offer more choices.

Figure 15: Definition of Iterative-node.

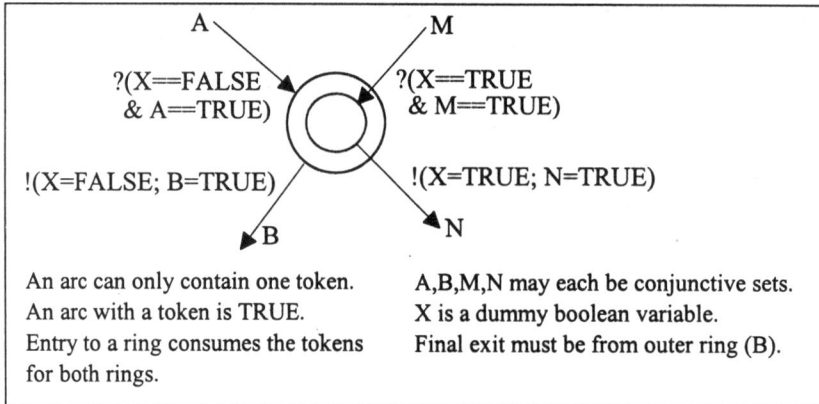

A	M
?(X==FALSE & A==TRUE)	?(X==TRUE & M==TRUE)
!(X=FALSE; B=TRUE)	!(X=TRUE; N=TRUE)
B	N

An arc can only contain one token.   A,B,M,N may each be conjunctive sets.
An arc with a token is TRUE.   X is a dummy boolean variable.
Entry to a ring consumes the tokens   Final exit must be from outer ring (B).
for both rings.

If Figure 15 is a little unclear, a possibly simpler description of the Iterative-node is that it has multiple rings, and only one ring is active at any one time. First entry is always to the outer ring when all messages to the outer ring have arrived, exit can be from any ring, and subsequent re-entry must be to the same ring as exited from.

To re-enter a ring, the normal synchronous dataflow rules apply; that is, all (synchronous wire) messages for that ring must have arrived. Messages to other rings do not matter, and they are consumed and discarded upon re-entry.

In keeping with synchronous dataflow, upon exit from any ring, all output (synchronous) wires from the exited-from ring must have messages.

Clarification on wire types

I kept on putting the qualification "synchronous wire" in the above comments. If you look back to Figure 2, you will see that there are also asynchronous wires. These do what their name suggests, that is, the execution scheduler does not take any notice of them when deciding which node to execute.

The OS must deliver all messages, synchronous and asynchronous, even though its scheduler component ignores asynchronous messages. My TERSE OS looks in the message buffer and extracts all messages addressed to a particular node when that node is to be executed next and knows nothing about rings. See the above comment about messages to all rings being consumed for Iterative-nodes. TERSE simply identifies each input wire as arriving at a uniquely numbered terminal, so rings are a higher conceptual level.

Deadlock avoidance

Figure 14(a) shows tight coupling with node 5, as the preferred method for conducting a dialogue, handshake, or *rendezvous* (an Ada term), with another diagram; as the mechanism that allows return paths to avoid the possibility of deadlock, and as a discipline for ensuring deterministic behaviour. Of course, node 2 could send message C to node 5, without requiring a reply.

Rephrasing this in English, node 2 sends a message to node 5, and node 5 replies to the same place that called it, not elsewhere. Obviously, if the return message D came back to someplace earlier in the diagram, before node 2, there is the possibility of a deadlock, because that someplace-earlier will be waiting for message D, which cannot come until node 2 has sent off a message to node 5.

Scheduling of Iterative-nodes

I wrote the TERSE operating system specifically for executing GOOFEE diagrams, and the following notes are related to that.

An important point about the above-mentioned mechanism is that node 2 has to exit, to post message C, which gives TERSE the opportunity, if desired, of scheduling another node on the local diagram (if node 5 is on another processor) — the designer has total control over this, by means of the OS Scheduling Table.

Be aware that I am talking here in terms of cooperative scheduling, in which the OS will not preempt nodes. Look at Chapter 3 for more detail on this. I do have a version of TERSE that has timeslicing, but it is between *virtual machines*, and within each virtual machine there are GOOFEE diagrams that are scheduled cooperatively. For now, don't worry about these issues; just be aware that a node must run to completion before the OS can schedule another node.

TERSE looks in the message buffer to see what messages are there and uses those to calculate a *signature* ("checksum"). The signature is unique for every unique permutation of messages, so for the purposes of constructing the Scheduling Table, you have to ensure that there is a unique signature generated everytime, even if it means posting dummy messages. The only time that you would want TERSE to calculate the same signature as at an earlier time is if you want to re-execute that same node.

This is really more of an implementation issue, and other RTOSs will have different approaches to scheduling. TERSE is analysed in detail in Chapter 5.

However, it is useful to be aware of the TERSE approach, because it has been designed to implement everything that GOOFEE is capable of expressing.

Reiterating the above discussion, an exit from the inner ring of node 2, with message C (Figure 14(a)) constitutes an actual exit from the node as far as TERSE is concerned. All that TERSE knows is that a node has exited, and TERSE looks in the message buffer, computes a signature from the messages waiting in it, looks in the signature-to-node translation table, and fires the next node. In this case it will (probably) be node 5.

Similarly, when node 5 exits, message D will be in the buffer, causing TERSE to fire node 2 again. Thus, TERSE is very simple and knows nothing about the sophisticated GOOFEE concepts, yet is able to implement them.

Node 3 is also a local iteration. The loopback wire allows optional exit and re-entry from and to the inner ring as many times as required. Of course from the low-level viewpoint of TERSE, it sees message F, so re-fires node 3, and if TERSE sees messages G and B in the buffer, not F, it fires node 4. With signature scheduling this is very easy to realise.

Shared resources

Figure 14(b) shows how shared resources can be represented, which gets back to my idea of I/O-centred design. Nodes 12 and 13 are the simplest case. The technique is object oriented, in that nodes 12 and 13 (usually) share the same code, which the notation shows by placing them touching (or by use of Joining-bars).

Mutual exclusion

Mutual exclusion, or rather non-concurrency of execution of the clone nodes, can be specified by choice of the appropriate "clone relationship". To see the options, refer back to the Joining-bars in Figure 2.

Persistence of ownership

Nodes 6 and 7 show (optional) extended ownership of a resource, allowing a dialog, or many transitions of X and Y, between node 7 and its caller. The loop-back arc indicates this. At the TERSE operating system level, the loop-back places a message in the message buffer that re-schedules that node, locking out the other one.

The wire Y/X is shown going to both rings, which fires the outer ring on first arrival of Y (when the outer ring is active), then fires the inner ring when Y and W both arrive (and the inner ring is active). Shown as a 2-way wire, the implication is also that X will issue from whatever ring is active and from the outer ring on final exit.

The double-headed arrow is a convenient short form, instead of drawing two separate wires.

Persistence of ownership is perhaps a bit exotic at this point in the book, so if it isn't clear, don't worry. I haven't had any application so far in which I have needed to use the double-headed arrows; it is one of those things where I can see the *possibility* of a need. The simple clones as shown by nodes 12 and 13 (Figure 14(b)) are all you need to understand for now.

Interprocessor messages

Figure 14(c) is concerned with messages that arrive from another processor. These are the crux of the problem with distributed systems, as they can, potentially, arrive at any time. Even if there is only one processor, if the RTOS supports timeslicing, the same situation can exist. My x86 TERSE emulates a distributed system by running multiple GOOFEE diagrams in virtual machines. These virtual machines execute in a time-sliced manner, and messages posted between virtual machines arrive at any time, just like a distributed system. Really, whether the implementation is one processor or distributed over many independent processors is not so important at the design phase, and the GOOFEE diagram can map to either.

The random arrival of an inter-processor message immediately upsets the Signature Table that I use for scheduling in TERSE, as one remote input can theoretically double the size of the table. Also, they introduce the probability of "chaos", because there is the chance of a signature being generated that causes a false "hit" in the lookup table.

This probability is $1/(2^n)$, which for a 16-bit signature is 0.0000152. The only way to ensure total determinism is an exhaustive simulation.

Repeating again, if runtime variation of node scheduling is required, you need to look at some kind of executive or OS, and my product is TERSE. The technique I have used is to examine the set of messages awaiting delivery and from those calculate an 8- or 16-bit number, that I call a signature, and this signature is used as a lookup into a table to select the next node to fire. It's a simple principle, with what could be referred to as bounded-runtime-determinism of scheduling, thus highly desirable for predictable systems. However, this nice idea is upset when remote input messages arrive randomly as the number of possible signatures generated explodes. That is, the *ordering* of messages in the buffer affects the generated signature, not just what messages are there.

To solve this problem, I developed a modified scheduling algorithm, that handles remote messages without the signature explosion problem, yet still allows full flexibility for scheduling. This technique is very powerful and is referred to as MESS scheduling. It is described in Chapter 5.

One fascinating aspect of Signature Scheduling is error recovery.

If TERSE calculates a signature but fails to find it in the lookup table, it means that the system has got into a pickle, and TERSE defaults to calling node 0.

Thus, any unpredicted state is detected, which is a very important feature for mission-critical applications.

Notifications

Two techniques for remote input messages, that is, messages from another processor, are shown in Figure 14(c). Message U is a normal synchronous input, and would be scheduled as described above. Message M is called a *Notification*, or *asynchronous* wire, represented by a wavy line. A Notification is a message that TERSE ignores, and it does not take part in the signature calculation; however, TERSE still delivers it to its destination.

Another important distinction between Notification (asynchronous) and ordinary (synchronous) wires, is that Notifications can *queue n-deep*, whereas normal wires (straight lines, solid arrowheads) can only queue 1-deep.

With regard to the software bundled with this book, I had immense difficulty trying to figure out how to draw wavy lines, so the software uses a different representation, being a straight line with a perpendicular line near the arrowhead.

Notifications can also be local, i.e., within a processor.

Only message N is required to satisfy initial schedulability of node 9.

Notifications are invaluable for sporadic messages, such as error messages. In a later case study, I use the Notification to deliver button-presses from clients wanting to ride on an elevator. These button-presses arrive asynchronously and can queue, until the destination-node executes and consumes them.

The pure synchronous dataflow model cannot handle this kind of sporadic behaviour, so the Notification extension is invaluable.

Figure 16: Time bound of callee/caller.

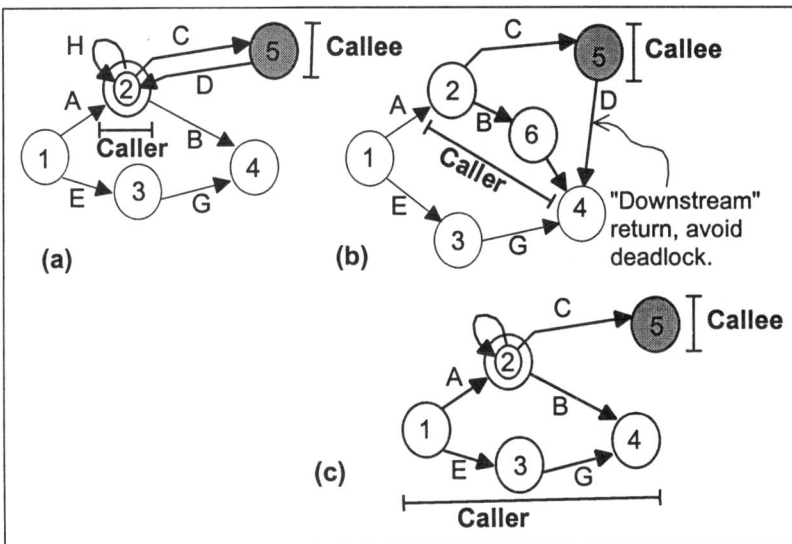

Normal synchronous messages can only queue 1-deep, which is in keeping with the synchronous dataflow model. If a system is constructed around this constraint, there is an interesting outcome — the receiver-diagram (callee) of a message, must always have a quicker cycle time than the sender-diagram (caller). If this parent—child cycle time requirement is met, messages will always arrive "in context", and runtime deadline analysis can be performed, simply by flagging a deadline overrun if more than one remote message arrives.

The callee—caller timing constraints are summarised in Figure 16.

Local and global variables and time

A local or global variable is a shared resource and can be implemented by a Notification (asynchronous wire). The Notification has the advantage that the variable cannot be read randomly, but only when the node that "owns" it decides to post the Notifications. There is a context issue here, as the recipient-node of a Notification may or may not have received the Notification message when it fires — this can be taken in a very positive sense, as the recipient will know if it has to work with old data.

Alternatively, local and global variables are represented by rectangles, as shown in Figure 2. Usage of these, following appropriate rules for data hiding, is described later in the book, in particular Chapter 4.

Structured cyclic design

For design of well-structured GOOFEE diagrams, there are a very small number of rules to follow. I promised you simple A, B, C steps, so here they are. My emphasis is on practical application, so these rules are very few and are expressed in plain language. Do take the time to study them.

They are as follows, for a system in which X is the caller and Y is the callee. X and Y can refer to individual nodes or to subdiagrams, so to generalise this, Figure 17 shows them as clouds.

Figure 17: Callee/caller generalised messaging.

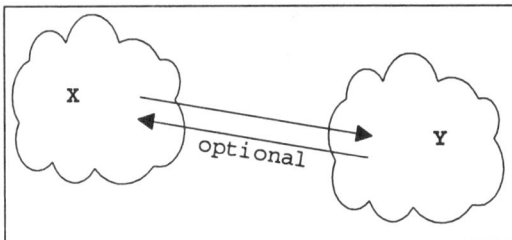

1 There will be no other dependencies between X and Y.

2 Any other access to Y, from any diagram with a dependency with X, must access a clone of Y.

3 Y must always have a quicker cycle time than X.

4 Optional return to X, must be "downstream".

5 GOTO scheduling is discouraged.

Points 1 to 5 summarise the discussion of this chapter; if clarification is required, read carefully from the start of the chapter.

Notifications (asynchronous wires) are not bound by these rules, and usage should be minimised. This is a cyclic model, not interrupt-driven, but MESS scheduling employed in TERSE goes a long way toward giving prompt response to quasi-random arrival of remote input messages.

Also, interrupts can be handled as they go directly into a node. All access directly into the code inside a node, to and from hardware resources and memory, is shown in GOOFEE by I/O wires, shown in Figure 2. These have nothing to do with scheduling of the diagram.

Clarification of I/O wires

So far, I haven't written much about I/O wires, as originally shown in Figure 2. There is really not much to say about them. They go between the code inside a node and resources and have nothing to do with dataflow scheduling or message delivery. TERSE knows nothing about them.

If, for example, you have an I/O port, say output to a printer, you can show it by a rectangle and draw an I/O wire from a node to show that the code in that node writes to that port.

However, do note that the printer port then becomes the property of that node and is visible only to that node; resource visibility is developed in Chapter 4.

Please think about the above points 1 to 5 very carefully, as I have reduced real-time distributed/multiprocessor/emulated-multiprocessor/emulated-distributed microcontroller design down to such a simple and small list of rules. These are all you will need to build very sophisticated systems.

These rules are invaluable for constructing safe structured systems, and can be expanded very easily to object-oriented designs, as developed in Chapter 4. Chapter 3 is a diversion into issues relevant to real time, that you may prefer to skim through, depending on your knowledge level.

3

Real-time systems

Preamble

We need to know something about the terminology and the issues involved with embedded applications before putting together flow diagrams. This chapter starts with terminology and moves into looking at issues, controversy, and solutions.

You may find some of the opinions expressed here to be idiosyncratic. I give them anyway. Also, depending on your background, you may find nothing new in this chapter, in which case you may wish to skim through.

The terminology

Real-time

Microcontrollers are usually used in what are called *real-time* applications, which means that the system has some kind of time constraint. That is, there are *deadlines*, within which certain things must happen.

Embedded

Also, microcontrollers are usually used in *embedded* applications, which simply means that the micro is hidden out-of-sight, inside a piece of equipment. All you see is the piece of equipment, and you are not necessarily aware that it even has a microcontroller inside; for example, a washing machine.

Distributed

An aircraft may have dozens of embedded microcontrollers, and they may all be communicating over some kind of network. Such a system, in which the processors are physically separated but communicate, is a distributed system.

Multiprocessor

One feature of a distributed system is that each processor has its own memory, and there is no common memory. Systems in which two or more processors can directly read and write a shared memory, i.e., they are connected to the same bus or the memory is multi-port, are called *multiprocessor* systems.

It is possible for a design to be implemented in either distributed processor or multiprocessor hardware. For example, later in this book an elevator control system is developed, and the design consists of logically independent parts that, in the case study, are mapped onto a distributed system. However, it could also be mapped onto a single processor system, with virtual machines, or some combination.

A real-time application for an aircraft, motor vehicle, or factory can become incredibly complex. If you've ever been involved in a large project, you'll know what I mean. We need to have some idea what those problems are before we can look at solutions. Some of the major problems are:

Resource conflict

Resource conflict is when two or more different parts of the system both try to use the same physical or logical device at the same time; for example, a RAM memory area. This relates to the classical mutual exclusion problem.

Deadlock

Deadlock is when the system is in some kind of endless loop, most usually in the context of two or more parts of the system waiting for the other to release some resource.

Mutual exclusion

Mutual exclusion refers to the techniques of preventing more than one part of the system from having simultaneous access to a physical or logical device — enforcement of mutual exclusion is also related to deadlock.

I also use the term *non-concurrency* in this book to refer to the same thing in relation to clone nodes. See the definition of concurrency below. Referring back to Figure 2, the Joining-bar can specify non-concurrency of clones, which means simply that execution can only be in one of the nodes. Even on a purely cooperatively scheduled system, this can be an issue, as a Composite or Super-node is composed of many nodes, and the OS can schedule any node after one has exited.

Deadlines

Deadlines are when something should happen within a certain time. For example, "Gizmo-A" may interrupt a microcontroller and expect to be serviced within a certain time. Or, if the boiler tells the control system that it is overheating, it should be shutdown within a certain time frame.

There are many issues here, in particular the meaning of "time" itself. All time is relative to something and has a certain granularity.

Concurrency

The simplest real-time system is one in which everything happens *sequentially*, i.e., one thing after the other. This is well suited to a microcontroller, which executes instructions sequentially, but it is a problem if the microcontroller has to do two or more "things" at once. For example, it may have to keep an eye on some critical parameters while simultaneously perfoming some other control function.

Multitasking

A key point from the identification of these problems — resource conflict, deadlock, mutual exclusion, deadlines, concurrency — is that they are all caused by the application having a non-sequential requirement. That is, two or more things have to happen apparently at the same time.

If we were to break an application down into code modules and specify that each module be sequential code inside, then the concurrency issue is relegated to the module level.

We could call these modules tasks, threads, processes, jobs, or whatever. In this book, I call each module a *node*.

A module is a portion of a program that does one particular job, such as monitoring the temperature of a boiler, calculating some mathematical relationship, or sorting an array — in fact, anything that you can program strictly sequentially. If you need to keep monitoring the boiler temperature, while at the same time calculating a mathematical equation, then you have two "concurrent" modules. In fact, what you would have is known as *multitasking*.

Actually, you can't *really* have concurrency with only one processor, because it is inherently sequential, so you have to simulate concurrency, which takes us into the controversial realm of *task scheduling*. Because you have these "concurrent" modules, they may have to synchronise so that they start and stop at the right times, and they may have to send messages between each other. Oh boy .... this is where we start to look toward an operating system for help.

Real-time operating system

Some kind of software kernel can help us juggle these "concurrent" modules, and it can range from something very simple that you "cook up" yourself, to a very sophisticated operating system. Ready-made operating systems designed for real-time applications, from microcontrollers up to large workstations, are referred to as *Real Time Operating Systems*, or simply RTOSs.

At the bottom end, the RTOS may be so simple that you may not even want to call it an operating system — an *execution executive* may be more appropriate.

Whatever you call it, nearly all of these RTOSs have one thing in common — they provide multitasking. Furthermore, they achieve multitasking by various techniques of scheduling the modules. There are two broad classifications of scheduling: *preemptive* or *cooperative*.

Preemptive versus cooperative scheduling

Actually, there are more rigorous treatments of the various scheduling techniques, and I would like to quote from Brian Brown's excellent on-line tutorials, at:

`http://www.cit.ac.nz/smac/cbt/hwsys/`

Note that Brian is now charging a small fee for access to these materials.

Another excellent treatment of scheduling issues, highly relevant to embedded applications, is *μC/OS: The Real-Time Kernel*, by Jean Labrosse, published by R&D Books.

I want to avoid a lot of classifications, so I am defining just these two: preemptive and cooperative. Let's look at Brian's definitions:

Cooperative

"Tasks give up the processor voluntarily at some stage in their execution cycle. This normally occurs when waiting for data arrival or device-ready signals. The design is to free the processor for other tasks that are not waiting on devices.

Preemptive

"A real-time clock interrupts the processor at regular intervals, and a kernel executive forces switching of the processor between tasks. This system enforces regular task execution, thus response times can be calculated. Tasks will be in various stages of execution, and the kernel executive schedules tasks for execution according to preset criteria.

The vast majority of RTOSs are of the preemptive nature; however, they usually have some cooperative features. The version of TERSE that I wrote for the 8051 is purely cooperative, whereas my version for the x86 is cooperative with preemptive features. In other words, I have come from the opposite direction of most other RTOSs, but my x86 TERSE is still fundamentally rooted in the cooperative way of thinking, somewhat at variance to other RTOSs. Why should I buck the trend?

Ok, let's pause and get a second opinion. What follows is a message posted on the Internet to newsgroup COMP.ARCH.EMBEDDED during August 1995. I don't know if the author would object to his name being printed in this book, so it shall remain anonymous:

Start email message ...
Having worked on embedded real time systems for 13 years, and having written a number of embedded operating systems on various platforms, I am not a huge fan of pre-emptive scheduling.
I see a lot of companies selling whiz-bang 'Real Time' Operating Systems that have complex priority and

preemption schemes; especially true with the
Unix-compatible systems, where non-realtime and realtime
tasks are mixed (IMHO put the real time tasks where they
belong — out of Unix and into embedded systems...)

The complexity of these systems is mostly (I say again,
mostly, not *always*) unwarranted and often add to the
overall cost of the system (in terms of money, CPU,
software cost etc.). In the truly embedded world, it is
often better to simplify the OS and make the
processes/tasks running under it 'co-operative', so that
timing contracts are met. My point of view is that it
is never as simple as the preemptive OS vendors would
have us believe.

Preemption and priorities are a slippery slope; once you
are on them, you quickly slide down into a sticky swamp.
Why? Prioritisation implies preemption — there would be
no point in having a higher priority task if it did not
preempt a lower priority task.

The message continues, but a comment is in order here. Preemption means
that one task can interrupt another task, and quite logically, the interrupting
task must be assigned a higher priority (even if that priority is only because
a task is "due" for scheduling, i.e., has higher priority by virtue of having
waited longest, as in a round-robin system). Therefore, such an RTOS must
be driven by an interrupt — how else can the RTOS break in to a running
task, put it on hold, and run another task?

If you have preemption, then you have a problem with
synchronisation and locking, especially with shared data
structures such as lists and queues. Fine, you then add
semaphores, messaging and mailboxes so that you can
overcome the locking problems, but you have to ensure
that preemption works properly and that tasks do not get
switched in the middle of critical sections. So you add
monitors, or have the concept of privilege (privileged
sections do not get switched), and then after each
monitor/semaphore you have checking for preemption...
and then you find that your real-time operating system
has grown too big and slow for your real time processing
needs, since it spends all its time locking and

messaging and semaphoring and preempting, so you have to
buy a bigger processor with more memory...

Let me break in again. I don't want to take you on a journey into the dark
woods of semaphores, mailboxes, critical sections, monitors, privilege .....
because my TERSE operating system avoids all of that (even my time-sliced
x86 version). However, if you would like further details, Brian Brown's
above-mentioned tutorial has further details. Continuing ...

A good real-time design with co-operative switching will
beat a poor design that relies on pre-emption, under
most constrained embedded systems. I guess preemption
allows you to be more sloppy in the design or
implementation, so perhaps that is a Good Thing.
It all depends on your bent; I tend to be a minimalist,
so I see the extra baggage as overhead, others tend to
see the baggage as extra facilities and tools to help
get the job done faster and better. I have no problem
with that.
I have come to the conclusion that preemption is to be
avoided *if at all possible*, since it carries a lot of
baggage with it. But having said all that, it certainly
has its place outside of the hard real time world,
especially in systems that require some aspects of real
time behaviour, such as responding quickly to user
input, yet sharing CPU resources fairly amongst
competing processes, where some processes are considered
higher priority (e.g. the X server responding to
mouse/keyboard events, yet while processing large bit
images). Threads will help a lot.
Only my opinion, of course.

End email message.

Perhaps the most appropriate conclusion is to say "if the hat fits, wear it". I
don't want to become bogged down in the preemption versus cooperation
argument. TERSE is built upon a simple cooperative dataflow principle,
and I find it works for all real-time applications investigated so far.

However, the word "cooperation", as applied to TERSE, is a special case of
Brian's aforementioned definition, in that my building blocks are nodes
rather than tasks.

TERSE cooperative scheduling

A node can never be preempted, and will always run to completion. Upon completion, the RTOS can schedule another eligible node.

The exception to this is my virtual machine extension; however, this is constrained so as not to interfere with the cooperative philosophy. A complex project can be divided into sub-diagrams that run independently in a distributed environment or single-processor time-sliced environment, but this is a transparent implementation detail.

More specifically, any program, or task within a program, must be decomposed to nodes that always run to completion. Therefore, what Brian conceives of as a task may be composed of one or more nodes.

TERSE has none of the complexities of preemptive RTOSs, is even simpler than other cooperative techniques, and is incredibly easy to use; yet, I hope to convince you, in the course of studying this book, that TERSE will do anything and do it better than the "hard-core" preemptive route.

Note however, that TERSE is my "baby", so quite naturally I'm peddling its virtues. The exercises I have performed with GOOFEE have mostly been mapped either onto TERSE or to constrained designs that have no underlying RTOS. It is quite viable to map the nodes of GOOFEE onto implementations running on preemptive RTOSs, and I am keen to obtain feedback from people experimenting in this direction.

Of course, for many applications, it is impractical to discard interrupts, but still, that does not mean that you need preemption. An interrupt routine interrupts the current task, but doesn't have to preempt it. With GOOFEE, I place interrupt handlers inside nodes, and the results are available when the RTOS eventually gets around to scheduling the node.

An improvement on this is for the interrupt routine to be able to post a Notification (asynchronous) message before exiting. These messages can queue, and this ensures that nothing is lost.

Just in case you missed the point, TERSE itself *does* have an interrupt routine; to handle remote input messages. Messages between processors or virtual machines must never get lost and must be delivered to the message buffer of the target processor/virtual machine. In the case of a distributed system, it is possible for some hardware support here, such as a network coprocessor, that shares memory with the main processor, possibly even doing away with the need for an interrupt routine.

Tiny time-sliced RTOSs

I do feel the need to quantify the preemption/cooperation issue introduced above. I don't, however, want to imply that GOOFEE is tied to just the cooperative route, as the current versions of TERSE are really a different issue.

Time-sliced or preemptive RTOSs are also cooperative, that is, support voluntary yielding, because it is inflexible to be totally one way or the other. Always, some compromise is best.

There is one commercial RTOS that comes to mind, tiny by comparison with most others, at only 900 bytes for the 8051 microcontroller. It has simple round-robin time-slicing, without priorities, and only six operating system services. Those services are for a task to

1 create another task

2 "go to sleep" or *block*

3 wait on a signal from another task

4 be destroyed

5 remove a signal that has already been posted to another task

6 have an interrupt service routine post a signal to it.

This RTOS doesn't do much for 900 bytes, and the *context switch*, which is the switch between tasks, takes between 100 and 700 clock cycles (about 7 to 47 instructions or 6 to 46 microseconds for a 16MHz clock), depending on how much stuff the tasks have on the stack. Basically, a task switch involves saving current registers and stack contents of the task that is being stopped and loading previously saved register and stack values for the task that is to be scheduled next. This of course means that a RAM area is required to save this data.

Although 46 microseconds doesn't seem like much, the processor will be rotating continuously around the tasks. If there are 5 tasks, and you require them all to be executed in 1 millisecond, there will have to be 5 task switches, so switching overhead is 5 x 46 = 230 microseconds, or 0.23

milliseconds, leaving 0.77/5 = 0.154 milliseconds for each task. What is very misleading about the simple switch-time figure, is that it gives the impression of speed — but what is all that 900 bytes of code doing? Just sitting there? Obviously, any practical application has to make lots of calls to the OS, and that 900 bytes will be very busy with all those semaphores and critical sections, and stuff, as mentioned in the peviously quoted email message, hence the time overhead of a practical task will be far beyond the 0.23 milliseconds calculated above. So, taking the worst-case context switching time of 700 clock cycles for the point of comparison with TERSE is, I think, rough but reasonable. In fact, I will add on another 20 instructions, or about 20 microseconds for a 16MHz 8051, for a per-task OS overhead of 66 microseconds.

The same software company has a bigger RTOS, of 8 to 9 Kb, that has more functions and *priorities*. The latter feature will make the above scenario somewhat more palatable. It does have CAN network support, but even so, 9Kb is a lot to stuff into a single-chip microcontroller.

Comparison with TERSE

Consider a 150-byte uniprocessor 8051 TERSE RTOS (supplied on the Companion Disk). It can also send signals between tasks, but, unlike the tiny RTOS described above, TERSE can send 8- or 16-bit messages or pointers to blocks, which are only offered by the bigger above-mentioned RTOS. A simple round-robin string of GOOFEE nodes will achieve the same effect as the time-sliced round-robin RTOS, and TERSE will have an overhead of about 70 instructions per switch, which is about 70 microseconds. This compares with about 66 microseconds for the time-sliced RTOS, as explained above.

Thus, TERSE comes out about the same. The TERSE "task-switch" also passes a message and performs runtime scheduling calculations — the notion of priorities and task creation and destruction can be implemented without any more overhead.

However, with TERSE, a *node* does not necessarily equate to a *task*. In fact, a task may be decomposed into two or more nodes, thus imposing the 70 microseconds on every node transition within a task.

Figure 18: TERSE comparison with time-sliced RTOSs.

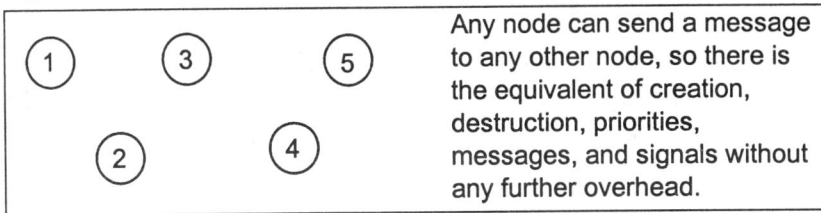

			Any node can send a message to any other node, so there is the equivalent of creation, destruction, priorities, messages, and signals without any further overhead.
(1)	(3)	(5)	
(2)		(4)	

Someone said that "engineering is the art of compromise". I also remember someone else saying "engineering is the art of approximation". Both are true, but more so the former at the moment.

In the above analysis, I wrote that a task may be composed of two or more nodes, but if the sequencing of those nodes within a task is fixed, you can simply hand tune the transitions to bypass TERSE's scheduler. TERSE consists of two parts, a message delivery module and a Signature Scheduler, and you can bypass either or both as required.

If you want to go from one node to another, without any runtime variation, then just post any data directly and jump straight to the next node. Or, if TERSE has other pending messages for the next node, you can go via the OS message delivery module.

So, why do we need TERSE? The fact is, if scheduling is *totally static*, i.e., fixed, or if runtime variations can readily be decided from within each node, *TERSE is not needed*. GOOFEE is still a superb way of designing the system, but it resolves down to a fast dedicated application without any OS overhead.

However, TERSE also performs message delivery, and you can still use this, without the scheduling part of TERSE.

TERSE's scheduling part is needed when scheduling has some uncertainty. The ideal solution for typical systems is a compromise in which you design the system initially to use TERSE in the normal way, then at the end of the design, you look at the flow diagram. For all cases in which the scheduling is definitely, absolutely fixed and where the next node does not require any other input messages to be extracted from the stack, do a direct jump, bypassing TERSE.

Which language?

In this book I have used assembly language and C. Why not Ada or C++? Let this message, posted to the Internet Newsgroup COMP.ARCH.EMBEDDED on the fourth of October 1995, answer this question for me:

```
>I agree. Why isn't C++ good for small embedded
>systems. If you don't do more than you did with
>standard C, nothings lost. If your compiler isn't
>doing for you, you have to do it yourself.
>Why not using constructors and destructors. Why not
>virtual functions, or did you never check what your
>C compiler on the 8051 produces when you use "switch
> - case"?
```

Having seen C++ burn quite a few experienced fingers, I'd say that C++ is a dangerous language on many platforms, not just embedded platforms.

Whereas the code sequences produced by C are normally quite predictable, since C is a small and simple language, the same is definitely not true of C++. C++ is actually a very different language in that it has some very different semantics to C, though it virtually shares the same syntax. To my mind this is the biggest gotcha of C++, it is very deceptive.

For my money, ANSI-C is a much more suitable language for embedded work than C++. It has all the good stuff (like type safety) without all the big gotchas. Sure classes are useful, but I'd give them up so that I don't get landed with the rest of the horrors that go with C++.

"But!", I hear you yell, "I want re-use". Re-use doesn't come for free just because you're using C++. There is plenty of code out there written in C which is being reused every day (take the standard C runtime libraries for instance).

To quote Bjarne Stroustrup [loosely, and BS, I hope I spelled your name right] "With C you can shoot your foot off, with C++ you can blow off your whole leg".

Some guy [his name escapes me right now] wrote a book called something like "50 ways to improve your C++ programs". Of these, about 35 were things that you'd better be doing otherwise C++ would kill you with no warning from the compiler. Programming safe C++ programs is like walking point in enemy territory, you have to be forever vigilant. By the way, I highly recommend the book, but do yourself a favour; rip the cover off and put on your own called "35 ways to stop C++ frying your butt + 15 ways to improve your C++ programs".

>Sure if somebody programs without knowing what the
>compiler produces, you are lost in the RT or
>embedded world, but this is TRUE for standard C as
>well (just try to pass to or return a structure from
>a function instead of using struct * and you see
>what I mean).

In a recent C++ project that I worked on, we had 15 programmers hacking code for two years. At the start of the project, two had 3 yrs C++ apiece, two had 2 yrs and the rest had training 3 weeks - 6 months. All were graduates (lotsa As) and all had considerable C experience 3yrs to 10 yrs. Any of them could have spotted your example without even getting out of bed. None of them could spot some of the babies that our C++ code generated without hours of analysis with debuggers and a dose of the ARM.

It is possible to write safe C++ code, but to do so means that you need to avoid many of the seductive features such as operator overloading and the implicit construction. The worst offenders are the functions which get automatically generated for you by the compiler (copy constructor, operator =...). These have been added to C++ to make code easy to read.

It is very easy to read, unfortunately what the compiler generates for you is nothing like what you read and nasty code gets hidden from the programmer's view making it difficult to find bugs and performance problems. A simple a=b; looks very innocent, but in C++ it can easily blow up to many function calls and performance bottlenecks. We had a term for this in the army, hiding a horrible thing under an innocent looking item, -- booby trapping!

Putting C++ on any platform is crazy, but putting it on a small embedded system is even worse! C++ has a nasty habit of creating lots of temporary variables and loves doing dynamic allocation behind your back. This beats the hell out of most heap managers [that's why those nice folk at MicroQuill {??} make so much money out of SmartHeap]. Now most embedded systems, especially small ones on 8051 kit, are not going to have very savvy heap management. C++ will kill them.

Some of the above comments are very interesting!

Replacement for OOP?

There is a lot of hype about OOP, and it may be that interest will shift elsewhere in a few years. I suspect the next wave will be *flow-based programming*. In fact, *FBP* is an acronym for Flow-Based Programming, the name given to a particular technique that has been in use for the last 20 years, mostly for business programming at IBM. A key person in this area (ex-IBM) is Paul Morrison, the author of *Flow-Based Programming* (International Thomson Publishing, USA, 1993, ISBN 0-442-01771-5). There are many many other related papers, products, articles, oriented around the "flow" paradigm, and I mention Paul's book here because his thinking is that his FBP has been waiting in the wings for too long, and its time will come as a major competitor to OOP, possibly converging with OOP.

If you would like a jumping-off point on the Internet, there is an academically oriented "Dataflow home page", with lots of links:

http://odyssey.ucc.ie/www/user-dirs/oregan/dataflow.html

TERSE and GOOFEE are variations on the flow-programming theme, definitely not for business programming (though, I wonder ....?), and I would like to think that my tools will be part of that next wave.

Postamble

This chapter has exposed the problems of an OO language such as C++ for embedded work.

I have taken the approach that OO methodology can be applied at the analysis/design phases but does not have to be at the coding phase, which on the surface at least, would seem to offer the best of both worlds. GOOFEE diagrams can be as object-oriented as you want them to be; however, this is at the diagramming level. Any enforcement of OO principles can be done by the CASE tool. The code within the nodes only needs to be plain C or plain whatever.

Later chapters in this book show how this approach is practical and it works.

Some fundamental real-time concepts have been introduced and some issues discussed. Concurrency is a very difficult topic, and if you feel after reading this chapter that your questions are not all answered, my response is that I cannot give definitive answers. However, as you study further through this book you will develop some concrete feeling on the issues and how to tackle them.

The next chapter is very exciting; it exposes the "heart" of GOOFEE, the key concepts, at least as vital as the clone and Iterative-nodes introduced in Chapter 1. Now you will move into real OO design.

4

Unified object-oriented design

Preamble

This chapter develops a unified vision for object-oriented design (OOD) of computer systems based upon a single diagram and a single graphical notation, GOOFEE, which models every phase and every aspect of the development process.

Although the single-view approach can be applied to structured design, I have focused here on the object-oriented approach, because it has fundamental advantages.

This chapter explores the GOOFEE notation for representation of classes and objects, the distinction between them, and the relationships between and within them. The chapter clarifies some underlying concepts and builds toward showing how GOOFEE can represent nearly all views and relationships that can be expressed in *Booch* 91/94 notation. Booch is chosen as the reference, because it has emerged as the single dominant standard for OOD, with *OMT* tending to merge into Booch to form the new Unified Booch—OMT notation developed by G. Booch and J. Rumbaugh.

For those readers interested in doing some background reading on the Booch methodology, I recommend Grady Booch's book *Object Oriented Analysis and Design*, 2nd edition (Benjamin/Cummins: Redwood City).

The chapter builds toward elaboration of the underlying concept of the paradigm shift from multiple views to a single view, and shows the practicality of GOOFEE notation by developing infrastructure via a GOOFEE case study presented later in the book.

Genesis of the multiple-view paradigm

GOOFEE diagram structuring for inheritance versus messaging

Figure 19 states that PU2 contains node 19 and PU3 contains node 5, and nodes 19 and 5 are identical, each with their own copies of code and data and that concurrency of execution is allowed: these are the *Joining-bars* of Figure 2. Also, each node PU2 and PU3 has its own external arc connections. Note that the naming of Composite-nodes as PU2 and PU3 is not meant to imply that a Composite-node always equates to a processor: this is an implementation decision, and one processor could be composed of 0 to n Composite-nodes.

Because PU2B "clone" is in union (i.e., no separate copies of code and data) with PU2, it is appropriate that one of the Composite-nodes shows external wire connections; although in theory, it could be either one, or a mixture, i.e., some external connections shown on one Composite-node, some on the other. This is further clarified in this chapter.

PU2B and PU3B are *classes*, as clarified further in this chapter, and do not have external message wires. Point 'X' on PU3B is an example, with the external arc 'X' shown on the instantiation PU3. However, inheritance relationships can be shown directly, regardless of whether a node is a class or an *object* (or a node or Composite-node), as between nodes 19 and 5, PU2B and PU2, and between PU3B and PU3.

The physical separation between nodes exhibiting inheritance may be extreme. However, even if the Joining-bar (inheritance relationship) emanating from node 5 goes off the immediate screen, its presence shows that there is a clone relationship, and a computer tool could conceivably be made to point down a Joining-bar and rapidly travel to the other end.

Figure 19: Distinction between inheritance bars and messaging wires.

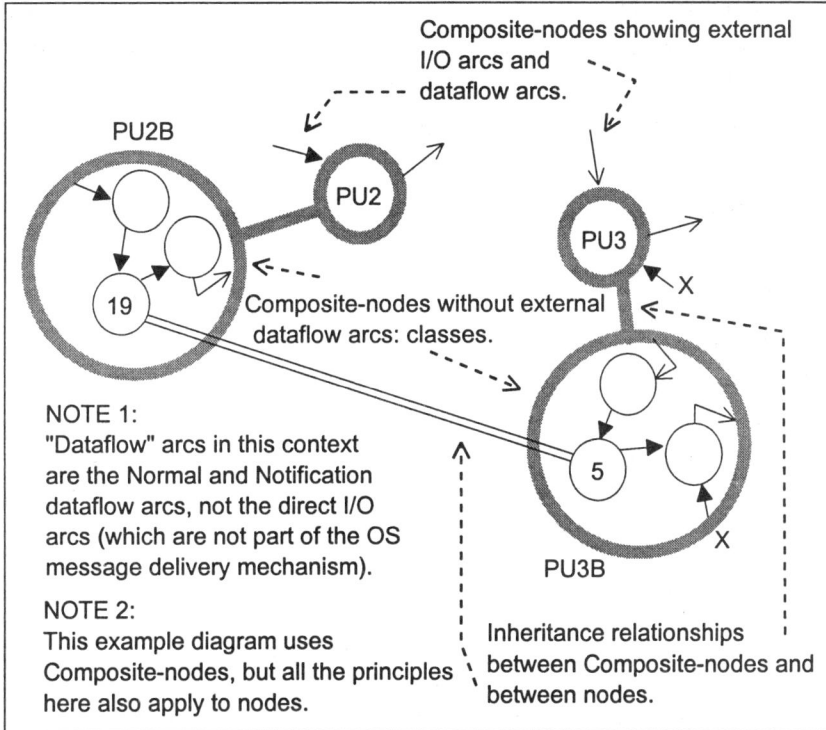

It should be noted that the *dataflow* wires are inherently different from the *direct I/O* wires. The former are of two types: *Normal* (synchronous) and *Notification* (asynchronous). Normal wires are synchronous dataflow wires, and Notifications have no effect on the execution scheduling of the destination-node. Direct I/O wires also have no effect on node scheduling and also have nothing to do with the runtime message delivery mechanism, as they are accessed directly from the code within a node.

The hierarchical alternative

Figure 20 shows a conventional hierarchical decomposition, mimicking the functionality of Figure 19. Each rectangle is a different view, or window, and the decompositions of Composite-nodes PU2 and PU3 are windows

PU2B and PU3B with each lower level window showing the internal diagrams.

The clone (inheritance) relationships between nodes 19 and 5 can no longer be shown directly and must be shown as a separate inter-window object—inheritance view.

In fact, if you think about this, you will realise that the root cause of this separation of views is the hierarchical decomposition.

Figure 20: Conventional hierarchical decomposition.

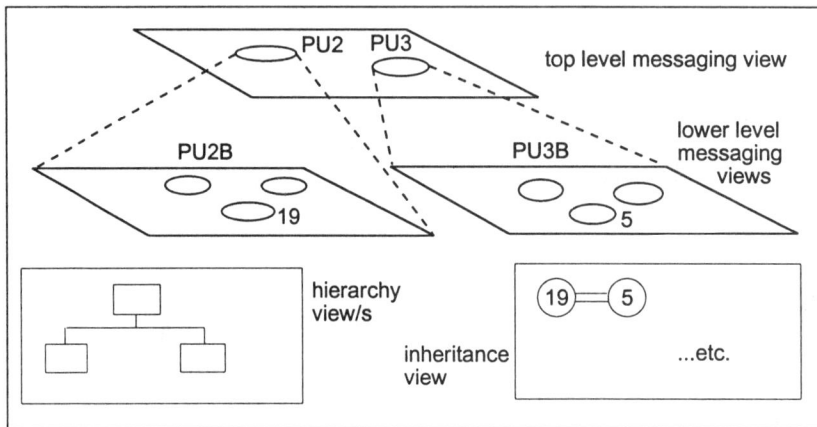

Specialised notations have developed, different for each view, and as each view is a partial picture of the whole system, the number of notational elements for each view has tended to proliferate. Different notations in different views may even have the same or overlapping meaning.

With GOOFEE, I have abandoned 3-dimensional hierarchy, and all design is in a 2-dimensional plane, using a single unified notation in which a node can be a class, an object, or a state (if we want to constrain it to these conceptual subsets), depending on the context in which it is drawn.

I have envisaged at-a-glance comprehension of how a system functions at any level of detail and immediate comprehension of relationships between any part of the system, and I would like to show that this is potentially augmented by only having one diagram to look at using my simplified notation.

Figure 21 shows an exacerbated situation. Node 19 has inheritance relationships with nodes 20 and 5. Node 20 is common code, separately instantiated data, concurrency allowed. In the hierarchical system, since the inheritance between 19 and 5 is shown in a separate window, it would be consistent to do the same for the relationship between 19 and 20, even though they reside in the same view, or window.

That is, all inheritance relationships are shown in separate views from messaging views.

Figure 21: Exacerbated inheritance example.

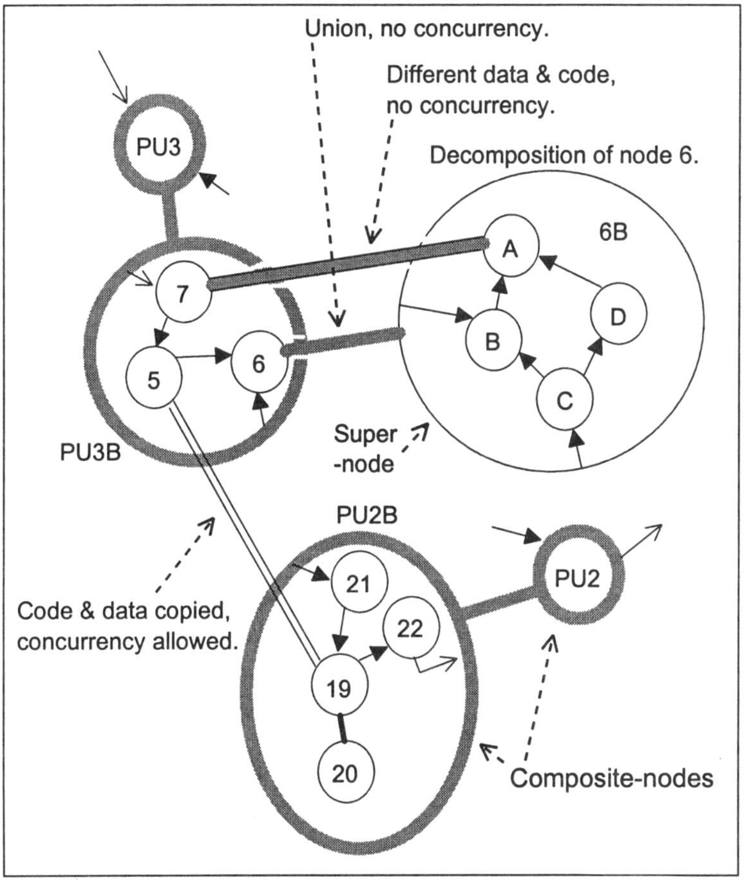

The separation is made in the hierarchical systems out of necessity. Only GOOFEE, being totally 2-dimensional, is capable of clearly representing both messaging and inheritance views in the same view. Furthermore, Figure 20 requires a separate hierarchy view to properly show decomposition of the messaging views.

Notice something important about Figure 21: Joining-bars are always drawn directly between the nodes they are concerned with. That is, node 7 has a Joining-bar directly to node A, NOT via node 6, despite the fact that node 6 is a Super-node object (and node 6B is a Super-node class). This is a vital difference from dataflow wires, which must never be connected externally to a class; they connect to the objects and by *implication* connect inside the class. Be clear on this difference.

What is a Composite-node?

Normal (synchronous) wires into and out of a node have synchronous dataflow behaviour, but this is not implied for the Composite-node, because it is just a composite, or logical, sub-division of the diagram, usually for inheritance and/or visibility/scope purposes.

An example of a Composite-node could be the diagram of a complete physical processor.

However, this does not mean that decomposition stops at the "first" diagram within a Composite-node, as nodes can decompose indefinitely. Figure 21 illustrates this, with the decompostion of node 6.

Also, Composite-nodes themselves can have Joining-bars, just like nodes, and can also be considered as classes and objects.

What is a Super-node?

Any normal node that expands as node 6 does is a Super-node. Node 6 is the object, and the expansion, node 6B, is the class. Although a Super-node, it still behaves like any normal synchronous dataflow node.

Notice that I have drawn node 6 and its expansion with a thin black boundary. You will find in other places in the book that I have used a thick black boundary. The thick boundary is not essential; it is an adornment that emphasises the node as a Super-node.

Classes versus objects

Conventional hierarchical systems must clearly distinguish between classes (templates of objects) and objects (instantiations), because they are usually shown in different views.

In Figure 20, the "inheritance view" would be a class diagram, whereas those labelled "PU2B" and "PU3B" are object views and, lower-down, are state diagrams.

GOOFEE class

In the case of GOOFEE, a class is any node, Super-node, or Composite-node without externally connected message (dataflow) wires and with a Joining-bar to show an inheritance relationship. Note that the word *clone* applies to a node that has a Joining-bar to another node (clone), and it can be a class or an object.

GOOFEE object

An object is any node, Super-node, or Composite-node without a Joining-bar, or if it has a Joining-bar it must also have externally connected message (dataflow) wires.

That's it, and they can be mixed in any way on the same diagram without confusion.

Dataflow messaging interconnections are always shown by wires with full arrows; direct I/O wires have open arrows, whereas the inheritance (Joining-bar) does not have an arrow.

GOOFEE blurs the distinction between class and object, and Joining-bars can be drawn between classes or objects (and they can be nodes or Composite-nodes). It is reasonable to show a Joining-bar between a class and an object; however, it is equally valid to show a Joining-bar between two objects (or two classes), as Figure 22 shows.

However, there are representational problems when a node has no apparent message wires, and when direct I/O-wires are used; the above definition would make them classes. Usually this is okay, but sometimes they may need to be instantiations, i.e., objects.

Any node without external message wires is instantiated if it is the only node in the diagram connected to a particular resource (by an I/O wire).

Figure 22: GOOFEE notational distinction between class and object.

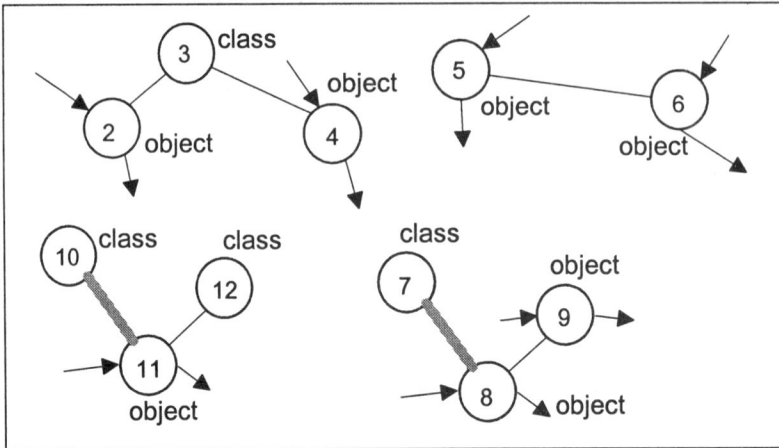

In Figure 22, node 3 is a class, but nodes 2, 4, 5, and 6 are all objects. Is there the danger of confusing node 3 with an instantiation? The notation is clear: there are no messaging wires (dataflow) to node 3, therefore it is a class.

Nodes 7, 8, and 9 are another example. Node 7 is a class, and node 8 inherits from node 7 with no separate copies of code and data. Node 8 is the object.

Node 9 inherits from node 8 with separate data and is another object.

Nodes 10, 11, and 12 explore further this notation. Node 11 is the only object, and 10 and 12 are both classes. Node 10 is a class that is identical to node 11, and node 12 is a *meta-class* with its own copy of data. Node 12 can be used as a class for other inheritance relationships.

GOOFEE meta-class

Any class with data that is different from its clone is a meta-class. This can be achieved by a Joining-bar showing copying of data or common code, or by connecting each clone to a different external resource.

Mixing of classes and objects

Why not clarify which nodes are classes by, say, dashed-line circles?

GOOFEE allows legal construction of diagrams in which classes and nodes intermix in a manner that may make such a distinction confusing.

Figure 23 illustrates class—object intermixing. XB is a class, and XA is an object. The fact that they are Composite-nodes does not matter, because inheritance relationships apply to either nodes or subdiagrams (Composite-nodes). However, XB contains within it, a diagram that does show instantiations — in reality, these objects reside in XA.

Figure 23: Mixed classes and objects.

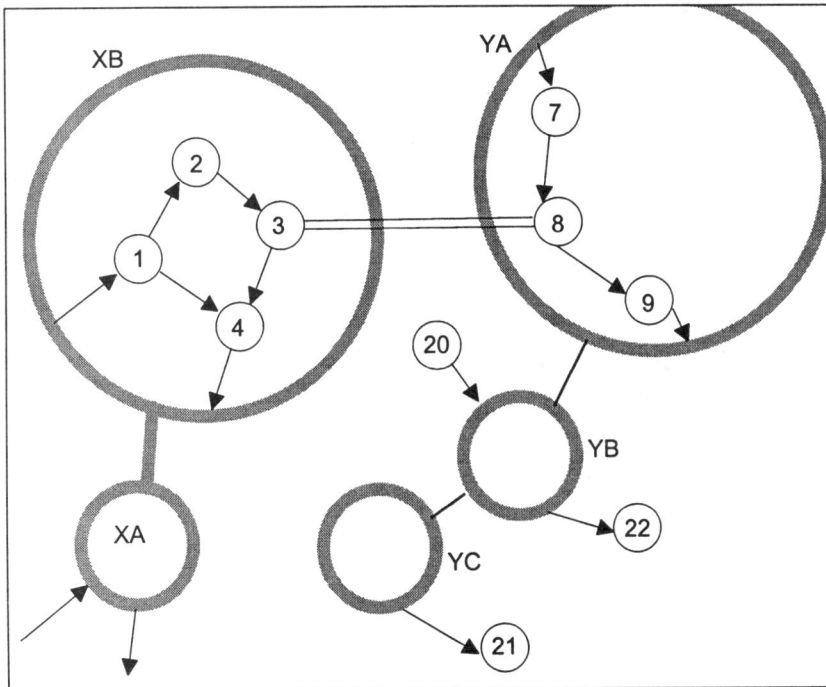

To make the diagram more interesting, there is also an inheritance relationship shown between nodes 3 and 8, and both are objects.

YA and YB illustrate another type of mixing that is legal for GOOFEE.

YC shows one external wire (from node 9 to node 21) but not into node 7. YB shows an external wire into YB's inherited node 7, and out of node 9. Both YC and YB are objects, because they have at least one external wire.

In fact the input to YC/node 7 will also be from node 20 by implication (which is an important feature to simplify GOOFEE diagrams).

When node 20 exits, it fires *two* tokens from its output arc to YC/node 7 and YB/node 7. The issue of multiple tokens is further developed later in the book.

Classes: comparison with Booch

Figure 24 compares relationships among classes for Booch and GOOFEE. Grady, my apologies if I have misrepresented your work in any way — let me know, and I'll see about getting your feedback (and anyone else's feedback) onto my home page. At the time of writing, you can find me at:

```
http://scorpion.cowan.edu.au/science/terse/index.html
```

If that link fails for some reason, it should be possible to trace my home page via the GOOFEE Systems Pty Ltd home page:

```
http://www.arrowweb.com/goofee/
```

In some cases there is no direct equivalent, and Figure 24 shows some of the mismatch. GOOFEE is able to represent more inheritance options by virtue of the five types of Joining-bar, and the uses relationships of Booch are not used in GOOFEE simply because they are redundant.

Booch notation targets conventional "procedure-based" OOP, which is a constrained subset of the generic dataflow OO model, as explained in chapter 1, so I have matched GOOFEE to Booch notation with some reluctance. Nor is Figure 24 a thorough comparison.

Figure 24: Notation for classes: Booch versus GOOFEE.

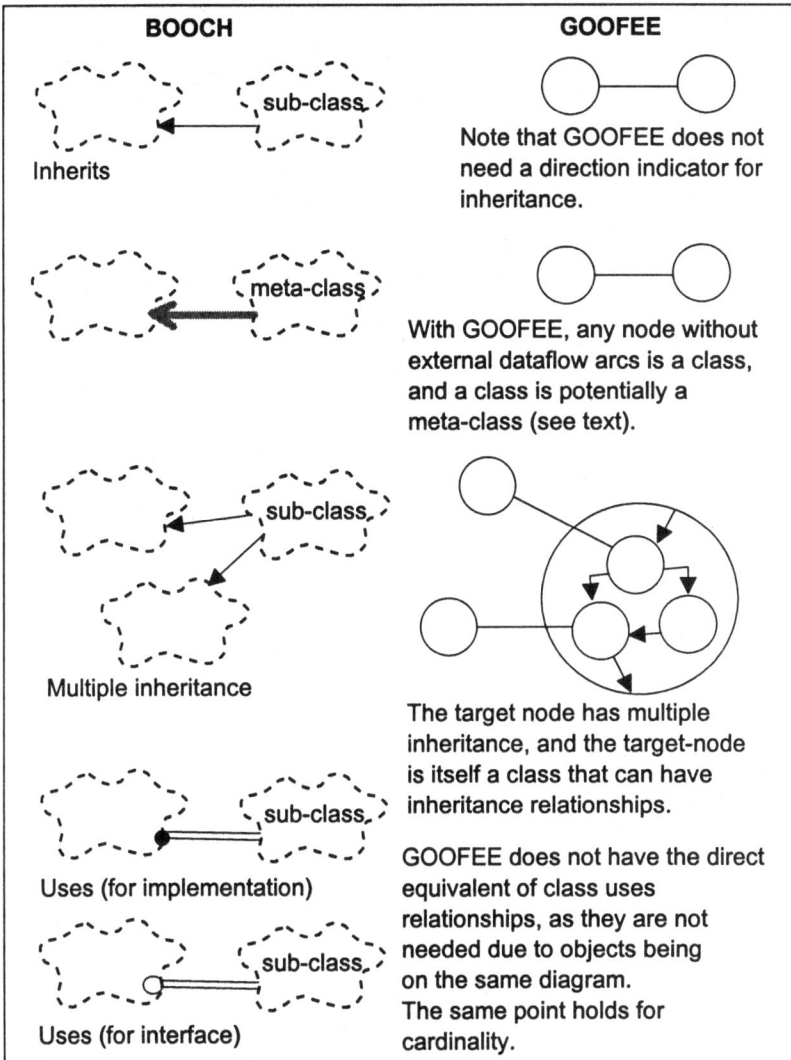

Objects: comparison with Booch

Within the bounds of a fairly restricted comparison, in particular missing out the dynamic behaviour of objects, Figure 24 shows that GOOFEE is able to represent equivalent functionality to Booch notation, and in fact, GOOFEE is more precise as regards the types of inheritance. However, to determine whether GOOFEE can substantially represent most possibilites of the Booch notation, it is necessary to examine object relationships, which is done in Figure 25.

Booch has two uses relationships, two instantiates relationships, two inherits relationships, one meta-class relationship, an undefined relationship for use between classes, six options for expressing cardinality, and the class-element itself.

The example of Figure 25, showing multiple inheritance, also illustrates how GOOFEE can implement the equivalent of Booch's contained classes or objects.

The examples given in Figure 25 utilise almost all of the notational elements of GOOFEE: the only ones left out are the Iterative-node, global resource, action:event, and some messaging types.

As GOOFEE integrates classes, objects, and hierarchy onto the same diagram, it is a little awkward to compare with Booch's divided views. However, the comparison must be done.

What is not shown in Figure 25 is the issue of *visibility*, which is covered below.

The only new elements introduced to GOOFEE (compared with Figure 24) are the timeout symbol and Notification, and Figure 25 introduces four synchronisation elements for Booch notation, the basic messaging arc (no arrows), and the object-symbol itself. There is also a return message symbol, introduced with Booch94 (see Figure 26).

For the asynchronous wire, the originator of a GOOFEE message may be an ordinary node, or an Iterative-node. It is messages that involve a reply that normally should be constrained to originate from an Iterative-node only.

Figure 25(a): Objects: comparison with Booch.

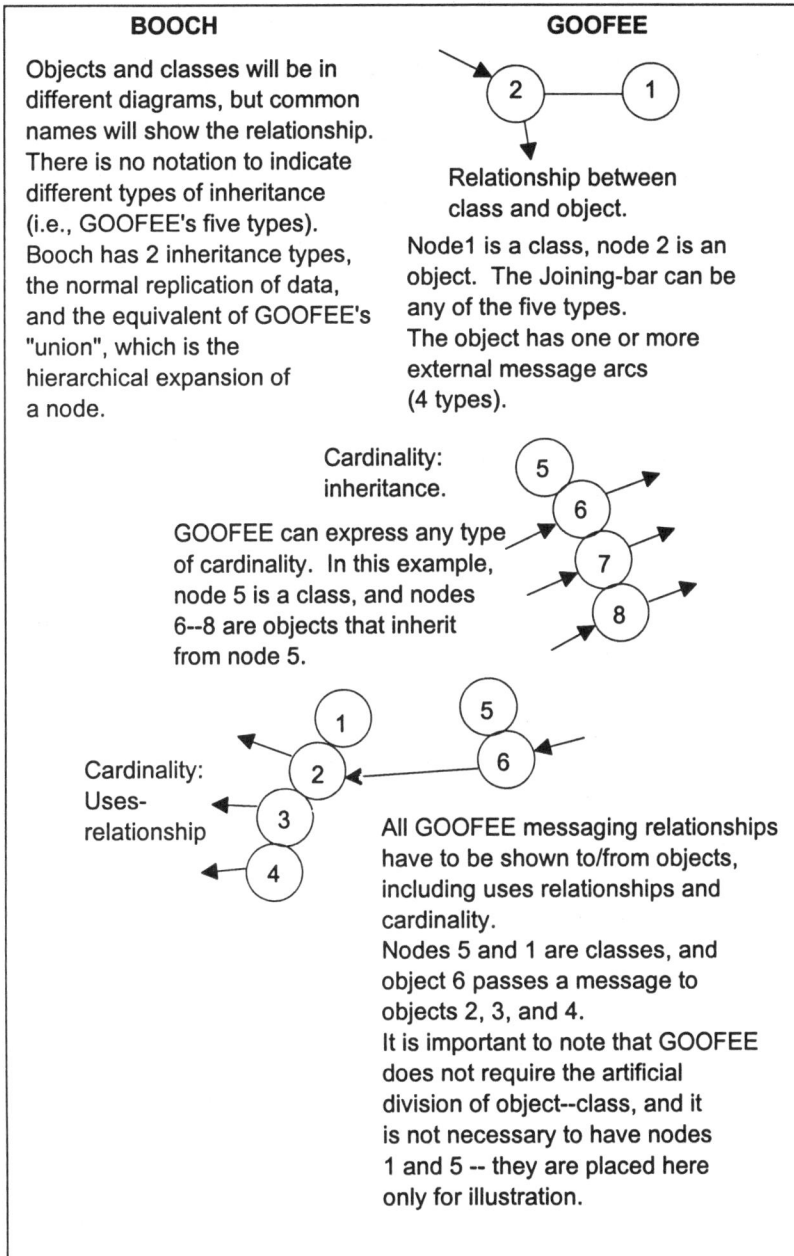

BOOCH   **GOOFEE**

Objects and classes will be in different diagrams, but common names will show the relationship. There is no notation to indicate different types of inheritance (i.e., GOOFEE's five types). Booch has 2 inheritance types, the normal replication of data, and the equivalent of GOOFEE's "union", which is the hierarchical expansion of a node.

Relationship between class and object.

Node1 is a class, node 2 is an object. The Joining-bar can be any of the five types. The object has one or more external message arcs (4 types).

Cardinality: inheritance.

GOOFEE can express any type of cardinality. In this example, node 5 is a class, and nodes 6--8 are objects that inherit from node 5.

Cardinality: Uses-relationship

All GOOFEE messaging relationships have to be shown to/from objects, including uses relationships and cardinality.

Nodes 5 and 1 are classes, and object 6 passes a message to objects 2, 3, and 4.

It is important to note that GOOFEE does not require the artificial division of object--class, and it is not necessary to have nodes 1 and 5 -- they are placed here only for illustration.

Figure 25(b) next page.

Figure 25(b): Objects: comparison with Booch.

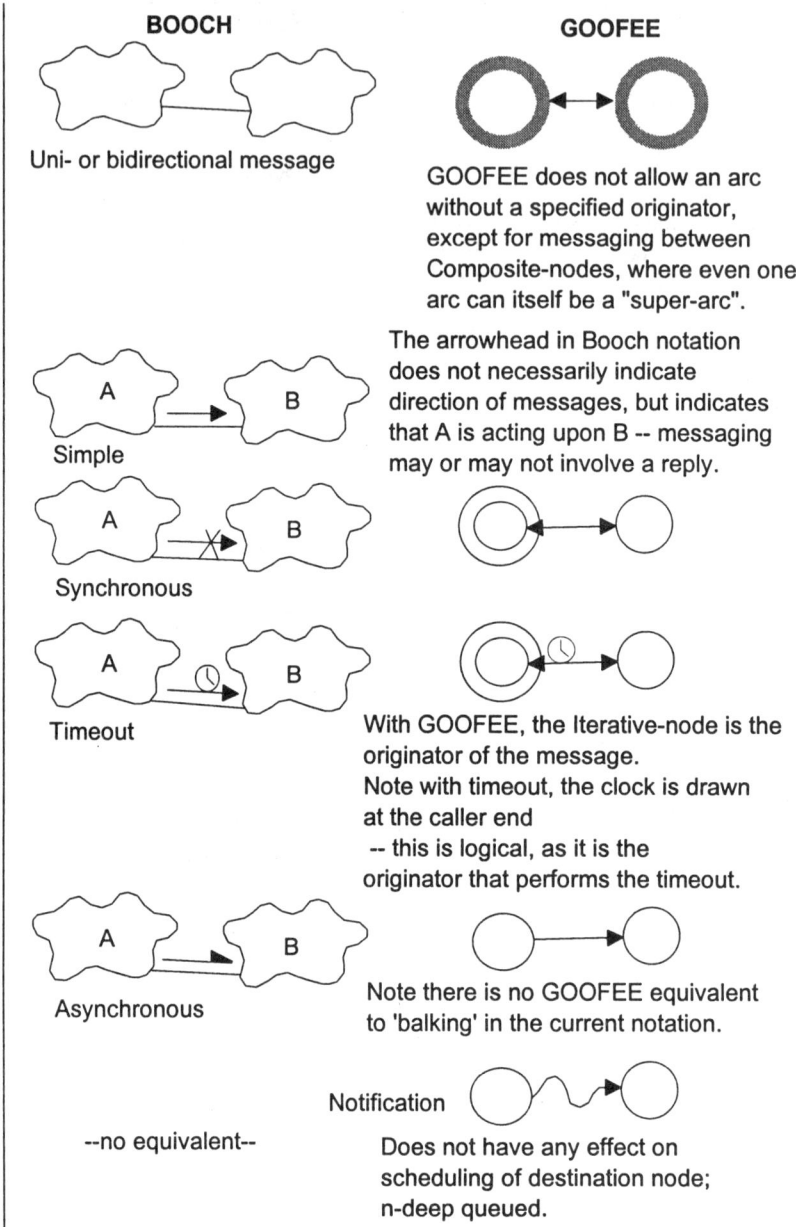

BOOCH

Uni- or bidirectional message

GOOFEE

GOOFEE does not allow an arc without a specified originator, except for messaging between Composite-nodes, where even one arc can itself be a "super-arc".

A → B

Simple

The arrowhead in Booch notation does not necessarily indicate direction of messages, but indicates that A is acting upon B -- messaging may or may not involve a reply.

A → B

Synchronous

A → B

Timeout

With GOOFEE, the Iterative-node is the originator of the message.
Note with timeout, the clock is drawn at the caller end
-- this is logical, as it is the originator that performs the timeout.

A → B

Asynchronous

Note there is no GOOFEE equivalent to 'balking' in the current notation.

Notification

--no equivalent--

Does not have any effect on scheduling of destination node; n-deep queued.

GOOFEE messages between nodes follow the synchronous dataflow model, meaning conjunction is required on all input and all output Normal wires at execution entry and exit, which provides multiple-arc synchronisation that is not expressed at the level of Booch's objects and classes.

In Booch notation, a link between objects will be adorned with synchronisation elements, textual description of messaging from the originator, and a return, if any. Typically, this will be as Figure 26.

Figure 26: Adornment of inter-object message link.

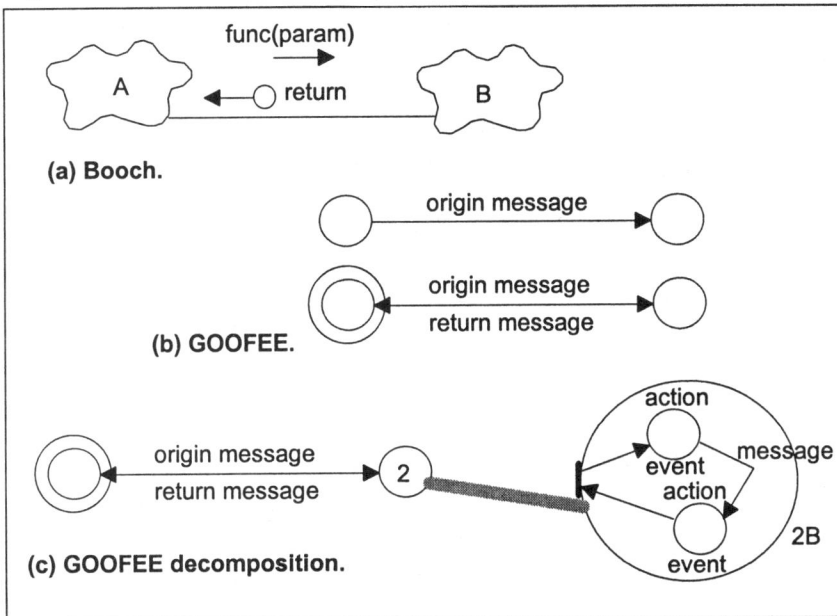

GOOFEE does not have any particular formalism for naming of messages between nodes, and various subsets are allowed, depending on the level of decomposition — this is clarified in Chapter 8. The inclusion of other information, such as a method to be invoked, is already implied if the destination-node is at the lowest "level" of decomposition, or, if not, the decomposition must be observed to see where the arc goes to, as shown in Figure 26(c).

In practice, node 2B can be constructed as a skeleton, to show the internal entry and exit nodes, as "stubs", which are filled out later.

Visibility

We tend to think of visibility and scope in terms of data, but it applies to any resource, and here I use the word resource to also include data.

Figure 27: Notation for visibility.

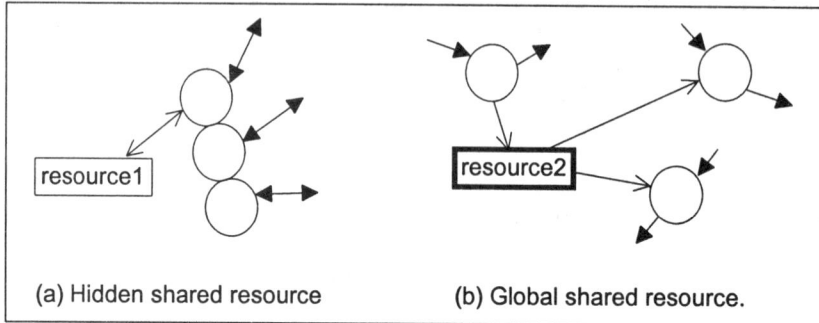

(a) Hidden shared resource   (b) Global shared resource.

Figure 27(a) shows the recommended clone technique for shared access to a resource. For a detailed description of "resource", see Chapter 8. Each of the three clones accesses resource1, and non-concurrency can be enforced by using the appropriate Joining-bar between the clones.

You may have a slight conceptual problem here, in that resource1 is only visible to the node it is connected to, despite being placed outside the node. This is done for consistency, because there are cases where resources must be drawn outside the node that encapsulates them. Again, see Chapter 8.

Figure 27(b) shows a shared resource, resource2, that is deliberately designed to be visible at the diagram level. This is a quasi-global variable, and is defined by a bold box. It is visible within the current Super-node or Composite-node, or, if not in any node, is visible globally.

All resources (including data) are made visible to the global diagram by the context in which they are drawn. A notational element, a bold outline, designates an intentionally bounded or unbounded global resource. A constraint is that a resource, hidden, bounded-global, or global, can only be written to by one wire.

The visibility of data equates to visibility of member variables in OOP terminology.

Just one element has been introduced to GOOFEE, the bold box, as a clarification of an intentional global resource, whereas Booch has six elements.

Dynamic behaviour within objects

Booch class and object diagrams do not fully describe the dynamic (controlflow/dataflow/synchronisation) within a class or object. This is done by state diagrams, which introduce more symbols.

GOOFEE diagrams also allow the internal behaviour of classes and objects to be expressed, but by the same notation, which also means that GOOFEE diagrams can be indefinitely decomposed. GOOFEE representation of State Machines is illustrated in Figures 3 and 4.

Note that the branching example for GOOFEE in Figure 4 is unstructured but appropriate for an FSM. If a CASE tool is to allow this unstructured construct, it should at least flag a warning.

Booch does not consider Harel's Statechart orthogonality to be required at the State Machine level within a class, but it is included in Figure 4 for comparison with GOOFEE.

Dynamic behaviour between objects

State diagrams do represent event-dependent behaviour, which can be associated with time; however, to quote Booch from his book *Object Oriented Design with Applications* (published by Benjamin Cummings, 1991, Redwood City, USA):

> "By themselves, object diagrams are static: they show a cooperative collection of objects that pass messages to one another, but they don't show the flow of control, nor do they show the ordering of events. The state transition diagrams associated with some classes don't help either, since they only show how state changes take place within a single object, not among a set of collaborating objects. To document the semantics of most mechanisms, additional information is vital. Thus we include in our notation three possible ways to document the dynamics of message passing in an object system.

The first technique Booch uses is to label messages in the form *order:message*, where order implies some order of execution but is useless for conditional execution. The other two approaches are a PDL and a timing diagram: the latter involves yet another view. The first method involves yet another notational element.

In the second edition of his book, in 1994, Booch dropped the above quote entirely and all references to PDL and timing diagrams and replaced them with *interaction diagrams*, which visually represent the ordering of passing of messages between objects, but not (directly) time relationships.

With GOOFEE, ordering can be implied by the rings of Iterative-nodes, such that the innermost ring is exited from first, moving out, until final exit is from the outer ring. If there is to be runtime variation of that ordering, it can be expressed by the *event,event, ...* notation, as shown in Figure 4, or, if the internal decisions are too complex, by a pop-up edit window (into which the complete code for the node can be typed). Thus, GOOFEE allows the semantics of state diagrams to be expressed anywhere, including in relation to runtime behaviour of objects.

It should be clarified that Iterative-nodes are objects, like any normal node, and can be treated in exactly the same way, as regards inheritance and expansion.

GOOFEE uses the same notation across all aspects of OOD. The constructions given in Figure 4 are available between objects and classes, eliminating the problem of expressing dynamic timing relationships.

Textual adornments

Figure 4 shows the GOOFEE textual adornments as "action, event, name, message".

- *Action* is taken upon entry to a node and is optional, specified at the State Machine level.
- *Event* is what causes exit from a node and is again specified at the lowest level of decomposition.
- *Message* describes what is passed on the wire. At the lowest level, this could be an immediate-value, or variable.
- *Name* is the name of a node or resource. Node names and resource names have scope only within their boundary of visibility.

Table 1: Booch94 textual adornments.

	BOOCH94	GOOFEE
Common to all	name	name of node
	definition	text inside node
Class/object specs	attributes: list of attributes	visual: direct I/O wires to named boxes
	operations: list of operations	visual: node decomposition
	constraints: list of constraints	*
	category name	visual: inside a Super- or Composite-node
	responsibilities: text	text inside node
	State Machine: reference to State Machine	visual: node decomposition
	export control: public/implementation	visual: inside Super- or Composite-node*
	cardinality: expression	visual: Joining-bar
	parameters: list of formal or actual	visual: conjunctive wires to a node
	persistence	visual: default static, dynamic icon*
	concurrency	visual: qualify by Joining-bar/sync. dataflow
	space complexity	memory management*
Operation specs	return class: reference to class	visual: node parent known visually
	arguments: list of formal arguments	visual: dataflow wires
	qualification	text inside node
	export control: public/prot/private/impl.	visual: inside a Super-node or Composite-node
State Machine	state icon: name, actions	name
	state transition icon: event, action	action, event
Object	context: global/category/class/operation	visual: inside a Super-node or Composite-node*

The variety of textual adornments in Booch diagrams is extensive and summarised in Table 1.

The outcome of Table 1 is that the textual adornments of GOOFEE, being action, event, message, name, defined above, are all that is required: all other specifications are provided visually.

The qualification to this statement is that GOOFEE may not be quite so well developed in terms of a few C++-specific specifications and those identified by an "*".

Conclusions

With regard to the section on visibility, making all resources visible on the diagram, even though they are "hidden", will enhance future extension of GOOFEE into resource management, in which contention will be able to be identified (and avoided) on the same diagram. The Author envisions a return of the very old-fashioned project management technique of pinning the project plan onto the wall, so all participants can see the overall picture at a glance — even having unique colours for each resource will be extremely helpful.

GOOFEE visibility and scope is explored in depth in Chapter 8.

GOOFEE cardinality is explored in depth in Chapter 7.

Booch has various other views, such as the timing diagram or interaction diagram; however, he has not developed this aspect very well with regard to time constraints. GOOFEE has the advantage of its synchronous nature but also needs more development with regard to time constraints.

The timing element introduced in this chapter is the "timeout" for synchronous messaging, which Booch does have, and this has been implemented in the TERSE testbed. Although this is important for real-time systems, further constraints may be required for hard-real-time.

GOOFEE scheduling and time relationships are treated in-depth in Chapter 9.

This document has shown that most of Booch's notational richness is also in GOOFEE, with examples on both sides of notations and constructions that the other cannot represent. Some elements of Booch's notation have not yet been fully mapped onto GOOFEE, and in some cases it will not be done, because GOOFEE, in the immediate future, targets the embedded systems market, particularly ROM-based code.

Booch94 has semantic extensions beyond Booch91, to much more closely match the capabilities of C++. This may be a problem with translation to GOOFEE, as the intention is to use conventional procedural code within GOOFEE nodes (such as C and assembly).

One important outcome of this chapter is that GOOFEE has been mapped onto Booch with only *eighteen* visual and textual elements in total, whereas Booch has approximately 36 visual elements (not counting some advanced features, such as module and process icons) and a "few dozen" textual elements.

Extension of GOOFEE into more complete descriptions of runtime behaviour of dynamic objects, is an important issue for scaling-up, and Chapter 7 goes into this in more depth.

A potentially awkward aspect of GOOFEE is that it is capable of representing dataflow, controlflow, concurrency, structure, and object orientation characteristics, and the correct construction for the current OOD context must be used. For example, some of the constructs of Figure 4 are only appropriate at the greatest "level" of decomposition of nodes, yet may be helpful to express runtime behaviour between objects at a "higher" level.

A little note to guide you as you read ahead. If you are interested in the TERSE RTOS, then it is appropriate to read Chapter 5. If the RTOS is low on your list of concerns, you may prefer to skim quickly through and focus on Chapter 6, which introduces implementation issues for GOOFEE. Beyond Chapter 6, if you find the material becoming too esoteric, you may find it most appropriate to jump ahead to Chapter 10. I wrote Chapter 10 as a pragmatic guide for developers using simple tools such as C and assembly, and it should equip you with enough understanding to "get going" using GOOFEE on your own project. However, do study Chapter 6 before Chapter 10.

We don't slog all the way through a book in one go anyway; we revisit the book as we need specific questions answered.

5

TERSE

Preamble

I have developed an operating system for distributed microcontroller systems, named *TERSE* (Tiny Embedded Real-time Software Environment). The operating system provides underlying support for a dataflow/controlflow system, by delivering messages between nodes and by scheduling execution of nodes. It must be emphasised that the focus has been on *microcontrollers* with limited RAM and ROM, and that scheduling issues examined in this chapter relate only to scheduling of execution, not creation, destruction, or relocation of nodes, nor memory management of any kind. TERSE to-date does not preempt nodes, allowing switches between threads of execution only after a node exits; however, I do have a time-sliced multiple-virtual-machine version, that is designed to carefully constrain preemption between independent diagrams. Also, the network is interrupt-driven, for handling remote messages and allowing urgent messages to override current execution.

Static versus dynamic scheduling

Basically, cooperative scheduling can be placed into two groups: *static* or *dynamic*. The former implies that scheduling is fixed at compile-time, and the latter implies run-time variation.

Static scheduling is to be found in various specialised application areas, such as digital signal processing, that are not *reactive*.

Dynamic scheduling in the context of TERSE is concerned only with choosing which static node to fire next (the word "static" in this context means the node is permanent, i.e., always exists), based upon meeting certain criteria determined partly at runtime. A static-scheduling system will choose a next-node based purely on which node has just finished; however, a reactive system is concerned with events in the external world and may have alternative next-nodes, based upon the interaction with those external conditions.

"Dataflow" implies that wires carry data between nodes, and a *synchronous* dataflow system is sometimes thought to mean that all output dataflow wires will produce tokens, or messages, when a node exits, and there must be conjunction of input, meaning all input wires to a node must have messages before it can fire. "Controlflow" nodes and wires are thought of as a mechanism to override the strictly synchronous behaviour.

GOOFEE/TERSE relationship

This chapter develops my solution to optimal flow-based scheduling for an embedded reactive distributed microcontroller system; however, TERSE cannot be considered in isolation to understand the rationale presented here. I have also developed a discipline, or rules, for construction/design of well-behaved systems, and this has resulted in a dataflow/controlflow notation called *GOOFEE* and basic rules for constructing GOOFEE diagrams — which is, of course, what the book has been about so far.

Notifications are asynchronous wires that carry messages that can queue n-deep and do not take part in TERSE's scheduling. *Normal* synchronous messages are those that can only queue one-deep and do take part in the execution—scheduling.

Therefore, a partial specification of the scheduling problem for TERSE is that a node is eligible to fire when all of its Normal inputs have arrived, and when a node exits, it produces messages on all output wires (on that *ring* — see the *Iterative*-node in Chapter 2, Figure 15).

TERSE has nothing at all to do with *I/O* wires, as these are connected directly with code inside nodes.

Eligibility to execute may be established, but choice of next node to fire in a reactive system may require knowledge of past history of execution of the program and on priorities of external inputs. A scheduler that can automatically decide on an optimal choice at runtime, amongst a set of eligible nodes, is the topic of this chapter.

The term *Signature Scheduling* has been coined to describe the unique scheduler I developed, that goes beyond anything else that I have been able to locate in published form.

In this chapter, I will wander through a bit of background thinking, as you might find it useful, and it may suggest further avenues of research.

Scheduling based on execution trajectory

In the first quarter of 1995, I worked on the idea that the decision of which node to fire next could be influenced by knowing where execution has been, and the idea developed to feed each node number, as it executes, to an accumulative "signature generator", like a CRC code, that gives a number unique to each past history or trajectory.

Based upon this signature, a table could then provide a list of candidate-nodes for firing, and these could be scanned for eligibility (all inputs arrived) and a choice made, with perhaps a reference to a priority table.

Figure 28: Flow diagram, showing contention.

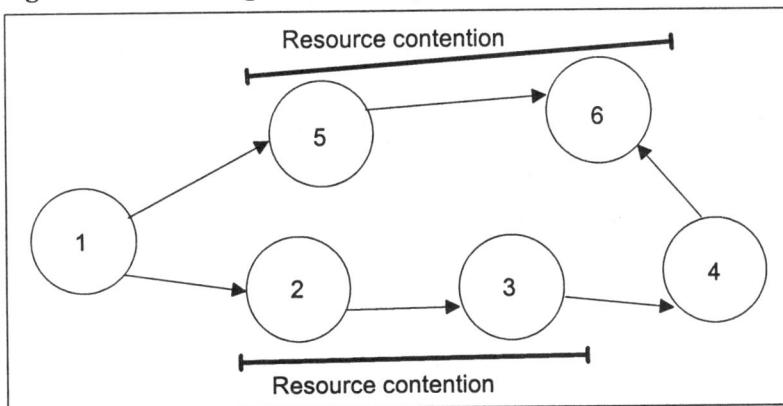

The first version of TERSE used this principle.

The problem illustrated in Figure 28 is that when execution is in the region of nodes 2 to 3, it is not allowed to be in the region of nodes 5 and 6. Furthermore, a deadlock situation is shown, because if execution goes through 1, 5, the system is stuck, because node 6 cannot execute.

	Relevant to TERSE v1.0 only

Table 2: Signature Scheduling table.

Trajectory	Potential next nodes															
	16	15	14	13	12	11	10	9	8	7	6	5	4	3	2	1
0 (start)																✓
1>														✓		
1>2>													✓			
1>2>3>											✓	✓				
1>2>3>4>											✓					
1>2>3>5>												✓				
1>2>3>4>5>								✓								
1>2>3>5>4>								✓								
1>2>3>4>5>6>																✓
1>2>3>5>4>6>																✓

`<----------------------------- ROM ---------------------------------->`

A Signature table is shown in Table 2 in which each row represents a particular signature. For clarity, the actual signatures are not shown here. Instead, the trajectory is shown symbolically, such as >1>2>3>5> to mean that the trajectory went via nodes 1, 2, 3, then 5 (and 5 has just finished).

The row of the table shows ticks for all nodes that are potential candidates for next firing; thus, choice of which nodes to scan for next execution is determined by execution history.

It is easy to fill this table in manually, directly from the diagram, or it can be done by automated means. As the user fills in the ticks, any blank row means that the diagram cannot complete. If there is at least one tick in each row, the diagram is guaranteed to complete under all circumstances. Consider a wrong choice — you make a row with signature >1> and put in ticks under nodes 2 and 5. Then, you insert a row for >1>5> but find that after exiting from node 5, nothing is eligible to fire, so the row remains blank. You would then go back and delete that row and the tick that led to it. Very simple.

Notice the row with signature >1>2>3> — it has two ticks, meaning that nodes 4 and 5 are potential candidates for firing. It is easy to assign a priority to the order in which TERSE scans these nodes by ordering them in the table such that the higher-priority node is indexed earlier in the table — or there could be a separate priority table.

Table 3: Diagram table.

Relevant to TERSE v1.0 only

Source		Destination		Input message			Token
PU	Node	PU	Node	Config.	Pointer	Size	
1	1	1	2				
1	2	1	3				✓
1	3	1	4				
1	3	1	5				
1	1	1	5				✓
1	4	1	6				
1	5	1	6				

<------------------------ ROM ------------------------>   RAM

Message passing

A table is required (with this first design) to identify starting and ending nodes of each arc, including those with source/destination that are remote, the type of arc, and a token indicator. TERSE version 1.0 refers to this as the Diagram table, and it is illustrated in Table 3.

Basically, TERSE version 1.0 uses the Diagram table, along with another table called the Node table, to quickly look at the wires coming into the node currently being scanned, and check for suitability for firing. Note that the actual data associated with each message is not in the Diagram table, as it is in ROM, but it is pointed to by the "pointer" and "size" fields. A penalty is that even if the data is one bit, it requires this overhead. The configuration field specifies whether the arc is discrete/continuous, and asynchronous/synchronous and its addressing mode (byte/bit/indirect).

Table 4: Node table.

	Destination node					
	1	2	3	4	5	6
arcptr	0/0	0/1	1/1	2/1	3/2	5/2
asyncptr						
syncptr						

Relevant to TERSE v1.0 only

<------------------------------- ROM ------------------------------->

In the Node table, note that "arcptr" entries are in the form index/size, where index specifies an entry in the Diagram table, and size specifies how many entries are in the Diagram table. Index/size points to all wires coming to the node indexed in Node-table. Index/sixe = 0/0 means no wires come to this node. Index/size is 5/3 bits, so the maximum is 16 nodes, 8 wires/node. "asyncptr" & "syncptr" point to the code for each node. This table is only for local nodes.

Table 5: Remote Node table.

	Remote destinations
	Index/size
remoteptr	0/0

Relevant to TERSE v1.0 only

<------- ROM -------->

Note that the Remote Node table is an add-on to the Node table and indexes the group of wires with remote destinations in the the Diagram table.

Please do note that Tables 2—5 are placed here as an outline of the origins of TERSE, and the description is not complete. Unless you want to conduct research into the above technique, do not bother with detailed understanding of these tables. Move ahead to my later work ...

Signature explosion

The historical sequence is that the above notes describe the absolute-trajectory signature technique, which was used in TERSE version 1.0. The chronological sequence is that I then conducted an analysis of signature explosion and the means of reducing it, and that work is presented below. Some awkward problems associated with timely response to external messages remained unresolved at this stage, until early in 1996, with *MESS* scheduling presented later in this chapter.

This chapter is written to show the historical progression, and the early analysis of signature explosion is presented in this section.

As can be seen in Figure 29, TERSE51 (for the 8051) version 1.0 has a problem with simultaneous parallel threads. Nodes without any dependencies, as in Figure 29(b), are not a problem, because the Signature Scheduler would normally treat each one as a new signature when it is launched; i.e., these nodes are really independent diagrams. The problem arises when the parallel nodes must all complete, to complete the cycle, as in Figure 29(c). For this case, the absolute signature, that is, a signature that tracks execution from start to finish of the cycle, has $2n!$ options, where n is due to the parallel nodes, and 2 arises at the conjunction.

Figure 29: Number of worst-case absolute trajectories for various node configurations.

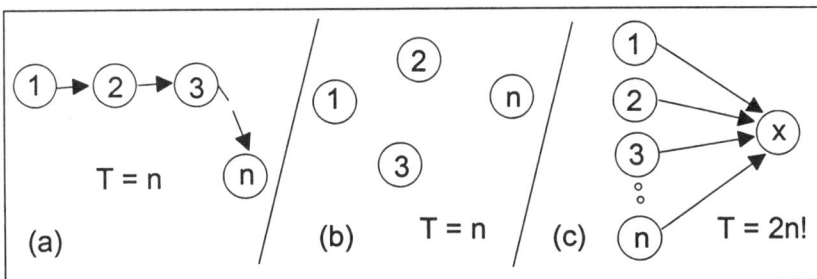

For example, if $n = 4$, then $T = 48$. That is, the Signature table requires 48 signatures. If the diagram has just the 5 nodes, the size of the table will be 96 bytes (TERSE v1.0).

Short-term memory (partial history trajectory)

One possible solution to this is for the trajectory to have "short-term memory", such as only remembering the most recent nodes. Consider that the signature calculation is based upon the last two nodes only (refer to Figure 29(c)). If the signature is >2⅋3>, for example, it may or may not mean that node x is ready to fire. The scheduler does not know if any of the other nodes have already fired, so for example, if node 1 has already fired, the scheduler may scan it again, and fire it, because there are no input dependencies to stop it.

There are two caveats here. The scheduler will have to scan node x after exiting any of the nodes 1 to n, and the diagram needs to have *one* starting node to supply tokens to the nodes 1 to n.

Figure 30: Number of trajectories, with memory of two nodes.

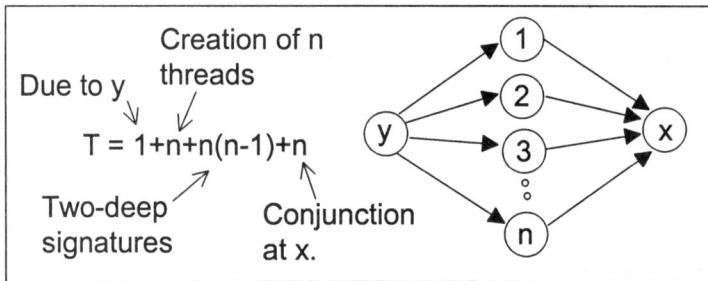

The expression in Figure 30 simplifies to $T = n^2+n+1$. Applying this to $n = 4$: $T = 21$. Thus, the Signature table, with 6 nodes, will only be 42 bytes in size.

There is also a third caveat with a two-deep signature, being that the optimum nodes to scan may have some relation with execution further back in the diagram.

Constrained full-history trajectory

Is an absolute trajectory really necessary? One usefulness is that it proves *reachability* of all nodes for the cycle to complete. If it is desired to retain absolute trajectories, a question that then arises is, is it possible to somehow constrain the *2n!* explosion of trajectories shown in Figure 29(c)?

In practice, a "constrained" Signature table is easy to implement. The rule to follow is to always minimise the number of potential next-nodes to be scanned to one entry, or at most, two entries.

Figure 31: Constrained Signature table with absolute trajectories, to reduce number of signatures.

SIGNATURE	1	2	3	...	n	x
>	*					
>1>		*				
>1>2>			*			
>1>2>3>				*		
...						
>1>2>3>...>n-1>					*	
>1>2>3>...>n-1>n>						*

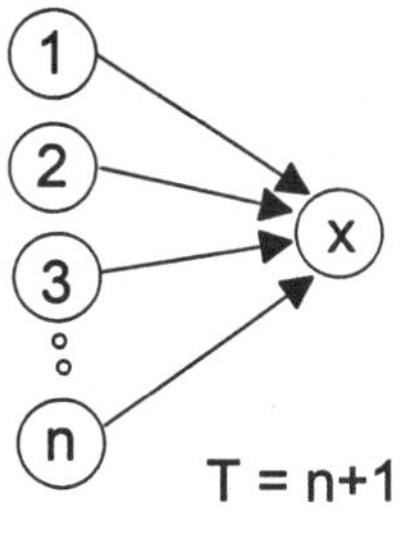

For the case of n = 4, T becomes 5. A positive aspect of reducing the scanning options is that scanning of a node is a time overhead. Also, in the particular case of Figure 31, the nodes have no input dependencies, so there is really no point to scanning them — in practice, there may be parallel threads with different dependencies, however.

The conclusion from this analysis is that absolute trajectories, as employed in TERSE 1.0, can produce a compact Signature table, although some attention has to be given to minimising the scanning options.

Signature generation

Various versions of TERSE have employed 8- or 16-bit Signature (CRC) codes, and it is necessary to analyse what size is required. Also, a fast algorithm is required. TERSE v1.0 used an 8-bit code.

A fast parallel algorithm

The algorithm itself is based upon a description given by T. Rajashekhara with further theory by J. Chan:

Rajashekhara, T.N. (1990) Signature Analysers in Built-In Self-Test Circuits: A Perspective. *Proceedings of the 1990 IEEE Southern Tier Technical Conference*. P. 275—281. New York.

Chan, J.C. (1990) An Algorithm of Diagnostics with Signature Analyser. *IEEE Transactions on Instrumentation and Measurement*. Vol. 39, No. 6, Dec.

This is best illustrated by a code extract (8051 code, see Appendix A):

```
calcsig:
;entered with r1=msg-header, r2=accumulated signature
; (starts =0)
  mov   a,r2
  jnb   acc.7,sig1  ;jump if bit a.7 is clear.
  xrl   a,#00100001b   ;exclusive-or, tapping points.
sig1:
  xrl   a,r1          ;exclusive-or.
  rl    a             ;rotate left one bit.
  mov   r2,a
  ajmp  loop3         ;out.
```

This code fragment accumulates a signature, with r1 bringing the next byte and r2 holding the accumulated signature. The tapping points are chosen in accordance with the desired encryption polynomial.

The code has been developed by me from the *Multiple Input Signature Register* (MISR) technique, which is described in the above references. This technique has significant speed and code advantages over other serial and table algorithms, including the serial algorithm used in the first version of TERSE51.

It is extremely interesting to note that it is a myth that a table-lookup method is faster than a direct calculation based on MISR. Also, the table lookup requires a very large table related to how parallel the calculation is to be, that is unrealistic for a microcontroller system.

The MISR technique applied to a 16-bit signature is listed below:

```
calcsig:
;entered with r1=msg-header, r7:r2=accumulated
; signature (starts =0)
  mov   a,r2
  mov   b,r7
  jnb   b.7,sig1      ;jump if bit b.7 is clear.
  xrl   a,#00010001b  ;tapping points.
  xrl   b,#01000100b  ;   /
sig1:
  xrl   a,r1          ;exclusive-or, result into a.
  clr   c             ;clear carry flag.
  rlc   a             ;rotate left through carry.
  mov   r2,a
```

```
mov    a,b
rlc    a                  ;rotate left through carry.
mov    r7,a
ajmp   main3   ;ret
```

An 8051 instruction can take either 12 or 24 clock cycles, and an instruction cycle is taken to equate to 12 clock cycles. Therefore, the above code, which includes loading from and saving to a variable that records the signature, is 14 instruction cycles.

Actually, this is really a 15-bit signature, as on output, bit 0 of "r2" is always clear.

The 8051 code should be easy to read, but of course asking an 8-bit processor to do 16-bit calculations results in long-winded code. So here is the same thing written for the Intel x86:

```
calcsig:
;entered with di pointing to 16-bit message-header,
;and dx=accumulated signature (starts =0).
       test dh,80h            ;test most significant bit.
       jz   calc1             ;jump if bit15 clear.
       xor  dx,0010010000010001b ;tapping points.
calc1: xor  dx,[di]           ;excl-or msg-header with dx.
       shl  dx,1              ;shift left 1 bit.
;ret ;note that lsb=0, sig. is 15 bits, bits 1--15.
```

Scheduling error

Errors associated with signatures are analysed in:

Frohwerk, R.A. (1977) Signature Analysis: A New Digital Field Service Method. *Hewlett-Packard Journal*. May. Palo Alto: Hewlett Packard.

Basically, there may be a probability of two or more different bit streams generating the same signature. In the case of TERSE, this will result in an incorrect node being fired. The formula developed by Frohwerk is:

$$\text{Probability of a clash, } P = \frac{2^{(m-n)} - 1}{2^{m} - 1}$$

where m = length of bit stream, and n = length of signature.

For example, for m = 160, n = 8, then P = 0.0039

That is, this is the statistical probability of two different bit streams producing the same signature.

What is of particular interest is that as m increases, the formula approximates to:

$$\text{Probability of a clash, } P = \frac{1}{2^n}$$

That is, the probability is independent of the length of the bit stream. For an 8-bit code, P = 1/256, which means that if a signature-scheduled system has 256 signatures, statistically there will be one clash.

For a system using the absolute-trajectory method of calculating a signature, it should be possible to examine all possible trajectories manually, to determine if a clash occurs, then modify a node number; however, this avoidance can only be done for number of signatures well below 256. As the number of signatures approaches 256, it will become increasingly difficult to manually find clear paths for all trajectories.

The next convenient step-up is a 16-bit signature with P = 1/65536, which is satisfactory for systems with a very large number of nodes.

The next scheduling technique developed and employed on the most recent TERSE is based upon calculating the signature from the current set of messages awaiting delivery, not upon trajectory. This technique uses the header of each message packet as the byte to feed into the accumulative signature calculator, and they are fed in the order in which they are waiting in the buffer. Thus, the signature is dependent upon the current "state", being the set of waiting messages, and the "partial history", being the ordering.

It is possible to manually examine all signatures, to determine if two or more different messages/permutations will produce the same signature; however, in the case of distributed systems, if remote input messages join the queue, they will do so at any time (unless constrained somehow), potentially raising the probability of a signature clash up to the statistical figure.

Jumping ahead, the second verion of TERSE had a 16-bit signature. It employed the "waiting set" technique of signature generation, with remote input messages being delivered directly into the message buffer.

Third and later versions of the 8051 TERSE went back to an 8-bit signature, because remote input messages were no longer fed into the message queue and no longer were directly involved in the signature calculation. However, for the x86, I chose a 15-bit signature. Also, in all verions of TERSE written for the 8051 microcontroller, the maximum number of nodes allowed was 32 (this being developed as a coarse-grain dataflow/controlflow system).

A serious problem is signature = zero. TERSE calculates a signature of zero when there are *no* messages on the stack, and it is vital that no other sequence should produce zero.

TERSE51 (for the 8051) uses byte-serial generation of the signatures, and each byte is the header of the messages on the stack (version 2.0 onwards). This header consists of the destination node number and the destination terminal number. The terminals are numbered 1—4, but stored in the header as 0—3. TERSE51 allows nodes 0—31.

An examination of the signature algorithm reveals that a value of zero can *only* appear in the shift register when an input sequence of all zero bits greater-than or equal-to the length of the shift register is fed in.

This never happens; therefore, there will never be a signature of zero generated.

Thus, it can be guaranteed that a signature of zero is generated under one input condition only, ensuring that the diagram will start, or restart, only when no messages are active.

"Waiting set" signature generation technique on 8051

Signature errors

With a finite-length signature, it is obvious that two or more different bit streams could generate the same signature. It is obvious that two different message-sets, or in other words, when the diagram is in two different stages of execution, that the same signature must not be generated, otherwise there will only be the one entry in the lookup table, and only the one next-node to execute.

From the above notes, if a TERSE application has a lookup table with 256 entries, that is, the diagram has 256 possible "states", then the probability of one signature clash is one.

Because TERSE51 has a maximum of 32 nodes, 31 if the error handler is ignored, it will have *at least* 31 states. It is very important to note that TERSE computes the signature from the current set of messages, which represents the current state, but they are order dependent, so a TERSE "state" is dependent on execution history.

The theoretical worst case would be a diagram of one starting node feeding 30 output wires to 30 nodes, i.e., 30 concurrent paths. The possible number of "states" (signatures) generated is $30! = 2.6525^{\wedge}32$.

In practice, this does not happen. Normally, node 1 would post the 30 messages in a fixed time order on the stack, thus generating only *one* signature. The only reason that node 1 would post the messages in different time orders is to have runtime control over which of the 30 nodes will fire next — in that case, it is only necessary to generate 30 different posting orders, and thus 30 different signatures.

Thus, what seems like a worst case only requires 30 signatures.

A totally serial diagram, without any parallel threads, would also have 30 signatures.

The possibility of needing more than 30 signatures may only arise for a diagram that is somewhere "in between", being a combination of serial and parallel paths. Consider five parallel paths, each with 6 serial nodes.

I have not been able to derive a mathematical formula for a realistic maximum number of signatures, as any design has constraints. I have resorted to analysing various typical diagrams, and think that a worst-case estimate of number of signatures = 2 * number of wires is "reasonable".

Therefore, a worst case "practical" diagram will have 60 signatures.

With 256 signatures, a clash has a probability of one of occurring. When the designer develops the Signature Scheduling table, such clashes become obvious and can be avoided. Avoidance is achieved by making a small change to one of the offending messages, such as changing its destination terminal, or by introduction of a dummy message.

Unfortunately, if all 256 signatures are already in use, there is "no room to play".

Therefore, the actual number of signatures must be some fraction of 256. Sixty signatures leaves 196 signatures free, and the probalilty of a signature clash is reduced to 60/256 = 0.23.

Thus, the designer needs to be aware of the 23% chance of one signature clash as the TERSE51 diagram reaches its maximum number of nodes. The designer may need to use one of the above avoidance methods, and there is a 23% chance of the alternative signature causing another clash, which is reasonable.

A probability of chaos

A problem that emerges from this analysis, however, is that of the error-handler. If any node has a "bug", or some other unforseen circumstance arises at runtime, and if an unpredicted message pattern is produced, TERSE will not be able to find the signature in the lookup table — at least, that is the required behaviour.

The requirement is that such false signatures should cause TERSE to call node 0, the error-handler.

Unfortunately, for a maximal diagram (TERSE51, 8051 version), there is a 23% probability that a false message permutation will produce a genuine signature. The result will be chaos.

Therefore, for mission-critical situations, this error-handling mechanism cannot be relied upon, and there must be other methods for detecting errors. If a node *knows* at runtime that an unrecoverable error has occurred, it can post a certain message that can vector to the error-handler via the lookup table. Having a 77% probability that an *unpredicted* error will be detected, is quite good, but not the 23% chance of it causing a pseudo-random response from the program.

It can be argued of course, that if an unpredicted error is not detected, there will be chaos anyway, so the 8-bit signature is deemed "good enough" for a range of applications.

However, for "mission-critical" applications, it is recommended that TERSE51 use a signature length far in excess of 8 bits. A 16-bit signature allows 65,536 signatures, and for 60 signatures in a maximal 8051 system, the probability of one signature clash is 60/65,536 = 0.000915, or 0.091%.

Thus, if the system experiences an unpredicted error, there is a 99.909% chance that it will be detected.

Unpredicted means that the designers did not think of it, nor has any code been designed to recover from it. Detection does, however, require that a node exit, in order for TERSE to discover the faulty condition. Detection is based upon the premise that the node has gone into an unpredicted condition and has not output messages in the correct order, or incompletely.

It would be a very interesting line of research to consider how to structure code inside a node, such that if anything unexpected happens, unknown to the program itself and unpredicted by the programmer, the node *will* exit, but in such a way that the message output is *altered*.

Practical notes

Perhaps the above analysis is a bit too myopic if you are reading this book for the first time to discover what GOOFEE is all about. An awareness of the issues of Signature Scheduling is required, however, as you get into actual projects. A concern that someone expressed to me is that he didn't want to use TERSE in case he forgot to put a signature into the lookup table.

That is, you are supposed to go through each stage of execution, and at each "state", when execution is between nodes, look at the current set of messages and compute the signature. But what if you forget about one message or get them in the wrong order? Then the table will be wrong, and when those states are reached, execution will automatically go to the error-handler.

Thus, the designer's oversight is automatically handled, and a generic error-handler can examine current system status and respond accordingly. The person's concern is not valid, quite the reverse.

Also, the above analysis is a worst case, and in Chapter 9 you will see that I have produced an extremely compact Signature table for a very complex elevator control system. The reason for this is that most of the sequence is serial in nature, even though it is a highly concurrent application. It tends to work out in most cases that you don't have lots of messages waiting in the buffer — only one to three, which is very easy to mentally keep track of.

Global synchronisation and signature explosion

As TERSE51 version 2.0 calculates the signature from the "active set" of messages, a message from another PU poses a problem. If the remote message arrives asynchronously, that is, at any time, then the required number of entries in the lookup table *doubles*. Two remote input wires will *quadruple* the table!

Figure 32: A distributed system in early GOOFEE notation.

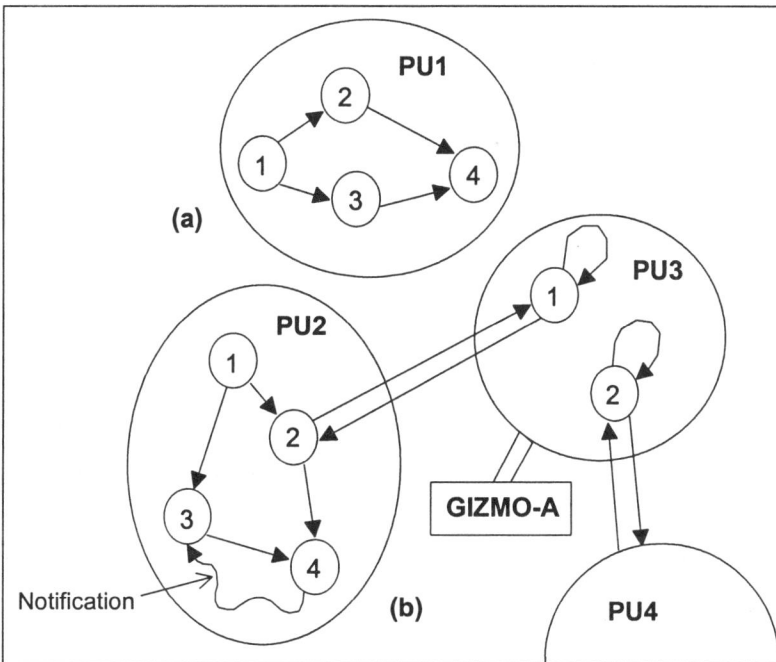

In one sense, this is very good, as there is a measure of "global time". That is, the exact arrival time of the remote message, relative to the current state of the local PU (Processor Unit), forms a unique signature. Thus, there is some measure of the state of execution of the local PU, relative to the state of execution of the remote PU.

The specific issue to be tackled here, however, is the problem of signature explosion. It may be that a remote message is to be responded to at a particular state of a local diagram's execution, so only one or two entries are required in the table, specifically for the remote message.

For example, in Figure 32, only after PU2/node 1 has posted a message to PU2/node 2, is node 2 in a position to fire, even though it may have received a remote message earlier. "Earlier" signatures will include the remote message, if it has arrived, but these signatures will reference the same next-node in the lookup table, as would the signature calculated without the remote message.

Solution #1

The remote message could be a *Notification* (asynchronous wire).

Therefore, the remote message will not have any input to the calculated signature. This will mean that nodes will fire due to local dependencies only, and it will be up the code inside a node to detect the Notification.

If the Notification has arrived, the node can continue as normal. If the Notification has not arrived, the node will have to post a "loop-back" wire that will cause the node to re-enter until the Notification arrives.

Solution #2

Limit the asynchronicity of the remote message.

That is, ensure that the local diagram will be in a state where it is already waiting for the remote message when it arrives. If the local diagram is not "ready", it is an error condition. Or perhaps the remote message can be delayed somehow.

This is a very interesting design constraint — the "downstream" diagram must always be in a certain state when the remote message arrives.

Solution #3

Spurious signatures can be allowed to fire the error-handler.

The error-handler will examine the messages in the buffer and determine if a remote message is present. If so, it has various options.

One option is to post the remote message off onto the network and return to normal TERSE operation. The remote message will be addressed to this local PU, so it will come back and be in the active set of messages again.

The technique of posting the remote message off around the network is simple and requires little additional code for TERSE. However, it does impose a network time overhead.

Solution #4

Automatically delay the remote message.

Version 2.0 of TERSE51, when it receives a remote input message, strips off the destination PU byte and places the header byte and data byte in the buffer. The header byte is thus used for the next signature calculation.

A modification is that the destination PU byte is not removed but is also placed on the stack. When TERSE is calculating the signature, if it finds a remote message that is addressed to this current PU, it will use that message in the signature calculation. Note that the normal behaviour of version 2.0 of TERSE is to ignore remote messages when calculating signatures, because remote messages are always addressed to another PU.

If TERSE calculates the signature, including the remote message addressed to this PU, and cannot find it in the lookup table, TERSE will simply recalculate the signature without the remote message.

Except, how are multiple remote input messages handled?

If the signature is not found on the first attempt, TERSE will need to recalculate the signature for each combination of remote signatures.

Solution #5

Reduce the eligible set.

When a remote message has arrived, TERSE could calculate the signature based purely upon messages with destinations to the same node as that of the remote input message.

If two or more remote messages have arrived, then the eligible set would widen accordingly.

This solution is not entirely satisfactory, because it is giving away some of the runtime control over scheduling.

Solution #6

Solutions 1—5 have various problems and are not gone into in any further detail; although at the time, they were subjected to considerable analysis. By far the most flexible technique for minimising signature explosion, while responding appropriatcly to all remote input messages, is by the *Modified by External Synchronous Set* (MESS) technique I developed, which scans for arrival of external messages.

MESS scheduling

There was a "lot of water under the bridge" before this technique was developed, and earlier techniques will not be further described as they are unsatisfactory, at least for distributed systems, and are distractions at this stage of development. TERSE51 version 3.0 implements MESS scheduling.

Figure 33: Scheduling problem of an external Normal input.

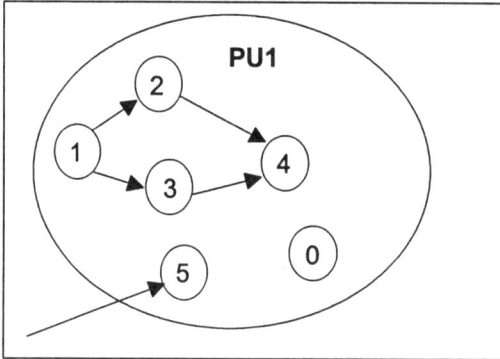

In Figure 33, if the remote message arrives at node 5, it is eligible to fire. Therefore, catering to this asynchronous behaviour will double the size of the Signature table (if the incoming message takes part in the signature calculation). The table could be reduced by constraining node 5 to only execute when the local diagram has reached a certain "state"; however, when the remote message arrives in the message buffer, a signature will be generated that may not exist in the lookup table, which will cause a fall-through to node 0, the error-handler.

Solutions 1—5 above tackled this and similar problems.

Solution 6 is to calculate the signature ONLY from the local messages, thus avoiding signature explosion and signature clashes.

Two major problem areas, when dealing with external Normal (synchronous) input messages, are illustrated in Figure 33, in which node 5 fires asynchronously to the rest of the diagram *or* has some dependency, as shown in Figure 34.

Figure 34: Node with remote Normal input has local dependency.

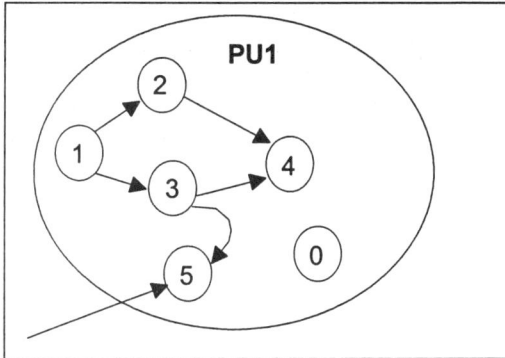

That is, node 5 cannot execute until BOTH input messages have arrived.

Figure 35: Exacerbated scheduling situation.

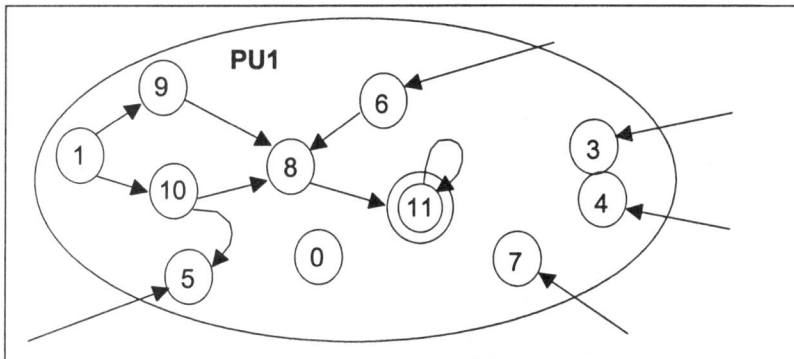

Figure 35 shows a diagram in which node 5 cannot fire until both local and remote input messages have arrived. Nodes 3, 4, and 7 have no local dependencies, so should fire as soon as their remote input Normal messages have arrived, although nodes 3 and 4 require non-concurrency (which would only be an issue if the OS supported time slicing between nodes, or if these nodes are Composite- or Super-nodes, that decompose to an underlying diagram). The same goes for node 6, that is, it should fire immediately upon arrival of its remote input message, but it produces a local output message to node 8, so node 8 cannot fire until all three local inputs have arrived.

The *Modified by External Synchronous Set* (MESS) technique handles all of these execution scheduling requirements.

MESS scheduling on the 8051

The technique is described here as actually implemented on the 8051. The following table is in ROM:

```
;TERSE51 version 3.0, MESS scheduling table.
WAIT          EQU 80h
signatures: DB 255, 0,136, 22, 152, 77         ;****
nodenum:    DB 0,   1,  2,  3,  4,   WAIT+126 ;*
extmsg:     DB 0,   0,  0,  0,  0,   02       ;**
numentries  EQU nodenum-signatures
nodeptr:                    ;these occupy 2 bytes each....
     ajmp node0         ;***
     ajmp node1              ;this must be in
     ajmp node2              ;ascending order
     ajmp node3              ;of node number.
     ajmp node4


*    last entry has a wait timeout.
**    flags alternative nodes,if ext.msg
*** 1st node in table is error-handler(always node-0)
**** starting node has signature=zero.
```

After a node exits back to TERSE, another signature is calculated from the local Normal (synchronous) messages on the local message queue and the signature lookup table is referenced (signatures) — the destination node is found (nodenum), but the extmsg entry is checked for any alternative nodes that may run if an appropriate external Normal input message has arrived. extmsg has 7 flags, extmsg.1—7, for each destination node 1—7 (as remote i/p messages can only go to nodes 1—7). If this entry is non-zero, it is checked against actual arrivals, extmsgwtg (logical AND), and the lowest numbered node is executed.

IT IS IMPORTANT to realise that if both nodes 1 and 2 are ticked in extmsg entry, and both have arrived, node1 will execute first, thus there is PRIORITY.

If no required remote Normal messages have arrived, execution defaults to the entry in nodenum.

Note that nodenum may contain WAIT, which causes a wait on arrival of an expected external message, but there is a timeout, given in the other bits

0—6 of the `nodenum` entry. A value of zero in these bits means wait indefinitely.

Note that if watchdog is turned off, timeout doesn't work either (i.e., will wait indefinitely).

Figure 36: Flowchart of TERSE.

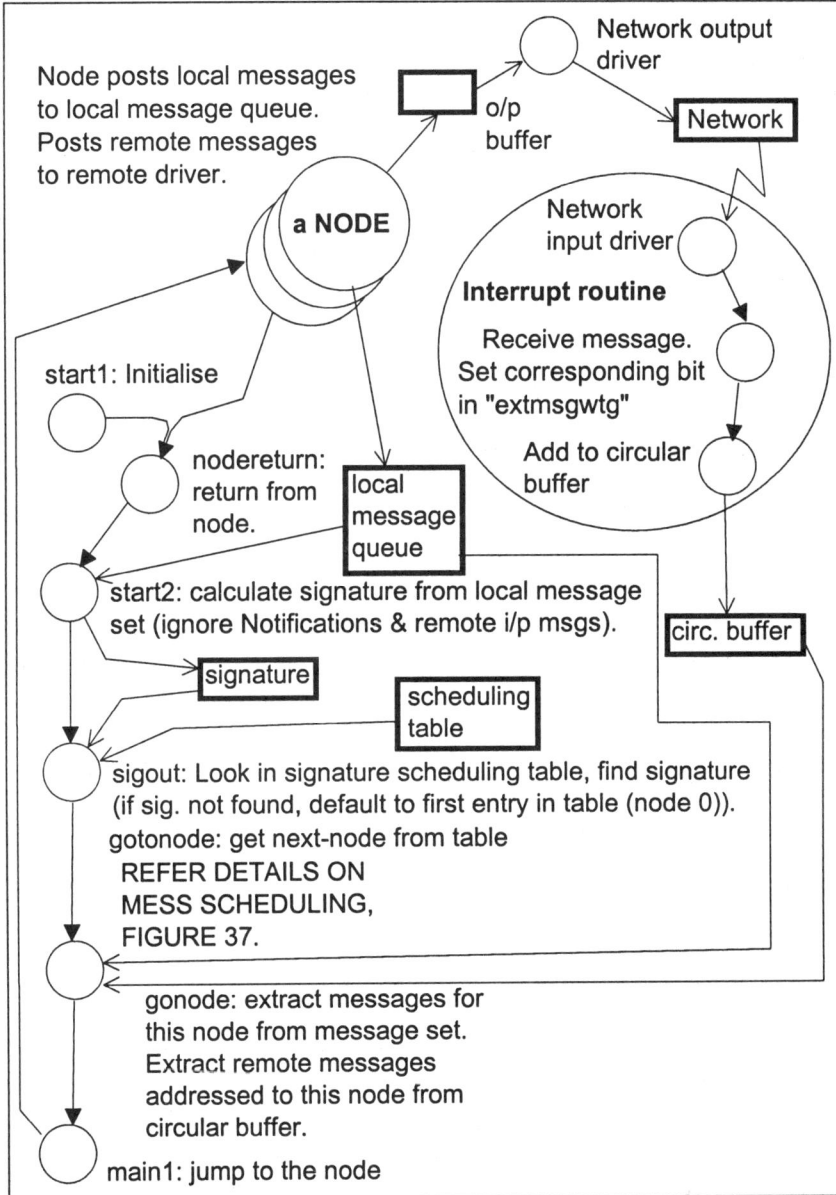

Figure 37: Unstructured flowchart of MESS scheduling.

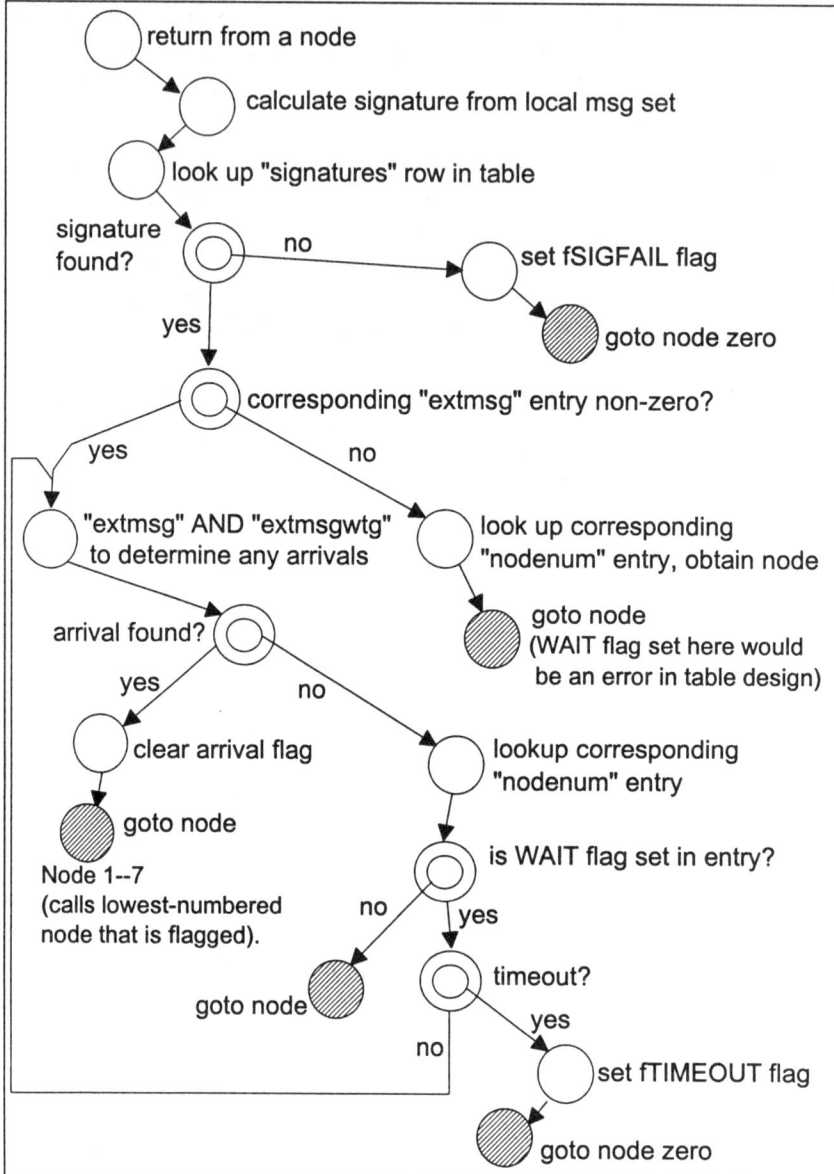

○ return from a node

○ calculate signature from local msg set

○ look up "signatures" row in table

signature found? ◎ — no → ○ set fSIGFAIL flag → ⬤ goto node zero

yes ↓

◎ corresponding "extmsg" entry non-zero?

yes ↙   no ↓

○ "extmsg" AND "extmsgwtg" to determine any arrivals

○ look up corresponding "nodenum" entry, obtain node → ⬤ goto node (WAIT flag set here would be an error in table design)

arrival found? ◎

yes ↙   no ↓

○ clear arrival flag → ⬤ goto node

Node 1--7 (calls lowest-numbered node that is flagged).

○ lookup corresponding "nodenum" entry

◎ is WAIT flag set in entry?

no ↙   yes ↓

⬤ goto node

◎ timeout?

no ↙   yes ↓

○ set fTIMEOUT flag → ⬤ goto node zero

The definition of extmsg

The concept here is very important, because it avoids signature explosion due to remote-input synchronous messages — they do not take part in the signature calculation. The flags of `extmsg` define what nodes are waiting on an external message and otherwise satisfy all input requirements needed to execute (i.e., all local messages, if any, have arrived at the node). A restriction is that only ONE remote Normal wire is allowed to go to each node, and also nodes 1—7 only.

For example, say that node 7 has ONLY ONE input arc, an external Normal message, which means that it satisfies all local scheduling conditions ALWAYS, so bit 7 must be set for EVERY entry in `extmsg`.

Design of MESS scheduling table

Having established a workable modified-signature execution-scheduling technique, it can be illustrated for various examples.

Figure 38: Example of MESS scheduling table.

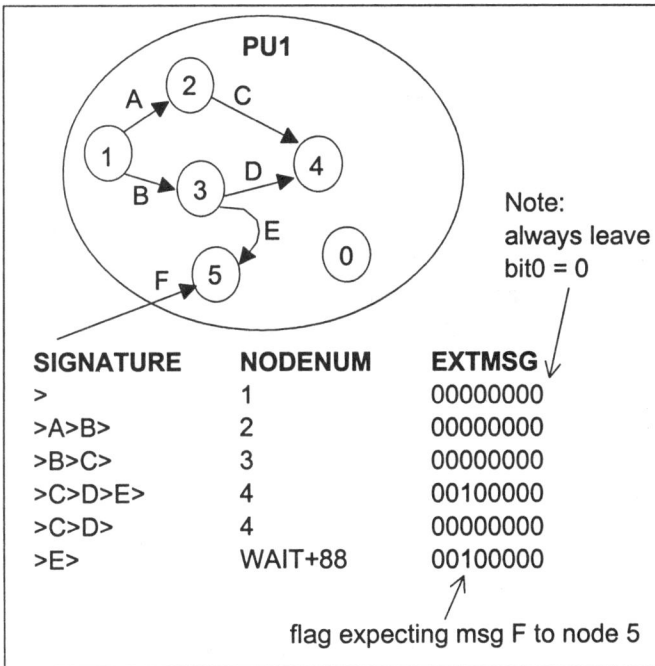

Notice in Figure 38 that execution scheduling is constrained to follow node sequences defined by the table only — thus, it is *bounded runtime scheduling*.

There is also a timeout built into TERSE51 while waiting on F.

Figure 39: Example scheduling independent node.

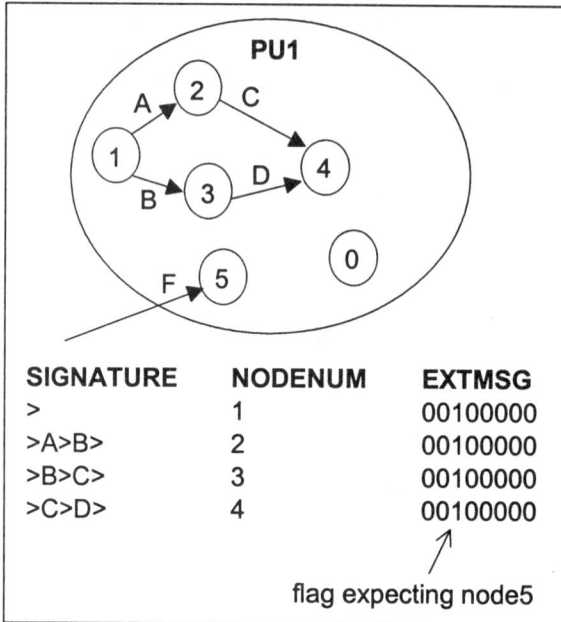

In Figure 39, bit 5 of EXTMSG is set for every entry, which means that TERSE will check for the arrival of F whenever execution is between nodes and fire node 5 if F has arrived. Note that the process of firing node 5 will clear bit 5 in the `extmsgwtg` variable, so the next node to fire after node 5 will be determined by the local `signature/nodenum` entries.

It is possible to constrain the execution of node 5 as required, for whatever reason, simply by clearing bit 5 in any of the EXTMSG entries.

Figure 40 shows that non-trivial scheduling requirements that can be expressed in GOOFEE can also be implemented by the underlying TERSE OS

Don't forget, as stated earlier, that when the WAIT flag is set, bits 0—6 of `nodenum` can also be zero, meaning indefinite wait. Of course, seven bits is not many for a timeout, and time-granularity is limited. It is, however, adequate for a large range of applications. My x86 TERSE uses a 16-bit `nodenum`, which is more flexible.

Figure 40: Exacerbated scheduling problem.

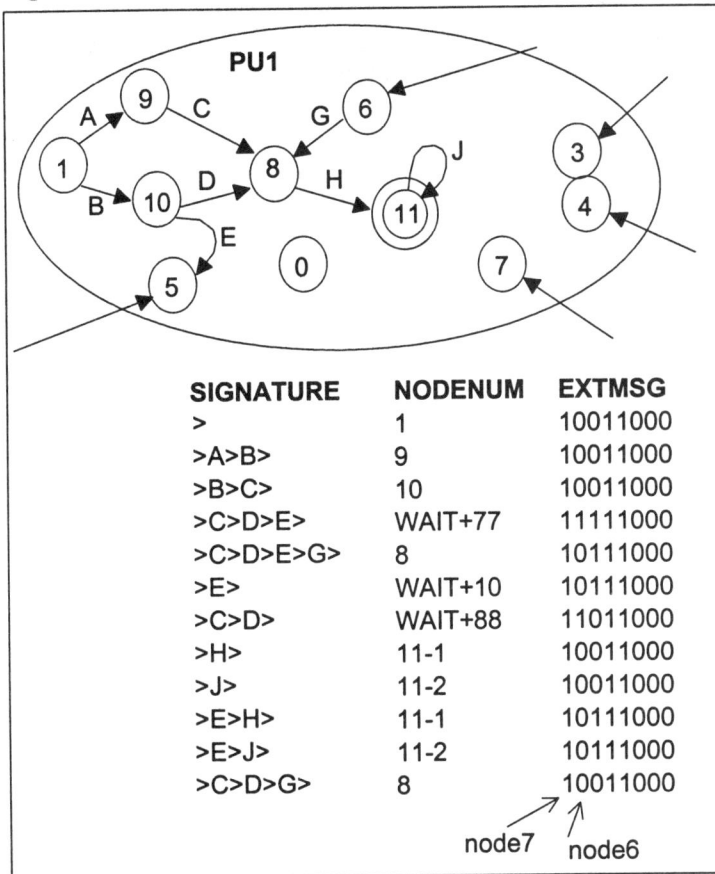

SIGNATURE	NODENUM	EXTMSG
>	1	10011000
>A>B>	9	10011000
>B>C>	10	10011000
>C>D>E>	WAIT+77	11111000
>C>D>E>G>	8	10111000
>E>	WAIT+10	10111000
>C>D>	WAIT+88	11011000
>H>	11-1	10011000
>J>	11-2	10011000
>E>H>	11-1	10111000
>E>J>	11-2	10111000
>C>D>G>	8	10011000

node7   node6

Fast code to test for external arrivals

Imagine the situation with my 16-bit x86 TERSE, in which the `extmsg` entry has 16 flags to be tested. It is vital that this be done as quickly as possible when the OS is executing between nodes. Shifting each bit out one at a time and testing it is incredibly time-consuming, as is performing an AND operation to test each bit.

This is the code from my x86 TERSE:

```
;extmsg entry in lookup table was non-0, so look for
; rem.i/p arrivals...
ext1:
  and  ax,extmsgwtg          ;compare with actual arrivals.
```

```
   jz   wtg1            ;no appropriate ext.msgs arrived.
ext2:
   mov  bx,ax           ;load destnode, clr bit in extmsgwtg.
   neg  ax              ;/ my clever code to extract 1 flag!
   and  ax,bx           ;/  /           ("rightmost" flag)
   ;ax has the bit I need to clr in extmsgwtg...
   xor  extmsgwtg,ax ;/  / exclusive-or.
   xor  bx,bx           ;/ now load destnode.
ext3:
   inc  bx              ;/  / increment
   shr  ax,1            ;/  / shift right one bit.
   jnc  ext3            ;/  / jump if no carry.
   dec  bx              ;/  / decrement.
   mov  destnode,bx  ;/  / destination node.
;Note, flag of lowest-numbered node has highest priority
; always, as the above code extracts the rightmost set
; flag in extmsgwtg.
   jmp  gonode          ;>>> execute the node.


;.......................
wtg1:
;some ext.i/ps are in-scope, but none have arrived...
```

Notice my very clever and fast code to determine the right-most set flag in register ax. Register ax has the in-scope remote inputs that have arrived on entry to ext2:.

What is still tedious, however, is the code at ext3:, in which I need to translate that flag into a destination node number. If anyone can do better than this, please let me know!

For the sake of completeness, here is the code after wtg1::

```
wtg1:                            ;8086 code!!!
;some ext.i/ps are in-scope, but none have arrived...
   xor  bx,bx
   mov  ax,csthispu ;it was in es, but got overwritten.
   mov  es,ax       ;/
   mov  bl,es:NUMENTRIESVAR
   shl  bx,1             ;* 2
   mov  ax,es:[si+bx]        ;get node.
   mov  nodenumsaved,ax      ;save it.
;If WAIT flag in nodenum =0, don't wait for rem.i/ps to
```

```
; arrive...
   test ax,8000h                   ;bit15 set if WX.
   jz    gonode
;.......
wtg2:           ;we have to wait, but bits0--14 of nodenum
                ; are a timeout...
   mov   ax,SEG dataISR
   mov   es,ax
   mov   bl,es:globaltime0     ;snapshot of globaltime.
   mov   bh,es:globaltime1     ;/    (we need this for calc
   mov   WORD PTR localref0,bx ;/        the timeout).
   mov   bx,WORD PTR es:globaltime2 ;/
   mov   WORD PTR localref2,bx ;/
;......
wtg3:      ;calc if we have timed out...
           ;granularity of timeout can be adjusted....
           ;let's use bits 14&13 as granularity field.
   mov   cx,nodenumsaved  ;nodenum entry was saved in this
                          ; variable.
   and   cx,1FFFh     ;mask off bits13-15.(15 is WAIT flag)
                      ;if nodenum timeout ==0, wait forever...
   jz    wtg4
   and   ch,01100000b
   cmp   ch,0
   jne   wtg3b           ;finest granularity ().
   mov   bl,es:globaltime0      ;this one not implemented.<<
   mov   bh,es:globaltime1
   sub   bx,WORD PTR localref0
   jmp   SHORT wtg3e
wtg3b:    cmp ch,00100000b   ;2nd finest gran (1mSec).
   jne wtg3c
   mov   bx,WORD PTR es:globaltime1   ;(timeout range 1mSec
   sub   bx,WORD PTR localref1    ;       − 8191mSec)
   jmp   SHORT wtg3e
wtg3c:    cmp ch,01000000b
   jne wtg3d
  mov   bx,WORD PTR es:globaltime2 ;(256mSec, appr 1/4sec)
   sub   bx,WORD PTR localref2    ;(range 1/4sec -- 2048sec)
   jmp   SHORT wtg3e
wtg3d:
   mov   bl,es:globaltime3 ;coarsest granularity (65.5sec)
   sub   bl,localref3             ;(range appr. 1min -- 256min)
   xor   bh,bh
wtg3e:    cmp   ax,bx
```

```
   jbe   wtg4                  ;check arrival rem.i/p...again.
;waiting on ext.i/p, have timed out...
   mov   fTIMEOUT,TRUE
   jmp   go4              ;re-execute previous node!!!! <<<<
                ;(i.e. don't update destnode)
;<<<< THIS IS DIFFERENT FROM FIGURE 37 IN TEXT <<<<<
;....
wtg4:  ;check if any in-scope rem. i/ps have arrived...
;NOTE again, we deviate slightly from Figure 37 in text
;as have repeated code rather than branching  back...
   mov   ax,extmsgsaved    ;previously saved extmsg entry.
   and   ax,extmsgwtg      ;compare with actual arrivals.
   jz    wtg3          ;no appropriate ext.msgs arrived.
   ;yes, a rem.i/p has arrived!!...
   jmp   ext2             ;translate rem.i/p --> dest.node.
```

Conclusions

TERSE was originally designed for very basic microcontroller hardware, and the scheduler does not preempt nodes (with the virtual machine exception, as already mentioned and elaborated on in Chapter 9). Interrupts can go inside nodes, but the current 8051 software does not allow the interrupt service routine to originate a message at the TERSE messaging level. It is probable that the x86 version supplied on the Companion Disk will support an interrupt routine posting an asynchronous message to the message buffer.

Reiterating the above comment, the non-preemptive nature of TERSE does impose limitations, such as not graciously handling independent tasks (perhaps with their own cycle times), and one solution is to scale-up by treating each task (which will be a diagram with one start and one stop node) as a "virtual processor" or separate machine, by utilising an underlying time-slicing mechanism. The messaging between these virtual processors would be remote messages, which have so far been described as being between physical processors. I have taken this approach with my x86 TERSE, TERSE86, filename TERS8631.ASM.

TERSE51 and TERSE86 were written as a public service and are conditionally freeware. MESS Signature Scheduling has been employed in the latest versions. As various versions get developed, I hope to put them onto my Internet home page at:

`http://scorpion.cowan.edu.au/science/terse/index.html`

You may also find them via the GOOFEE Systems Pty Ltd home page:

`http://www.arrowweb.com/goofee/`

You will also find various versions of TERSE on the Companion Disk.

Don't forget to peruse the Appendices of this book, as I have described various 8051 versions and an x86 version of TERSE. The 8051 versions come in uniprocessor and distributed flavors, while the x86 version is uniprocessor but supporting multiple virtual-processors. Dunfield C has been used with the 8051 TERSE, and Byte small C has been used with the x86 TERSE. Byte small C compiler is provided on the Companion Disk.

At the end of Chapter 10 you will find suggestions for further research and development of TERSE and GOOFEE. Preempting that list, I will mention some work that I am doing right now.

I am building a model elevator control system, using the superb AMD 186 microcontroller (see Appendix E) for the Supervisor processor and Atmel 2051s (see Appendix D) on floors and inside elevators. We are looking at using a star-configuration network, which suits the application and is extremely simple. That is, the Supervisor will be the hub of the star.

I intend to release modified versions of TERSE to support a star network.

Also, I am looking at simplifying TERSE even further by eliminating Signature Scheduling and keeping MESS Scheduling only. For applications with simpler scheduling requirements, this is feasible. It may also be feasible for the elevator application. I have so many good intentions, but it may be awhile before I get around to this latter project — maybe someone can preempt me on this?

6

Implementation

Preamble

The rest of this book focuses on application and develops an elevator control system in depth. This chapter generalises somewhat, by looking at how a GOOFEE diagram can be translated to code without requiring an underlying operating system — it is a somewhat idiosyncratic approach using GOTOs, so take it or leave it.

This chapter then introduces the elevator control system problem and outlines a solution. This is a "first pass" at a solution, and Chapters 7 to 9 examine the elevator system in myopic detail, while Chapter 10 winds up with a pragmatic solution.

This chapter looks at the most basic approach to the translation of GOOFEE diagrams to code, using plain vanilla C, with and without any kind of underlying executive or operating system.

Chapter 1 explained that conventional procedure-based OOP is a subset of the more generic dataflow object model, but if we design GOOFEE diagrams to conform as much as possible to the subset model, as illustrated in Figure 10, it becomes easier to translate the diagram to code without an operating system. Such a constrained diagram is also easier to map to an object-oriented language such as C++, if you wish to use C++ that is.

Skeleton C code for a node

Figure 41 is a basic section of a diagram with two nodes, labelled n001 and n002, which is how my CASE software automatically names nodes. My

CASE software gives each node a unique number, from 1 to 999 (though the maximum number of nodes allowed depends on the version). Double-clicking on a node invokes a user-specified editor and auto-generates a filename of Nxxx.yyy, where xxx = node-number and yyy = extension required for the language of choice.

In addition, a node may also have a 22-character text label, and either number or label may be displayed on the screen.

Figure 41 also shows a resource, and as described in Chapter 4 and illustrated in Figure 27, the resource, `res1`, is only visible to `n001`.

Figure 41: Skeleton C code.

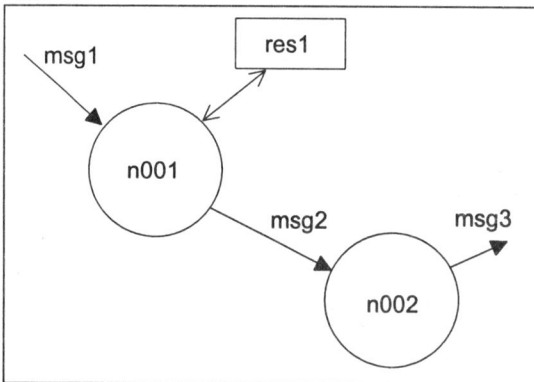

Code for `n001`

```
int msg1;                //input message.
int res1;                //data resource.
n001:
    . . .
    msg2 = msg1;         //pass msg straight thru.
    . . .
goto n002;
```

The above code may seem peculiar. After all, didn't I state back in Chapter 2 (see Figure 17) that "GOTO scheduling is discouraged"?

However, in this case, the structure is already in place, defined by the diagram, and GOTO is a convenient mechanism to implement the transitions between nodes.

Certainly the C program could have a mainline routine that sequentially calls each node, but this way, the decision about which node to execute next is made at the level of the node. This approach may be more appropriate for reactive systems, as long as such local decision making is kept strictly in accordance with the diagram.

`ret` is an arbitrary return value that could return an error or have some input to a choice of which next node to fire.

The function isn't doing anything useful, since this is only a skeleton, but I've put one statement in there to simply pass the value in `msg1` onto `msg2`.

Code for `n002`

```
int msg2;                    //input message.
n002:                        //execution entry point.
    ...
    msg3 = msg2;             //straight thru again.
    ...
goto n003;
```

Coding nodes with inheritance

Now it is getting interesting but still just as easy as the above code.

Figure 42: Coding nodes with inheritance.

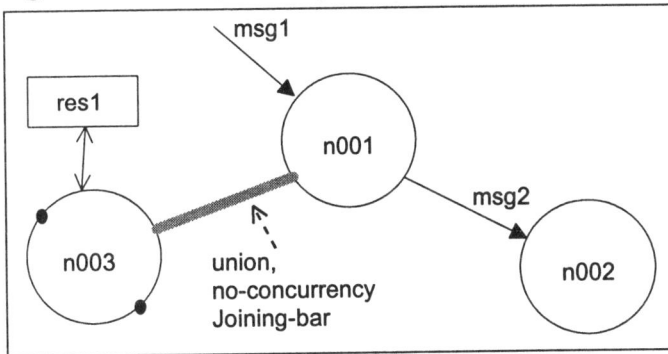

The Joining-bar is of the union, no-concurrency type, meaning that the data and code are common, i.e., only the one instance. But each node linked by Joining-bars has its own terminals. Also, remember that external connections are implied if there is an external wire on one clone but not on the other (further clarification in Chapter 7). Also, the node without *any* external wires (I/O wires not counted) is the class, i.e., is not instantiated.

You can see in Figure 42 that `n003` is the class, and `n001` is the object.

Code for n001

```
int msg1;                   //input messages.
n001:
ret = func003(msg1,&msg2)    //code for the node.
goto n002;
```

Code for n003

```
    int res1;               //static.
int func003(int x, int *y)
{
    int temp1;              //dynamic local data.
    static int var1;        //static local data.
    ....
    *y = x;                 //pass msg through.
    ....
}
```

The difference here is simply that I took the "template" information, or common code and data, into the class-node, n003. Any other nodes hanging off n003 can access the function, and consequently res1, in exactly the same way as n001.

Inheritance with copied data

Figure 43 shows a similar example, except now the Joining-bar is of the common-code, copied-data type (refer to Figure 2). What does "copied data" mean?

Figure 43: Inheritance with copied internal data.

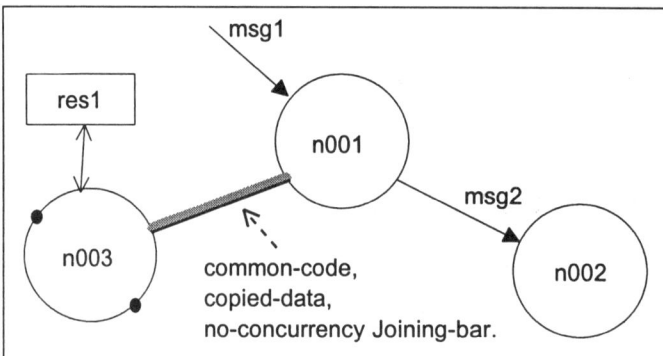

res1 is singular — it is a resource and cannot be "copied" — so copied data means the internal *static* data of the node (other than any externally connected resources, such as res1, that are declared as static). Static data is that which persists after the function has exited, so its values are still available the next time the function is called. There are many reasons why you might want each clone to have its own copy of static data.

Looking at the previous coding for n003, we cannot leave static data inside the function if it is to be copied for each node. One solution is to pass it as a parameter.

Code for n003

```
    int res1;                    //global to current file
int func003(int *z, int x, int *y)
{
    int temp1;                   //dynamic local data.
    ....
    *y = x;                      //pass msg through.
    ....
}
```

The only difference from before, is I left off the static var1 declaration and passed it as a parameter.

Code for n001

```
extern int msg2;
int msg1;                        //input messages.
int var1;                        //"copied" data.
n001:
ret = func003(&var1,msg1,&msg2)  //code for the node.
goto n002;
```

I am presuming here that the code for each node resides in a separate file so that global labels are only visible within the file.

Coding a mainline routine

GOOFEE can quite happily model a conventional structured program, including a mainline routine, as illustrated in Figure 44, based on Figure 9, Chapter 1.

Figure 44: Mainline routine.

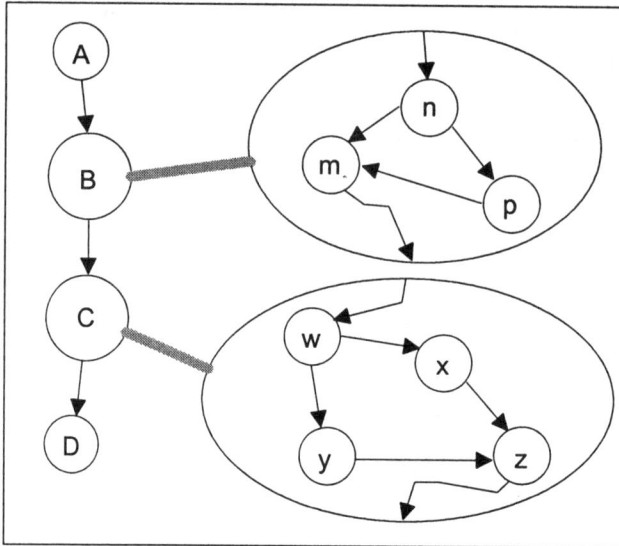

Another major device used in structured programming is the *Case* structure, or Switch, and this is just an extension of the Iterative-node. It is illustrated in Figure 45.

Figure 45: Modeling a Case structure.

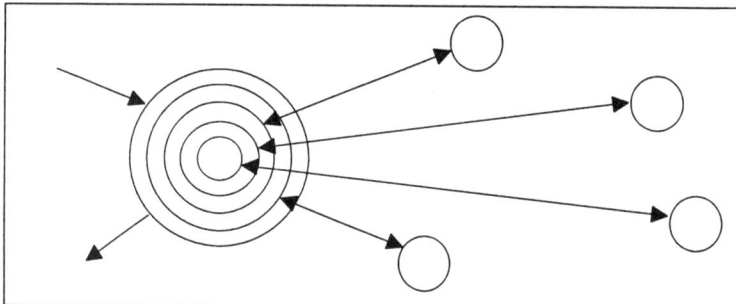

The constructs of Figures 44 and 45 are highly relevant to OO designs also, for decomposition of a Composite- or Super-node object, or as the "glue" code that ties together higher level node objects. It will be seen in the elevator control system how the Case structure is useful in the latter instance.

Of course, translating a diagram to code without utilising an underlying operating system means that you miss out on certain features. For example, the TERSE OS has built-in n-deep buffering for asynchronous messages, 1-deep buffering for synchronous messages, and bounded runtime scheduling with timely response to interprocessor input messages. Without an OS, you will have to work something out on an ad hoc basis, if you want these features.

If you want to use a wire with timeout (see Figure 2), you will need to work out your own code for that, such as by using a timer.

But this reinventing of the wheel is what programmers do all the time!

C programming with TERSE

Look in Appendix C for further details. The example is for Dunfield C, but it should be adaptable to other flavours of C.

This is an extract from Appendix C, showing skeleton code for the nodes. Note that I have made use of the infamous GOTO.

```
/*................................................*/
node0:
  EXITNODE
/*................................................*/
node1:

  POSTMSG(2,1,0,#34)   /*node2,term1,no-notif.,imm.-data.*/
  POSTMSG(3,1,0,#00) /*node3,term1,notnotif,immediate-data.*/
  EXITNODE
/*................................................*/
node3:
  POSTMSG(4,2,0,32)   /*node4,term2,notnotif,direct-data.*/
  EXITNODE
/*................................................*/
node2:
  if(TERM2flag) {  /*TERM2flag is a true/false macro*/
  /*a Notification has arrived... in register R1*/
  x=R1;
  }
  POSTMSG(4,1,0,#00)    /*node4,term1,0,immediate-data.*/
  EXITNODE
/*................................................*/
node4:
  POSTMSG(2,2,1,#11) /*notification, back to node-2,term-2.*/
  EXITNODE
/*................................................*/
```

EXITNODE is a macro that is a GOTO back to the OS.

A case study

The case study should answer, at least partly, some major questions: Will the unified notation and 2-dimensional representation become overly cluttered? Is it capable of representing classes and objects and relationships and messaging between them? Is it capable of stepping down and representing state diagram information within nodes? The list goes on. Actually, the last-mentioned point is interesting, as the unified notation should represent the design unambiguously, to the level at which coding can take place.

In fact, an interesting point emerges from this: other methodologies have a distinct "bottom level", such as the FSM, but the GOOFEE notation applies to all levels, which means that diagrams have no bottom level and can be decomposed indefinitely!

A serious problem with the presentation of this case study is the placing of sections of the diagram onto these tiny pages. You have to imagine what it would be like on an infinite page. The full diagram is on the Companion Disk, viewable by the GOOFEE Diagrammer program.

First pass at a solution

Figure 46 is the starting point, and the approach I have taken is to first draw the physical layout, showing where processors are located and to what resources they are connected. Then I made the decision that each processor will equate to one Composite-node. A CASE tool could have the ability to represent the picture of the elevator as a background bitmap image, maybe greyed-out, as a visual adornment. I made some early implementation decisions, as is often required in embedded systems.

The Composite-nodes in each elevator are identical, so you can see the type of Joining-bar I have used. Ditto for the Composite-nodes on each floor. However, each Composite-node has its own local "config" data that is explicitly shown. Note that the default behaviour for any resource/data connected to a node is that it is only visible to that node.

Note that the description here is my first pass, and any analysis/design is a circular process. I have included a lot of my thought process and the chronological evolution, in this chapter and through Chapters 7, 8, 9, and 10, as they are in themselves very instructive.

Figure 46: Elevator control system diagram.

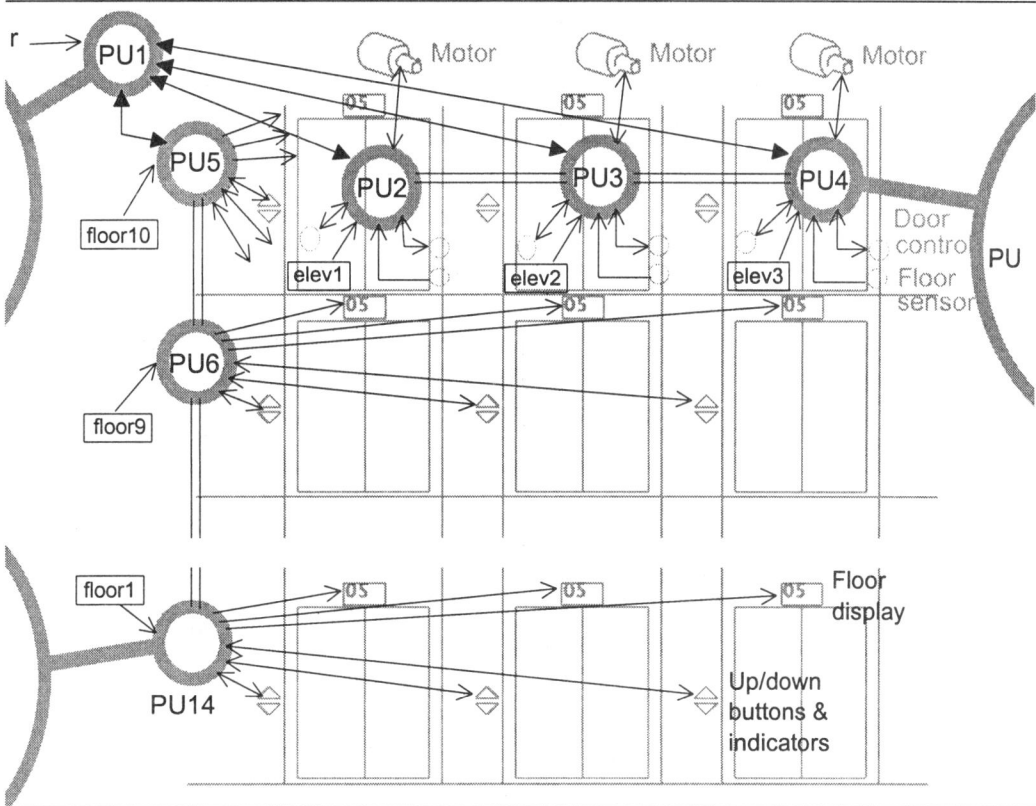

This "top-level" view has shown all of the physical connections, and now the decomposition can proceed on the 2-dimensional plane, as Figure 47 shows.

Because this chapter is a fairly short introduction to the case study, I want to avoid all possible distractions from the main issues, these figures are not adorned with all possible textual adornments, nor is decomposition necessarily complete. For example, nodes A, B, C, and D are joined by an implied union Joining-bar, and I have shown a union Joining-bar going off to the right, to indicate how further decomposition can proceed.

One thought that may occur to you is that I am being very repetitive, showing for example the connection to the motor in every elevator, when it

is really just a repeat of the same thing. Yes, the representation could be
refined, which I do in Chapter 7.

Figure 47: Decomposition of an elevator Composite-node.

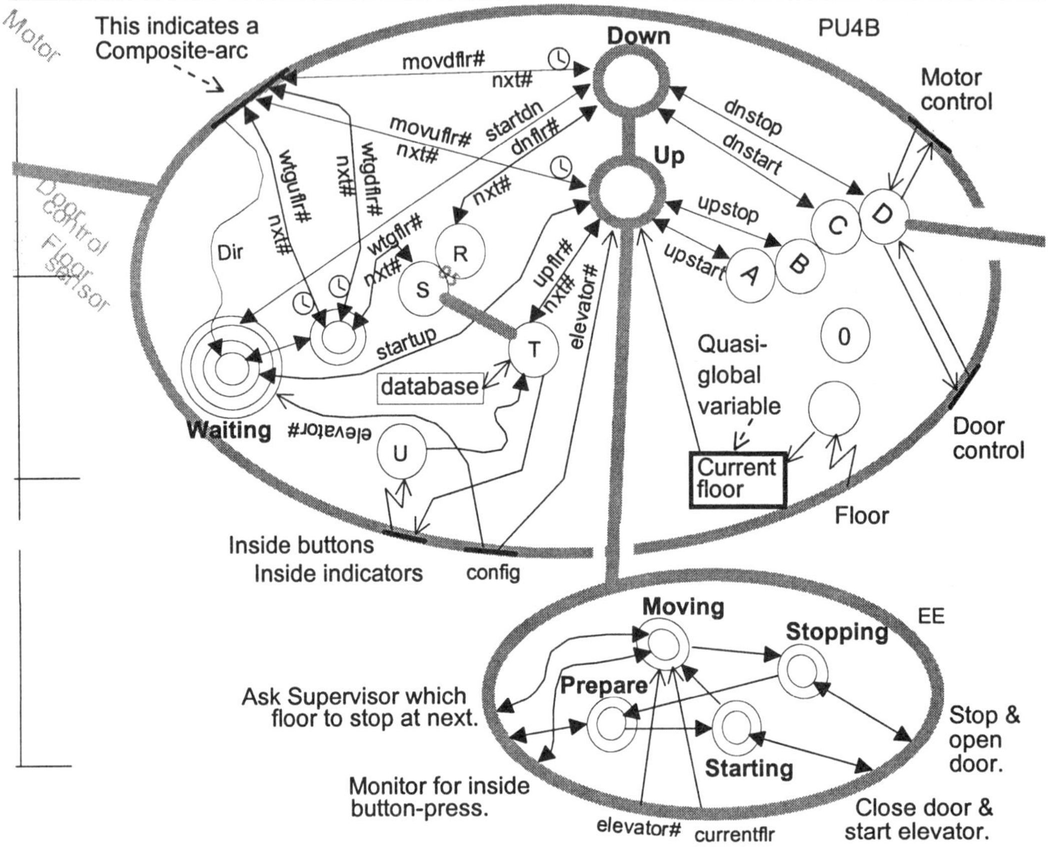

Nodes A, B, C, and D show the technique I recommend for accessing all
shared resources (even where non-concurrency of the clients is obvious). In
the case of the motor/door control, access to the resource from various parts
of the diagram comes in through its own access-node, or "clone" node. Ditto
for access to the local button database. Thus, we can see exactly how, and
when, a resource is being used, without needing another diagram or table.

The basic idea of the Composite-node PU4B of Figure 47 is that execution
starts at the node labelled "Waiting", requesting information from the local
button manager and from the Supervisor processor, which has the button

database for the floors. When a message comes back to go to a particular floor, the Iterative-node exits to either the "Down" or "Up" nodes, and what amounts to an FSM gets going: except that I chose to do it by structured programming principles (Composite-node EE). Exit from "Down" or "Up" takes control back to "Waiting".

Deciding which floor to stop at is a very time-critical operation, because information in real-time must be obtained from the Supervisor as well as from the local database. So I decided to implement "current floor" as a quasi-global variable, accessed directly by I/O wires; although do note that it is only visible inside the current Composite-node (or Super-node). Note that the Supervisor processor maintains separate up and down button databases, which simplifies the logistics of the system.

I decided to decouple the inside button-press interrupt via node U, to clarify mutual exclusion to the database, although node U could have been placed in the decomposition of node T. Node T will require further decomposition, but do note with all bottom-level decompositions that how you document them is up to you; you could do something like Node EE, or pseudo-code, or even direct code. A CASE tool will be expected to have a pop-up text editor for entering code into a node, or the tool could auto-generate code from a diagram.

Moving rapidly on, Figure 48 shows the decompositions of the other processors; although once again, some of the nodes could be further decomposed.

Look at node 1; notice that it has clones in a union/no-concurrency relationship, which also means that node 1 is exactly the same (internally) as its clones. If a message arrives at node 1 from the elevator-processor (right-hand elevator), requesting button information (message will have status, such as current floor), node 1 can access the database and respond with the next floor to go to.

Node 1's clones (Z and 4) can only execute when node 1 isn't (specified by the Joining-bar), so there are no problems with multiple accesses to the database: ditto for the other clones S2 and S1. Node N controls the firing of node Z and node V, and the latter two will unload the queued button data and update the database, whenever nodes 1/2/4/5 aren't doing it.

Figure 48: Further decomposition of elevator system.

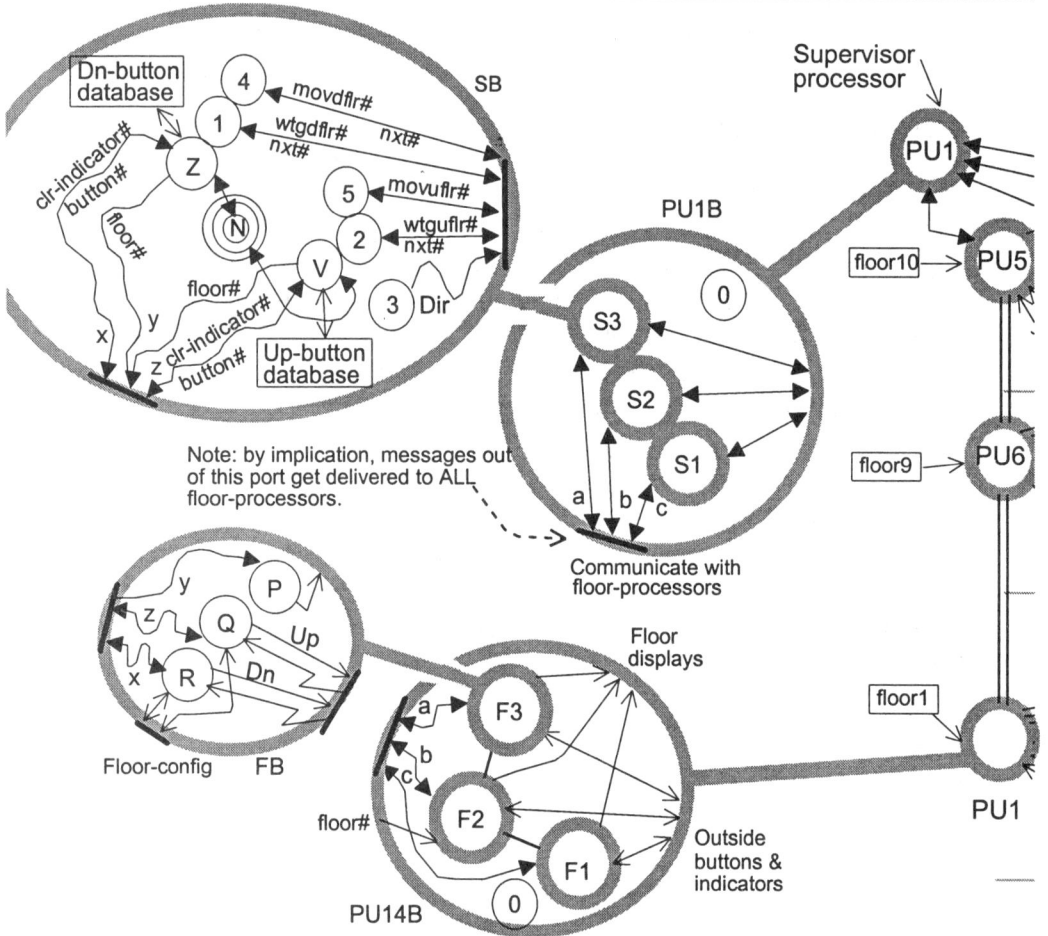

In fact, the floor processors chug away, sending information to the Supervisor as Notifications (asynchronous messages) whenever a button is pressed. Notifications can queue-up at the Supervisor until the Supervisor executes its node Z or node V (or a clone) to consume them. Nodes Z and V (and clones) can also post messages to the floors to update the floor displays, passing-on the current-floor information they receive from the elevator processors.

Notice the Super-arc from PU1 to PU5: it isn't shown going to PU6, etc. but it does, by inheritance implication. Messages out of PU1 are delivered to all the floor PUs. The reverse also is true.

Conclusions

I short-circuited the decomposition process somewhat, to try and keep it within 3 figures, so it is a bit more squashed than necessary, and some nodes need further decomposition. I have attempted to produce something that you should be able to look at to get an idea of how the notation is used and to see how decomposition can proceed in an orderly manner on a single plane without obfuscation. It is significant that in just 3 figures I have got almost to the point of being able to unambiguously describe the entire system and go to coding.

The case study also shows (mostly) how the one notation and diagram contains every aspect of OOD, including dataflow, controlflow, timing, synchronisation, classes and inheritance, objects and messaging, cardinality, resource handling, mutual exclusion, FSM, concurrency, multiple inheritance, exception-handling, meta-class, ... in fact, every buzzword you can think of.

For comparison, you might like to study the multiple-elevator case study in *Software Design Methods for Concurrent and Real-Time Systems*, by Hassan Gomaa (Addison-Wesley, 1993): he uses COBRA for analysis and CO-DARTS/DA for design.

Granularity

How far "down" do we go in a diagram? Theoretically, a GOOFEE diagram can be decomposed to the point where the complete code can be automatically generated, and I will probably develop my CASE software in this direction.

However, current implementations of TERSE for the 8051 and x86 have a coarse-grained approach. This is because there is an overhead involved in each transition between nodes, being the message-delivery module and the scheduler module. TERSE for the 8051 supports a maximum of 32 nodes.

This does not mean, however, that the GOOFEE designs have to be limited to 32 nodes, only that in the final implementation, the OS can only handle that many.

If the diagram is finer-grained, i.e., has more nodes, the "lower level" nodes have to be translated into procedural code. That is, they cannot be actual nodes in the final implementation.

By this I mean that GOOFEE can be used to model code flow/structure/algorithms. You can have a node on a GOOFEE diagram, expand it as a Super-node, with the understanding that the diagram inside the expansion models a code algorithm. In fact, in Chapter 10, which focuses on pragmatic issues, i.e., getting the job done with minimum fuss, the diagram can be constrained such that *all* Super-node expansions are below the OS messaging level and hence model code internal to the node.

Where to now?

Of course, a lot remains to be said. The book up to now has covered the basics of GOOFEE and TERSE, *almost* sufficient to get going on a project. As is always the case when tackling an actual project, all sorts of little problems emerge. Chapters 7 to 9 have been written to provide that myopic detail, so I recommend that you study them.

Chapter 7 focuses on cardinality, Chapter 8 on information hiding, Chapter 9 on timing, and Chapter 10, as mentioned above, focuses on "getting the job done".

If you are the kind of person who reads a technical book from cover to cover before utilising its information, go for it. If you are one of the majority, and want to immediately use the techniques and tools, skim through Chapters 7 to 9, and focus on Chapter 10. You may revisit the book in the future, as required.

GOOFEE is for everything. When next you have to describe a program, try GOOFEE diagrams instead, or alongside pseudocode or whatever it is you use. Discover for yourself how flexible GOOFEE is. If you have a complete project to develop, try GOOFEE alongside whatever you currently do, and compare. However, do at least read Chapter 10 for some pragmatic notes.

7

Modeling cardinality

Preamble

My flow-based object-oriented GOOFEE diagramming notation and methodology has its roots in the lower end of embedded design, particularly ROM-based target code, in which instances are fixed before runtime.

This chapter examines how GOOFEE can represent *cardinality* and explores possible limitations and solutions to those (possible) limitations.

First, of course, we need to know what "cardinality" is! A concise definition of cardinality is taken from a technical paper on the Internet at address `http://www.hatteras.com/c.html`:

> "The number of expected instances of an object relative to another type of object in a diagram.

Grady Booch, in his book *Object Oriented Analysis and Design*, 2nd ed. (Benjamin/Cummings, 1994, Redwood City, USA) has notation that allows *associations* between classes to express cardinality, as per this legend:

1	Exactly one
N	Unlimited number (zero or more)
0 .. N	Zero or more
1 .. N	One or more
1 .. 3	Specified range or exact number

I approached cardinality from a point of view that is totally different from all other methodologies. I developed the concept of the clone node and the Joining-bar; this approach has a number of advantages, including being

1 intuitive,

2 unambiguous,

3 understandable, and

4 clear in its timing relationships,

with relation to access of a resource by any part of the system, where the word "resource" is here used in its most general sense to apply to any physical or logical entity.

The next section summarises the clone-node/Joining-bar and their relation to cardinality, and the problem is then identified.

The GOOFEE "flat" model

In keeping with the embedded applications for which GOOFEE was conceived, design has an "I/O centric" approach.

I used my GOOFEE Diagrammer program to generate the figures in this chapter. Note that some clarity is lost as the Figures are printed as monochrome bitmap images, not reduced, while the original tool displays in colour.

Figure 49 is an extract of the elevator control system case study: a snapshot out of the "infinite" screen in the GOOFEE Diagrammer.

Nodes 007 and 008 illustrate use of clone-nodes and Joining-bars with access to a resource. The resource is "database", being a database of the states of the inside buttons of the elevator. The database is visible only to node 008, and the two together form an "object".

For the reasons enumerated above in the Preamble, and more fundamentally imposed by the dataflow-based approach, the problem of access to the database from different parts of the system is solved by the use of clone-nodes.

Figure 49: Extract of elevator control system case study.

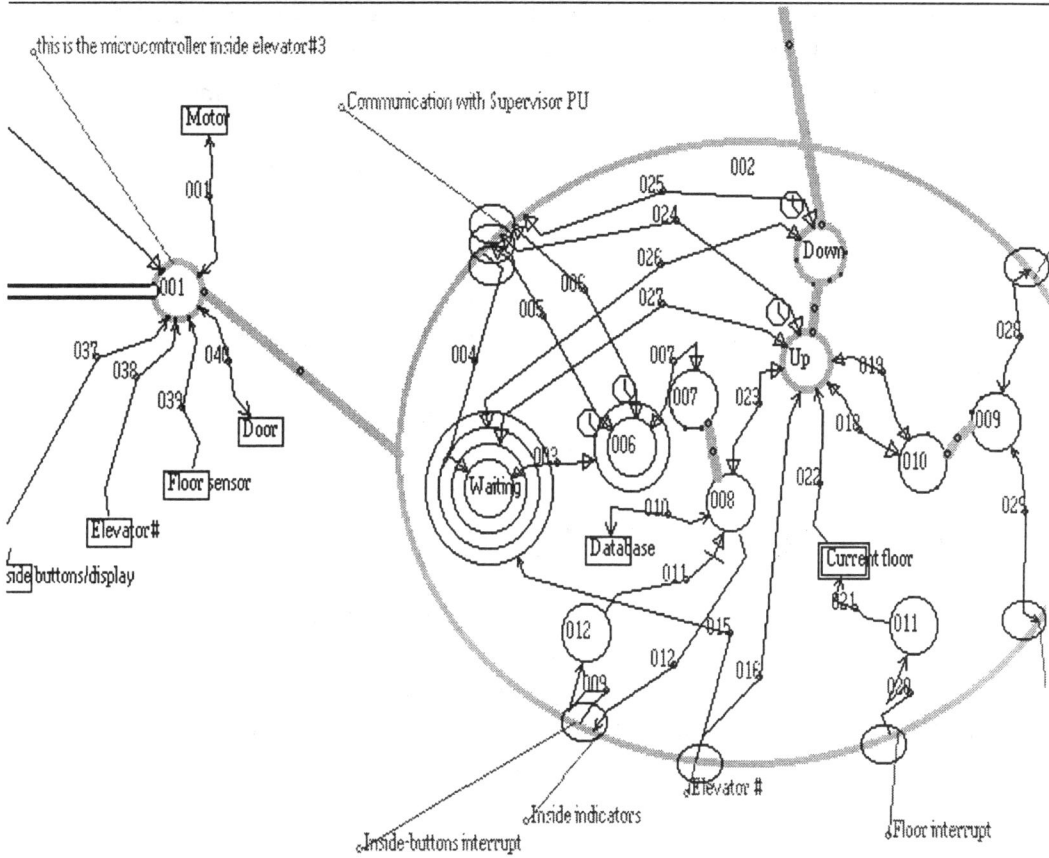

Node 007 is a "clone" of node 008, that is, it has some inheritance relationship defined by the broad line between them. The broad grey line denotes that the internal code (equivalent to the methods) and data (attributes) are only the one instance, and concurrency of execution is not allowed. This is just one of five possible relationships between clone-nodes (reiterating from Figure 2):

1 Union of code, union of data (resources), no concurrency

2 Union code, copy data (resources), no concurrency

3 Copy code, copy data (resources), allow concurrency

4 Union code, copy data (resources), allow concurrency

5 Different code, different data (resources), no concurrency

Relationship 1 is represented by a grey bar, 2 by an underlined grey bar, 3 by two parallel lines, 4 by a single line, and 5 by a grey bar with lines top and bottom.

The word "union" is a slight corruption of its common meaning in data structures and here can be read as "only one instance of". The word "resource" is used as an umbrella term for all physical and logical resources, including data items.

Thus, nodes 007 and 008 are internally only one node but have separate terminals. In keeping with the synchronous dataflow model, a message posted to any terminal is buffered until all messages for that node have arrived, at which time the node is eligible to fire. Therefore, the two accesses to the button database are clearly delineated.

It is easy to hang more clone-nodes off node 007, in a daisy-chain, for any other accesses to the database. Of course, although this expresses all access to the database with great clarity and precision, there must be an underlying mechanism at runtime to enforce the rules — for example, that of mutual exclusion, or non-concurrency of execution, of the clone nodes.

A point of clarification about node 007 is in order. Notice that it has little "blobs" on its boundary. These are terminals inherited from node 008. In accordance with the GOOFEE notation, if a terminal does not have an external dataflow wire connected, it will inherit the external connection from a clone, if there is one. Thus, all the various I/O wires shown connected to node 008 also go to node 007. This avoids clutter and is unambiguous.

Nodes 007 and 008 are "expressing" cardinality.

The multiple-elevator problem

In Figure 49, node 002, the large Composite-node (grey boundary) with a diagram inside is the equivalent of a class, and the grey Joining-bar to node 001 identifies the latter as an instantiation of node 002. This is developing the use of the Joining-bar and the relationship between classes and objects, somewhat beyond the above discussion. For further clarification, refer to Chapters 4 and 8.

The essential point here is that node 001 is the control system inside one elevator, while node 002 is the template, or class, showing what it consists of. Figure 50 shows that a Joining-bar, of the type indicating that both data and code are instantiated in each node, is drawn between each elevator in a three-elevator system.

Figure 50: Instantiation of control system for each elevator.

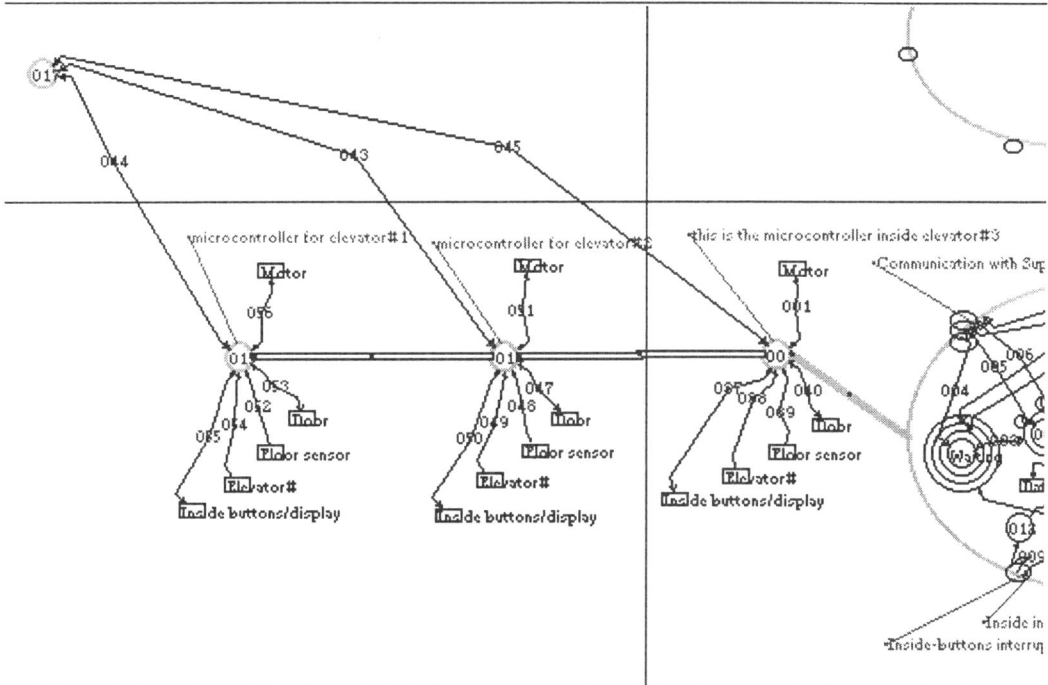

In Booch diagrams, cardinality is expressed between classes, but the GOOFEE notation is flat. That is, objects and classes intermingle on the same diagram. Therefore, there is no point in drawing cardinality relationships between classes when the objects are right there, alongside — object relationships can be drawn directly between the objects. However, note that the mind-set of GOOFEE-based design is different — the distinction between object and class is blurred. An object from one perspective may be a class from another. I do not even like to use the words "class" and "object", and the frequent usage in this book is somewhat of a condescension to readers with a traditional OO mind-set.

In Figure 50, there is a Supervisor processor, top-left corner, and it must send and receive messages from each internal elevator processor.

Cardinality is being expressed here also. The one Supervisor sends and receives to/from three different elevator objects. However, the cardinality is "hard wired" into the diagram, constructed as a fixed circuit with a wire or cluster of wires for each cardinal connection. This approach is alright for a wide range of embedded applications but starts to become limiting as we wish to scale-up. For example, if there were 30 elevators, there would have to be 30 instances chained together in Figure 50, all with wires to/from the Supervisor. How do we generalise the GOOFEE notation, as per Booch's "M ... N" textual adornment?

Actually, I am being a bit pedantic here. The first-pass solution given in Chapter 6 simply showed by implication that more elevators and/or floors can be added. Pragmatic and simple. In this chapter however, I am really "nit picking" and "nailing down" this cardinality issue with great precision. Please indulge me, as I voyage through a consideration of *sub-nodes ...*

Toward a cardinality notation for GOOFEE: the sub-node

I originally conceived of the sub-node as a mechanism for representing OO databases and for polymorphism.

Figure 51: GOOFEE sub-nodes.

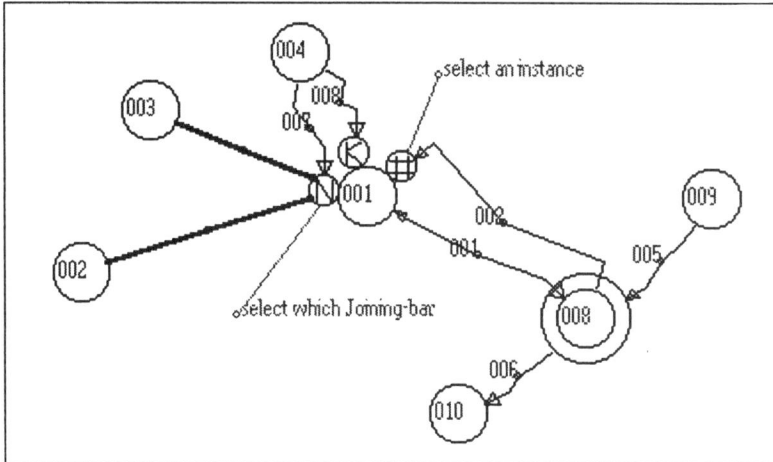

In Figure 51, the sub-nodes are N (New), K (Kill), and # (instance). The wires shown joining "N" to nodes 003 and 002 are Joining-bars, and the dataflow wire from node 004 "fires" the sub-node, selecting one of the inheritance sources as the template for node 001. The delaying of the action of the Joining-bars until runtime allows node 001 to be polymorphic.

Each time "N" fires, "#" can have as input an instance number, either a new number or a value that will cause overwriting of an existing instance. The normal operation of "#" is that it selects which instance is currently resident in node 001. This mechanism of creation and destruction of instances is for applications that are at least partially RAM-based, usually with a heap to hold the instances.

A design need not have all three sub-nodes. If node 001 has only the "#", it is not polymorphic, but it still has multiple instances. Conceptually, however, this is a deviation from earlier work, as the relationships between nodes (clones) is shown by the Joining-bar. Now, the "#" states that the node (with the one set of terminals) can have multiple instances internally — but the internal inheritance relationship is not specified.

Figure 52: Applying the Joining-bar to internal instantiation.

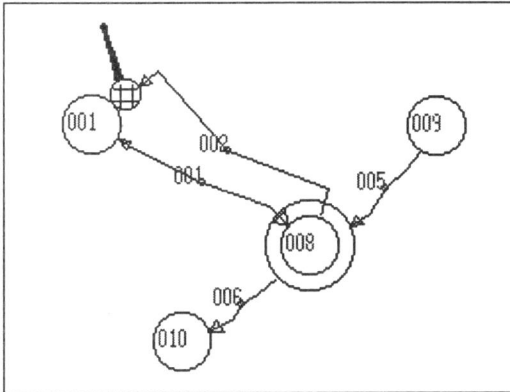

The "#" sub-node in Figure 52 has a Joining-bar going nowhere, to imply the inheritance relationship of internal instantiations.

This notation seems clear and in keeping with the synchronous dataflow model. It would seem to apply to a range of applications, in particular OO databases — node 001 could represent a record-object of the database. However, the notation has problems when applied to the elevator case study.

Bidirectional cardinality

Putting Figures 50 and 52 together, if node 001 in Figure 52 could be an elevator-object, i.e., a Composite-node encompassing all the functionality of the elevator, with a "#" sub-node attached, would scaling-up be easily represented?

Figure 53: Speculation, applying sub-nodes to the elevator system.

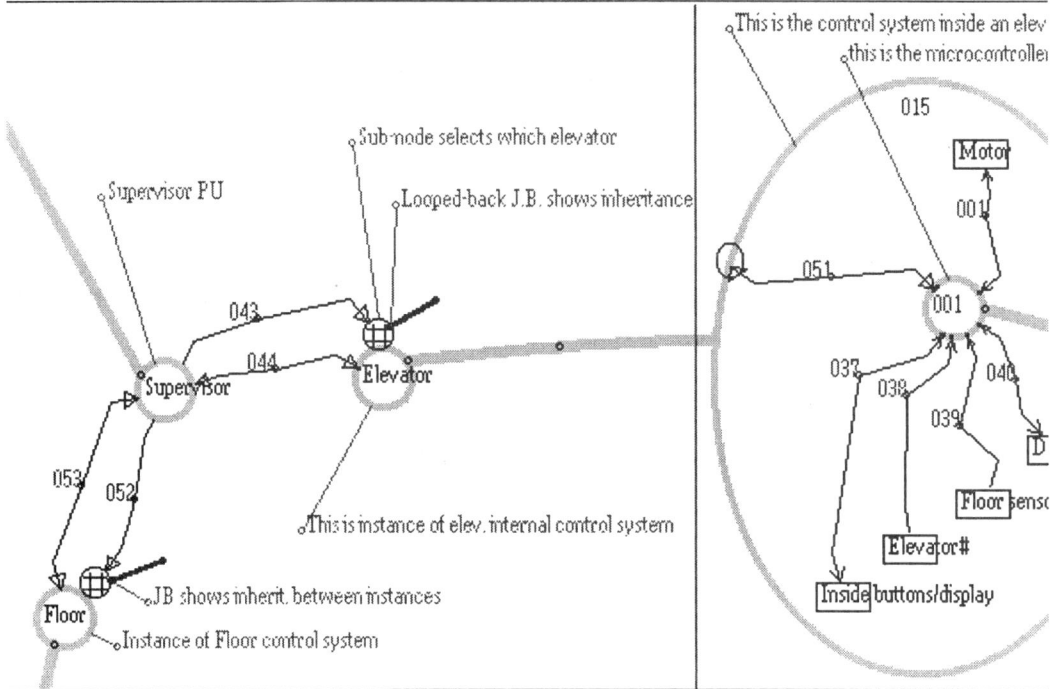

Figure 53 is not to be taken as a viable solution — it is speculation only. It illustrates all of the functionality of an elevator being encapsulated in a Composite-node, node 015, and instantiated to the left, by the node marked "Elevator" with a sub-node attached.

This is scalable, as the Supervisor can communicate with multiple elevator instances, however there is one fatal flaw — the cardinality is one-way only. That is, the Supervisor can select which elevator-instance to communicate with, but Figure 50 shows that each elevator can asynchronously send messages to the Supervisor.

The choice of an "allow concurrency" Joining-bar would imply that the internal instances are "active" (i.e., have independent threads of execution).

Figure 54: Generalising cardinality without sub-nodes.

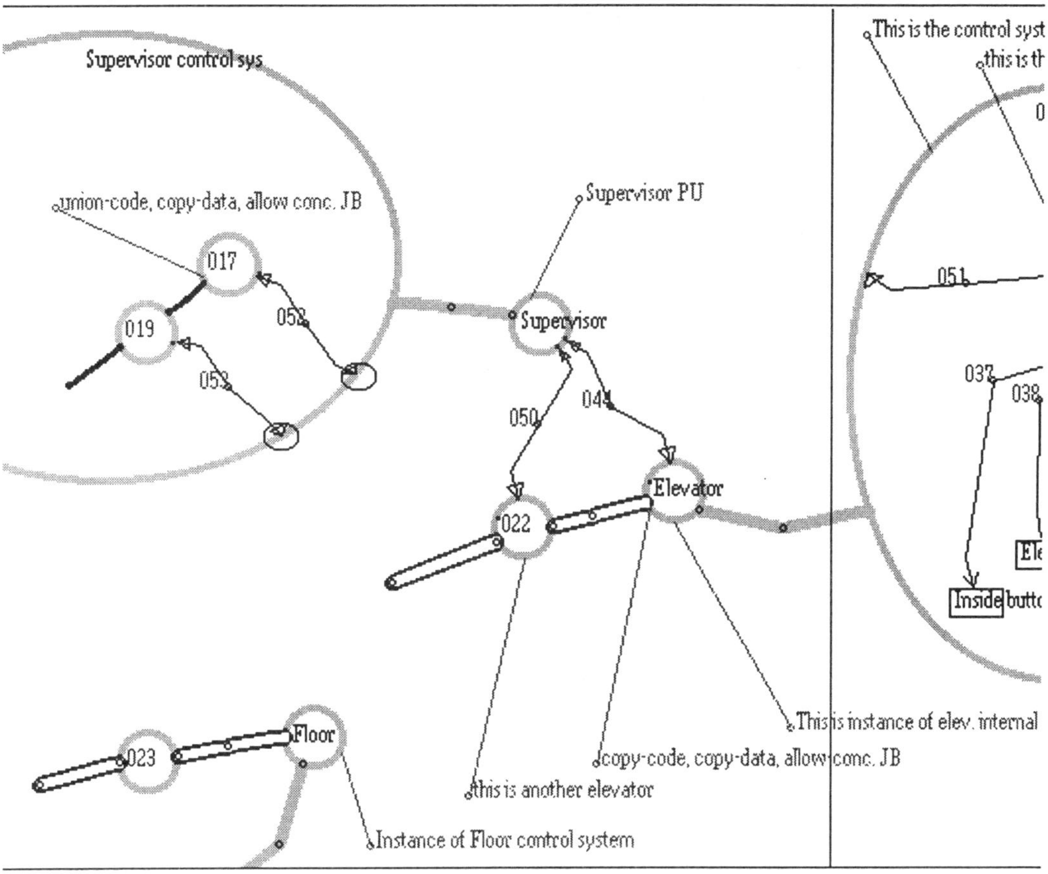

Figure 54 clarifies that the desired relationship between elevator-instances and the Supervisor is actually many-to-many. Figure 54 states that each elevator-instance communicates with an object-instance within the one Supervisor-instance. This is an extremely clear and unambiguous representation of what could be confusing to represent in other notations. The meaning conveyed is far beyond Booch's clouds with an association line and cardinality textual adornment.

It is suggested in Figure 54 that expansion can be beyond two elevators. The Joining-bars going "nowhere" designate this. Is this an adequate representation?

Complex many-to-many

"Many-to-many" can have another meaning that other notations also cannot convey clearly. Referring to Figure 54, node 017 is the clone responsible for servicing requests from one particular elevator, say elevator #1. Node 017 needs to send and receive messages to and from every floor processor. For example, elevator #1 will need to inform every floor processor to update the floor-level display outside the elevator #1 doorway.

Figure 55: A complex many-to-many relationship.

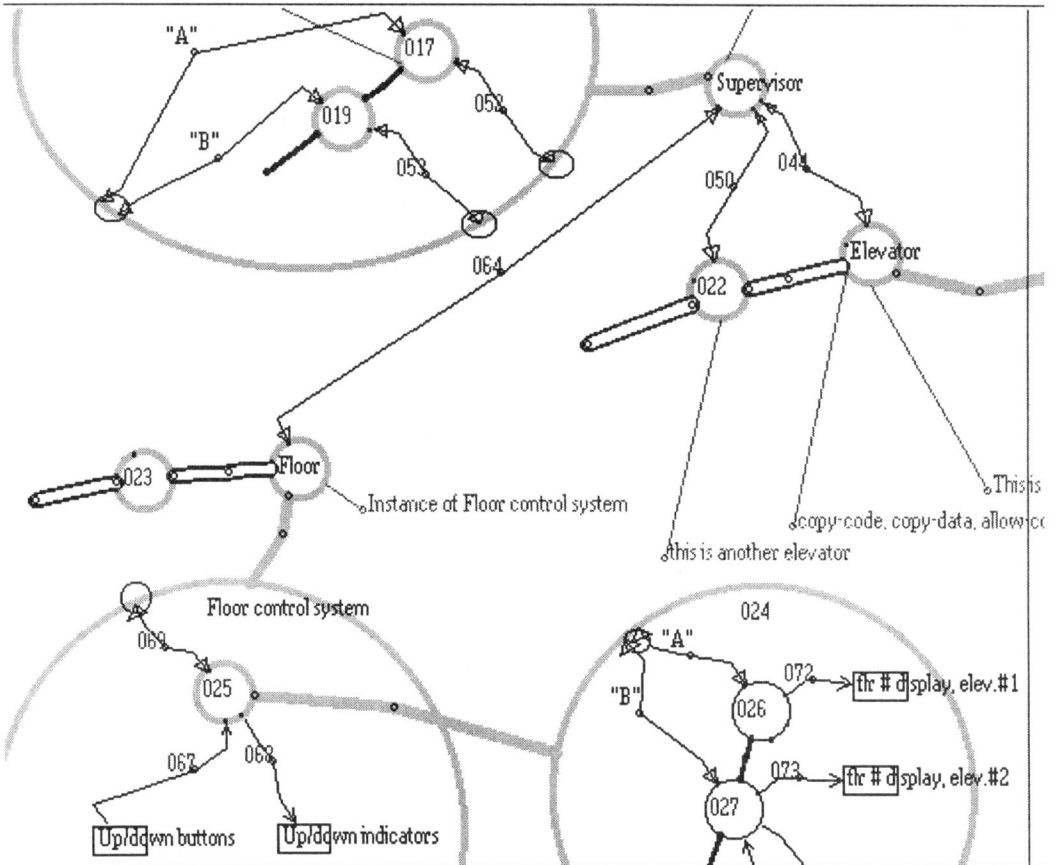

Figure 55 develops the messaging between Supervisor and floor processors. Take the scenario where elevator #1 wants to inform all floor processors of its current floor. A message via Composite-wire 044, and wire 052 will result in a message on the wire labelled "A". This will go onto composite-wire 064, which goes to the matching terminals of ALL floor processors.

For any floor-processor-instance, message "A" will end up at node 026, which is connected to the specific display for elevator #1. Note that nodes 026 and 027 represent the servicing modules for elevators #1 and #2, which can be expanded, as shown by the extra Joining-bar.

Although it is slightly off the figure, notice too that nodes 026 and 027 are BOTH connected to the buttons and up/down indicators of that floor.

Semantic consistency

The attempt to improve GOOFEE has lead away from the original pure concepts. Three major problem areas are:

1 One of the original concepts of GOOFEE was that a resource is explicitly drawn once on the diagram. Figure 55 modifies that by allowing a template, or class, to contain resources that can be instantiated from. For example, the "motor" in node 015, Figure 53.

2 The mechanism of clone-nodes was used for all sharing of code and resources. Clone-nodes are able to represent cardinality. Figure 55 still has clone-nodes, however some are nested within Composite-node expansions.

3 Potential confusion between Composite-node and schedulable normal-node and Super-node.

Referring to Figure 55, wires 044 and 050 are supposed to convey cardinality between elevators and Supervisor; however, this is only apparent within the expansions. Of course, a "solution" to this is to introduce either another symbol or some textual adornment. The vicinity of wires 044 and 050 is the part of the diagram that corresponds to the top level of a class diagram — "Supervisor" and "elevator" are the classes — and other methodologies, such as Booch, OMT, and Shlaer & Mellor, use various kinds of association lines with textual adornment.

A possibility with GOOFEE is to avoid the need for any extra symbol or text by retreating back to the original pure concepts.

With regard to point 3 above, there is potential confusion over whether a Composite-node is instantiated or not and its differences compared with normal- and Super-nodes. Quoting myself from Chapter 4:

"A *class* is any node, Super-node, or Composite-node, without externally connected dataflow message wires [I/O wires don't count] and with a Joining-bar to show an inheritance relationship.

"An *object* is any node, Super-node, or Composite-node without a Joining-bar, or if it has a Joining-bar it must also have externally connected message wires.

Is there a semantic inconsistency? In Figure 55, node 025, by the above definition, is instantiated. However, as it has an expansion, internally it is the expansion that is instantiated. With regard to the node 025 symbol itself, its terminals are instantiated.

By the above rules, the expansion, node 024 is not instantiated, yet the nodes inside it are. Thus, there are "objects" inside a "class" — now perhaps you can appreciate why a mind-shift is required regarding the distinction between object and class!

If node 025 is instantiated, it must be a schedulable node, recognised by the execution scheduler, and will have terminals from which messages can be delivered to and posted from. Because it has an internal expansion, at runtime there would need to be some "redirector" code in node 025. From the execution-scheduler's point of view, node 025 is scheduled differently from a normal- or Super-node (such as 026). Quoting myself again, to define the Composite-node:

"Normal (synchronous) wires into and out of a node have synchronous dataflow behaviour [I/O wires don't count], but this is not implied for the *Composite-node*, because it is just a composite, or logical, sub-division of the diagram, usually for inheritance and/or visibility/scope purposes.

Even though a Composite-node can be instantiated, it is different from the execution-scheduler's point of view, because it does not impose synchronous dataflow. This means that the arrival of any input message will make a Composite-node eligible to fire. Similarly, at exit, it is not required that all output dataflow wires should produce messages.

Cardinality: a special symbol

The above section identified three areas of concern in the interpretation of Figure 55; however, it is only cardinality that exhibits semantic inconsistency. Point 3 simply required further clarification, so that the reader will interpret the diagram correctly. Point 1 is a question of philosophy.

Focus on the essence of the cardinality problem — wires 044 and 050 to the top-level Supervisor-node. There are two possibly solutions:

1 Wire 044 could be connected directly to wire 052, and wire 050 connected directly to wire 053, completely bypassing the top-level Supervisor-node.

2 A new cardinality symbol could be introduced, probably at the juncture of wires 044, 050, and the top-level Supervisor-node.

The first solution seems contrary to the design process. The Supervisor and Elevator nodes are where design would start, and it is necessary to show relationships at this level. However, drawing the wires directly between lower levels will still "work" and is actually very meaningful, as it is not necessary to trace through a hierarchy of expansions to find where wires originate and terminate.

I am reluctant to introduce a new symbol; however investigation of necessity or otherwise of such a symbol is necessary. To cut a long story short, I do get around to determining, later in this chapter, that a special symbol is not necessary; however, these deliberations are useful. Also, the various sub-nodes and the special symbol described here are in my GOOFEE Diagrammer, so maybe you can find some use for them.

The Supervisor-node is instantiated, because it has external wires. However it is only a shell, or terminals and redirection (thunking?) code, as it is expanded internally. This is inefficient, and akin to a compiler replacing virtual function calls with direct calls. Optimisation during implementation will allow messages to be passed directly between ultimate source and destination, as per point 1 above.

Figure 56 introduces a proposed new symbol for cardinality: the *Composite-terminal*. Notice that node 015, the elevator template, has various messages to and from the Supervisor, combined into one

Composite-wire in wire 044 (and 050, etc.). The proposed Composite-terminal means "many terminals", and simply means that there may be many more terminals attached to the Supervisor-node than the two explicitly drawn. Similarly, those "many terminals" propagate into node 038. Notice that the original messages are "Dnreq", "Upreq", and "Pref".

Figure 56: The Composite-terminal.

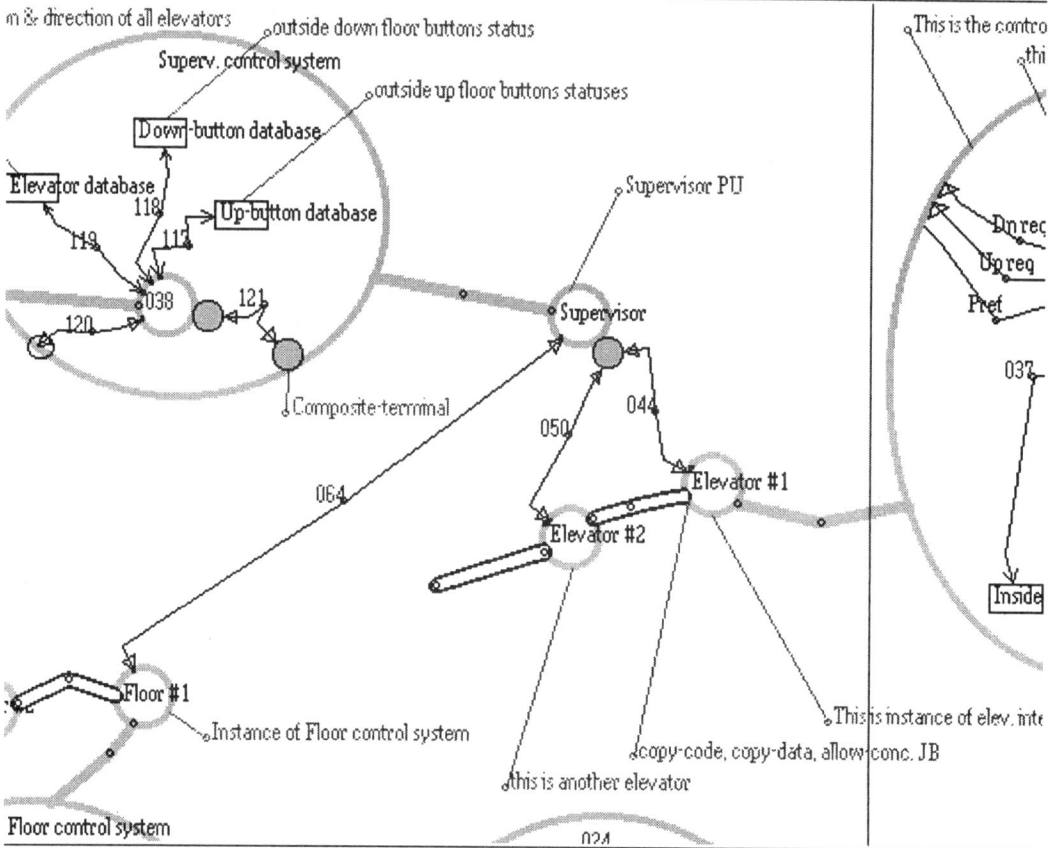

Figure 57 is a shifted view of the same diagram as Figure 56. The "Dnreq" and "Upreq" reach their destination. Wire 052 is a Composite-wire to the "service elev#1" node — does this reveal a semantic inconsistency with the new symbol? A Composite-wire is composed of a bundle of wires, so its terminating arrow implies multiple terminals, i.e., a special symbol is not required here.

However, where wires 052 and 053 meet the boundary of the "Supervisor control sys" node, they must combine with the special symbol. It seems inconsistent, even if only aesthetically.

Figure 57: Bundling and unbundling of composite messages.

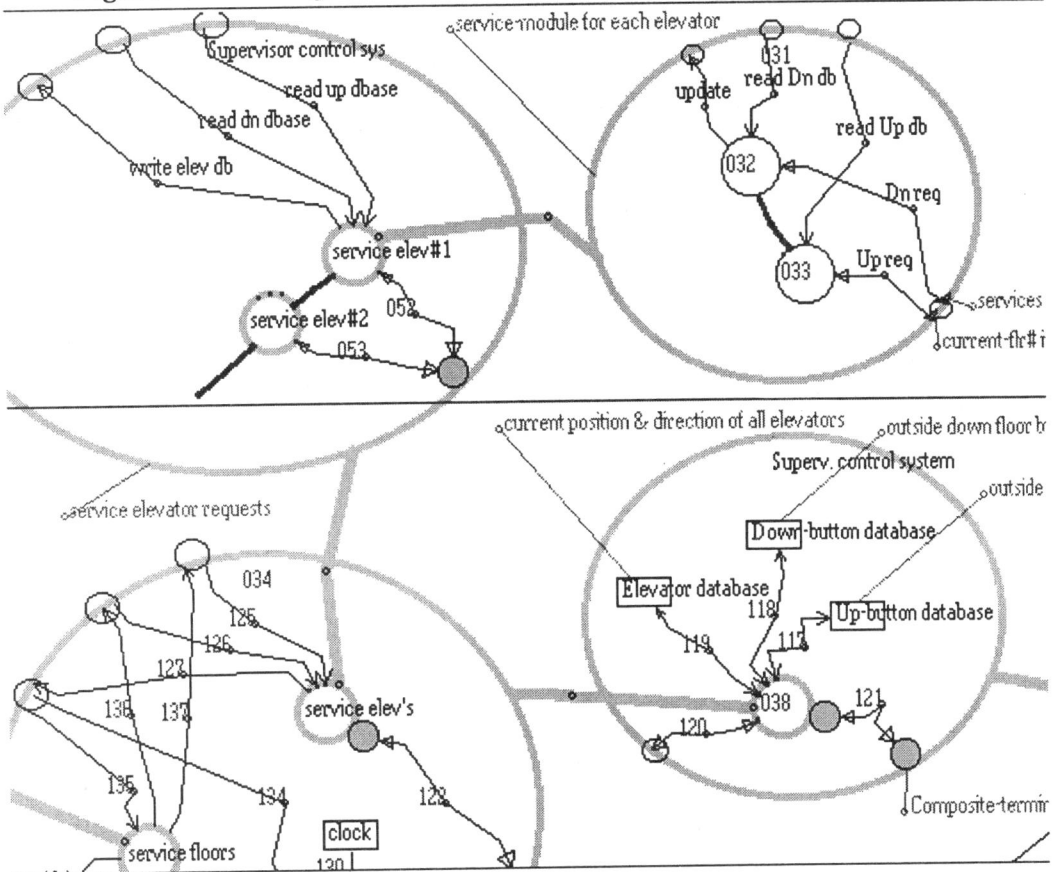

Achieving semantic consistency without a new symbol

Figure 58 is a fresh look, without a new cardinality symbol. Compare wires 044 and 050 with those in Figure 55. If these were individual wires, the meaning conveyed in Figure 58 would be that they connect to the same terminal. That is, a posting out of the "Supervisor" node is from the terminal and would go out on both wires. Similarly, messages into the terminal would overwrite each other in the case of synchronous 1-deep-queued wires or would interleave in the case of asynchronous (Notification) n-deep-queued wires.

Figure 58: The end result; cardinality without a new symbol.

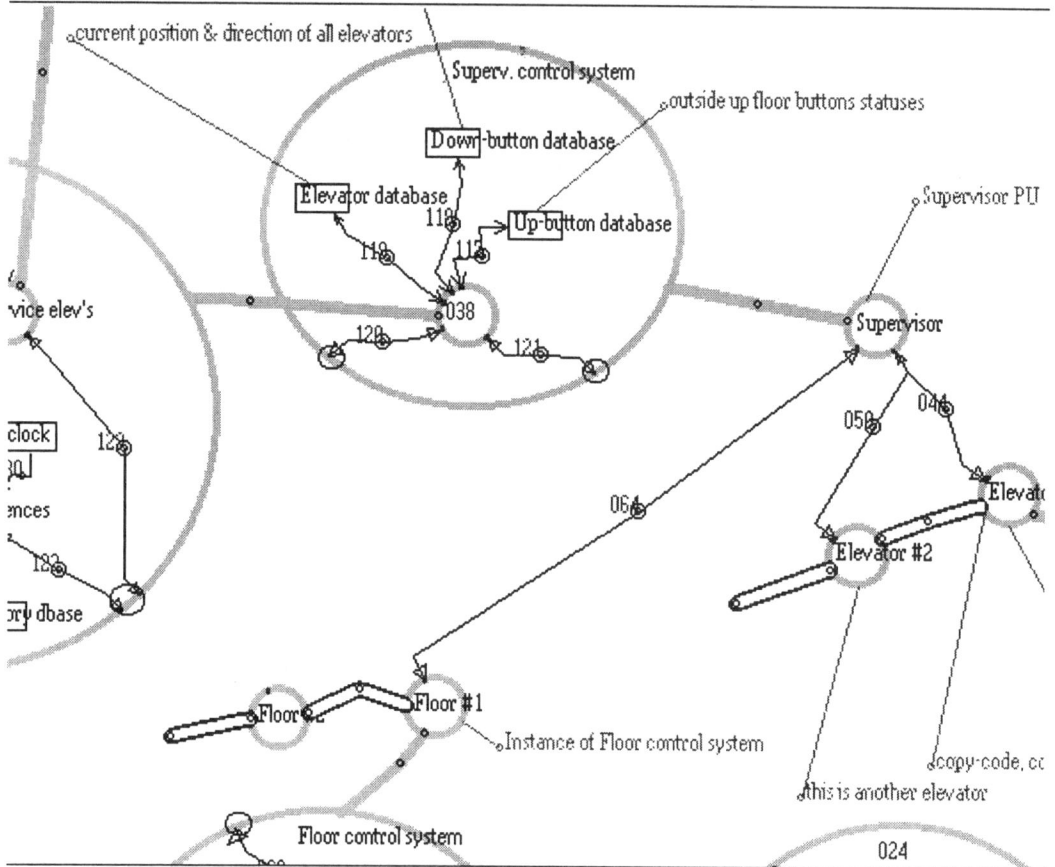

My previous thinking was that the principle would extend to Composite-wires, as in Figure 58, in which the actual wires inside the composite bundle would have coincident terminals. That is, if wire 044 is composed of "Dnreq", "Upreq", and "Pref", as is wire 050, the two "Dnreq" wires would join at the same terminal at the "Supervisor" node. However, this would have the same functionality as wire 064.

One of the fundamental principles of GOOFEE is embodied in the configuration of wire 064. It is a composite of wires (although it could be an individual wire) that, by implication, goes to "Floor #1", "Floor #2", etc. That is, a wire called "x" inside wire 064, if an output from "Supervisor", goes to matching terminals on all the floor nodes. In reverse, if wire "x" is an output from a floor node, it is also output from all other floor nodes and there is conjunction at "Supervisor" node. THIS IS IDENTICAL TO THE INTERPRETATION IN THE PREVIOUS PARAGRAPH.

Therefore, wires 044 and 050 require a different interpretation:

1 The conjunction of *individual* wires at a node implies conjunction of terminals also.

2 The conjunction of *Composite* wires at a node does not imply conjunction of terminals, only the bundling of the wires into a larger Composite-wire inside the node.

Figure 59: Continuation of final solution.

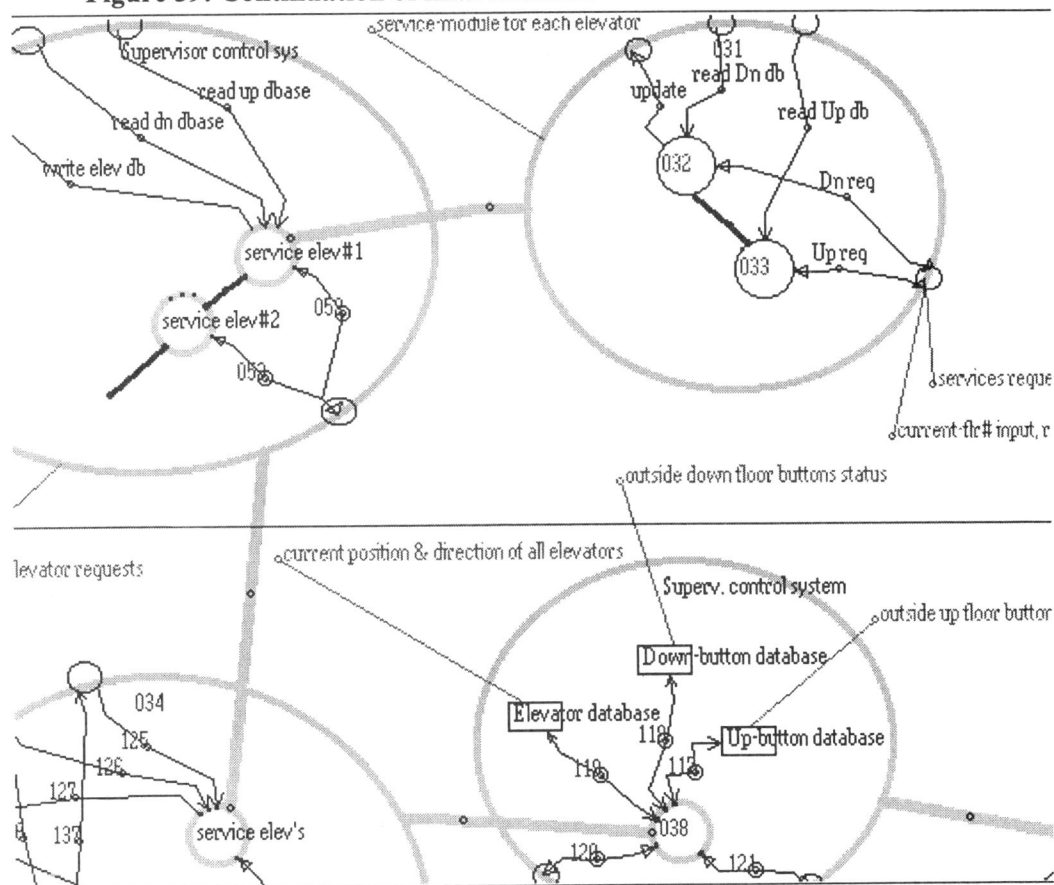

It does become more important to distinguish Composite wires from individual wires, and rather than use thicker wires, I have chosen to place a larger circle at the knee.

Figure 59 is a shift of Figure 58, showing the other end of "Dnreq" and "Upreq" (that were inside wires 044 and 050). Is the diagram now semantically consistent and unambiguous?

Wire 121 is a Composite-wire, that is a cluster or wires 044 and 050. Declustering occurs at wires 122 and 123 (Figure 58), but notice that these two wires do not have conjunction of the arrowheads at the boundary of node 034. The ellipse at the boundary is caused by wire 121, and the connection of multiple wires to the ellipse means that Composite-wire 121 is being decomposed. The point here may seem subtle — if the arrowheads of 122 and 123 are drawn in conjunction, it would imply that the cluster is being declustered to the original wires (044 and 050). The separation of the arrowheads implies a decomposition (or declustering) of the Composite wires (that were) 044 and 050 themselves.

By the above reasoning, the appropriate declustering at wires 052 and 053 (Figure 59) is by conjunction of arrowheads.

Node 031 shows the final extraction of "Dnreq" and "Upreq".

Conclusions

From the analysis of this chapter, it appears the sub-node concept has usefulness for a certain class of cardinality, namely the one-to-many type. It could be used for representing OO databases and for polymorphism.

However, complex cardinality relationships, particularly of the many-to-many type, appear to be beyond the expressiveness of the sub-node, and it appears adequate to imply expansion capability by open-ended Joining-bars. Composite wires can propogate implied cardinality without requiring a new cardinality symbol.

In other words, you construct a diagram by the simple application of intuitive common sense.

8

Modeling information

Preamble

This chapter examines how GOOFEE models information, with a focus on the information-hiding (visibility and persistence) aspect of OO design.

Referring back to Figures 58 and 59: for the OO purist, there is a fundamental ideological problem with these diagrams. The first expansion of "Supervisor" shows database resources attached to node 038. In accordance with GOOFEE terminology, the databases are visible only to node 038, which is in keeping with the principles of data hiding. If any resource is declared global, it becomes visible within the current Composite-node.

The ideological problem arises from the problem that the databases must therefore be visible to everything inside node 038.

Edward Yourdon, in his book *Object-Oriented Systems Design* (Yourdon Press, 1994), has an OO analysis of a similar elevator control system, and he extracts many resources as classes. This is his list of classes identified early in the OOA (Object-Oriented Analysis) cycle:

1   elevator
2   elevator motor
3   elevator door

4	building
5	floor
6	summons (or "request")
7	destination button (in elevator)
8	destination button light
9	arrival light
10	summons button: up versus down
11	summons button light: up versus down
12	overweight sensor
13	floor sensor

It would seem that any identifiable resource that needs to be shared, or occurs many times, is a candidate for a class. With reference to Figure 58, the databases are global inside node 038, and can thus be accessed in an ad hoc fashion. Even if we "know what we are doing" and access them in a safe and orderly fashion, the formalism of extracting them as classes and building read and write methods around them greatly clarifies and enforces the rules and restrictions of access.

Furthermore, these three databases may be structurally very similar, which leads the designer to think in terms of some kind of database parent class.

Although the diagram of Figures 58 and 59 will "work", it is necessary to develop the methodology to utilise the best principles of OO design in GOOFEE diagrams. This chapter develops the information-hiding aspect of OOA/D methodology, applied to GOOFEE diagrams, and examines the suitability of the graphical notation elements.

The designer of embedded systems typically thinks in terms of a resource as a resource, not as an abstract object. There may be a tradeoff here, as some inefficiency, and coding time, is involved with extracting a resource as a class. Where code efficiency and execution speed are paramount, it may be that some resources should not be "objectified". This tradeoff will also be examined.

Extraction of button databases as a class

What is information hiding?

Figure 60 removes an intermediary expansion, expanding the "Supervisor" node directly into node 034. By placing the databases inside this node, their visibility can be more carefully controlled. The basic idea of information hiding is that a resource will hide behind one or more methods that are the only ways of getting at the resource.

Figure 60: Extracting Up/Dn databases as a class.

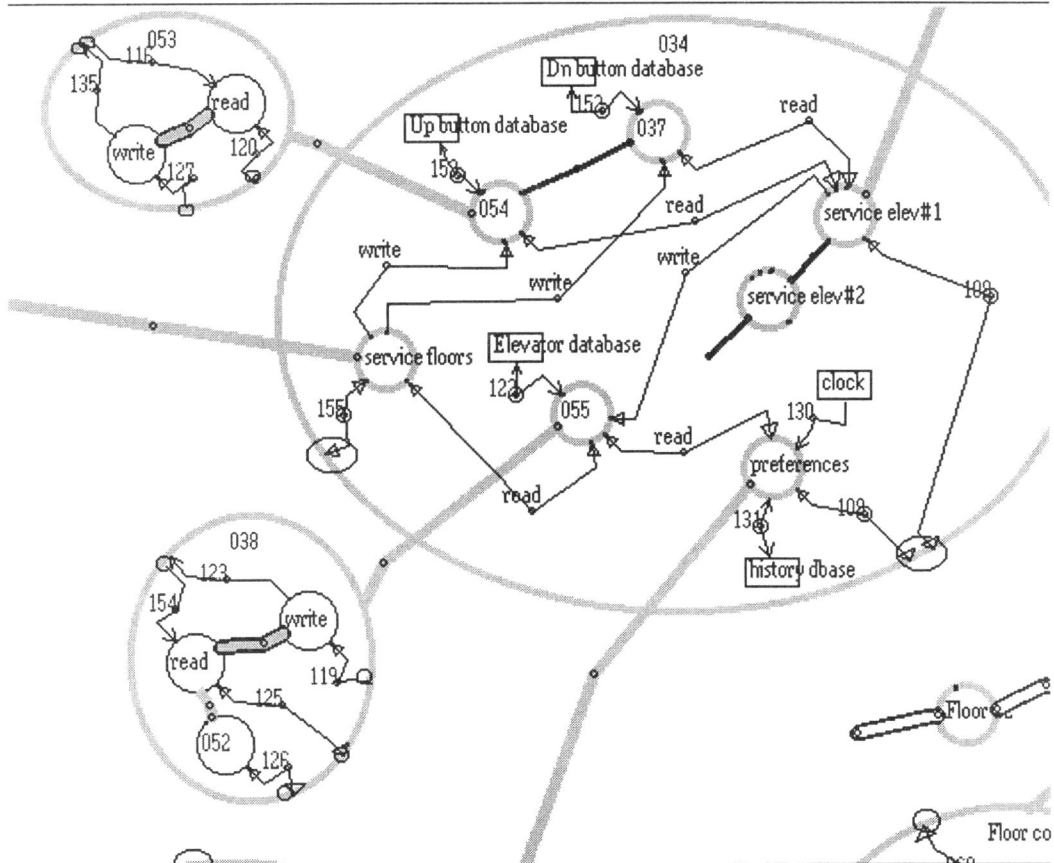

Thus, there is a standardised interface for communicating with the resource, and the interfacing details are contained within those methods — thus, any change to the resource or any improvement to the interface only needs change at one place in the program.

The above-mentioned advantages of information hiding are well known and explained in depth by Hassan Gomaa, in his book *Software Design Methods for Concurrent and Real-Time Systems* (Addison-Wesley, 1993). To quote:

> "With information hiding, the information that could potentially change is encapsulated (i.e., hidden) inside a module. External access to the module can only be made indirectly by invoking operations (e.g., access procedures or functions) that are also part of the module.

What is a resource?

Gomaa applies the information-hiding principle to internal data structures, access synchronisation, and to I/O devices. In GOOFEE terminology, the word *resource* encompasses both data and I/O devices. In fact, resource can be defined in a negative sense, as follows, to clarify its broad interpretation as I use it:

- *Resource* is any physical or logical entity without code.

Wiring by implication: danger

Figure 60 has a glaring fault. "Service elev#1" performs a "read" on "Dn-button database", but notice that the clone "service elev#2" is by default also wired to the same terminal on node 037. In fact, "service elev#2" should be wired to a clone of node 037. Also, a clone of node 054 is required, and all the wiring shown going to "service elev#1" needs to be duplicated for "service elev#2".

Consider, for example, that "service elev#1" posts a "read" request to node 037. When node 037 replies, the reply message will go to the matching terminals on both "service elev#1" and "service elev#2" by implication. Thus, next time "service elev#2" fires, it will have an inappropriate message already waiting. The designer might understand that a message posted from "service elev#1" should reply back only to the originator, but the diagram doesn't convey that.

This is the cardinality problem again. What is required is simplicity. The designer doesn't want a mess of wires going all over the place.

Figure 61: Logical grouping to minimise wiring.

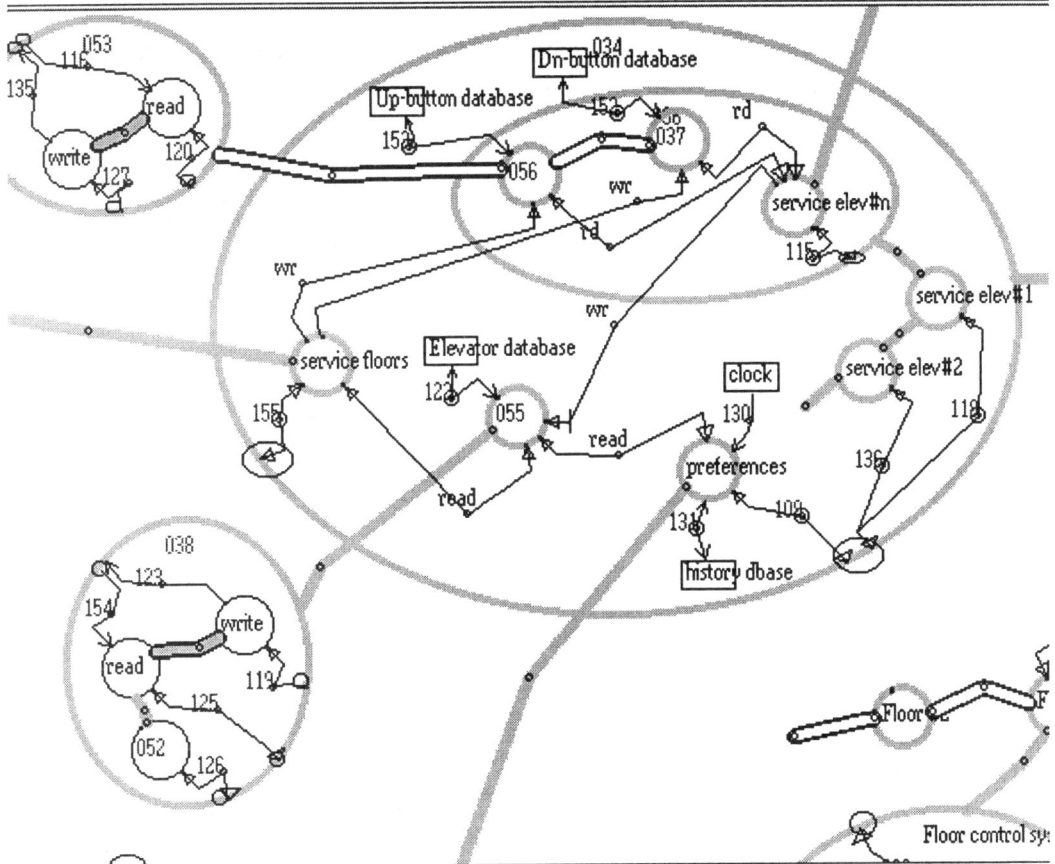

Figure 61 shows a simple mechanism for minimising wiring. The section of diagram to be duplicated encompasses nodes 056, 037, and "service elev#n" — these can be grouped and the group cloned. This does not prevent direct access to the nodes inside the group, as in the case of wires coming from "service floors".

Tracing the flow of execution

Notice that "service elev#1" and "service elev#2" are linked by total union and no-concurrency Joining-bars. This means that internally they are all one, but, each has its own terminals.

Therefore, a request from elevator #2 will arrive at "service elev#2", but due to the no-concurrency relationship with "service elev#1", the scheduler will only fire the former when the latter is not executing. When the scheduler does fire "service elev#2", the message delivered to the terminal will be forwarded to "service elev#n". Simple "thunking" code inside "service elev#2", written in any plain vanilla procedural language, can do this.

Notice too, the logical grouping of nodes, by using a Composite-node, does not impose any kind of restriction regarding wires crossing its boundary. Some wires terminate at the boundary, forming terminals, and some cross directly over.

Node 056 contains the only instance of the write routine to the "Up-button database", so it is quite sensible for "service floors" to send a message directly to it. An OO purist might think that a wire should go from node 056 to the boundary of the enclosing Composite-node, thus appearing as terminals on nodes "service elev#1" and "service elev#2". However, this introduces unnecessary complexity, and the cardinality problem comes back — a wire from "service floors" to one of the proposed terminals on "service elev#1" or "service elev#2" will by implication go to both. An awkward solution would be to feed a dummy input to one of those proposed terminals.

Thus, Figure 61 is a simple, understandable and very pragmatic solution.

Classifications of visibility

A GOOFEE node is an "object", because it may contain data as well as code. Data (and any resource) may be wired externally and still be visible only to the node it is connected to, as is the case with the "Elevator database" resource attached to node 055, in Figure 61 — therefore, it is visible to everything inside node 055. Data/resources may also be inside a node, and this includes dynamic data, or data with a lifetime only for the duration of execution of the node.

"Elevator database" could be made global, i.e., visible to everything inside the encompassing node 034, which is shown on the GOOFEE diagram as a rectangle with either a thick black boundary or a double-line boundary.

The classifications of visibility given in many textbooks can be summarised as follows:

    1 public,

    2 private,

    3 protected, and

    4 friends.

These pertain to both code and data and are well-established classifications throughout OOD. However, not all OO languages handle all four.

Friend data

With respect to resources, it is clear how GOOFEE models items 1, 2, and 3; however, item 4 is awkward. A friend resource is visible to a selected list of nodes in the system, regardless of where they are. It is possible that a "union" Joining-bar be used to explicitly make a resource visible somewhere else. That is, Joining-bars need not be restricted to defining relationships between nodes.

Figure 62: Friend relationship for a resource.

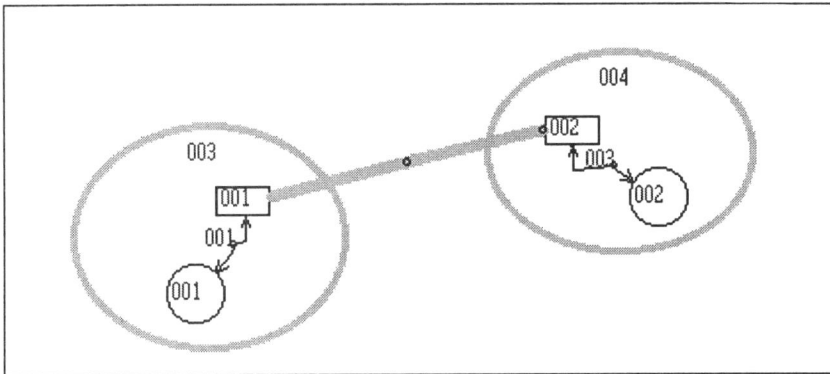

Figure 62 shows that resources 001 and 002 are joined by a "union" Joining-bar, which makes them internally only the one instance. Therefore, the same resource is visible inside two unrelated Composite-nodes.

From an ideological point of view however, using the Joining-bar to specify relationships between resources may be undesirable. What is desirable is that relationships be specified between objects and classes, which translates to nodes (in which resources are hidden). Presumably, the original idea behind friend data was one of efficiency, perhaps in terms of speed of access or code size. Therefore, it may have a place in the design of embedded applications.

Visibility of nodes

With GOOFEE, the limitations on visibility of nodes are not very explicit.

Figure 63: Friend node.

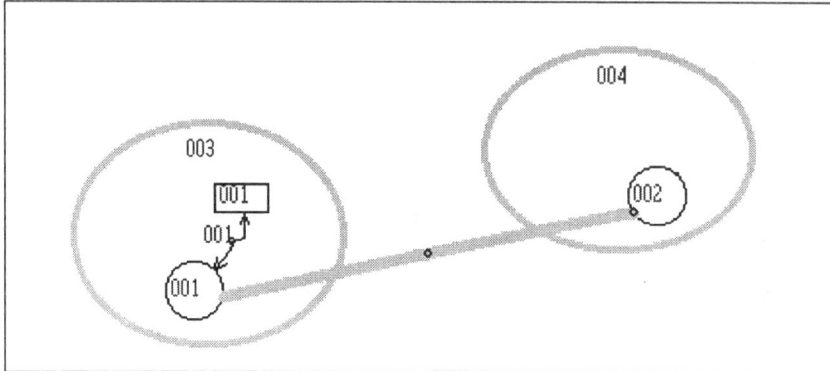

Figure 63 is ideologically an improvement over Figure 62. Resource 001 is accessable via node 001 or node 002. However, no visibility restriction has been imposed on node 001 in any earlier work on the principles underlying GOOFEE, which means that code in node 004 is free to throw a wire right across to node 001.

This "reaching inside" another Composite-node has advantages, as has been done in Figure 61, where "service floors" accesses nodes 056 and 037.

If the designer wants to impose visibility restrictions on nodes, as with data, there are various possibilities. The first is that only nodes with wires going to the boundary of the parent Composite-node are accessible externally. In Figure 61, "service elev#n" has a wire that is accessible outside, as is done by wires 136 and 118. Yet, the desirability of wires directly to nodes 056 and 037 has already been established.

One line of reasoning is that when Composite-nodes are nested, as in Figure 61, all nodes are visible right to the outer-most level. That is, node 056 will be visible anywhere in Composite-node 034, but not outside.

Another line of reasoning is that node 056 requires a "union" Joining-bar and a clone-node (see Figure 63) to make itself visible in node 034.

I favour the simpler diagram of Figure 61, so I propose the first rule should apply. Formalising this:

• Nodes are only visible (at runtime) within the enclosing parent node. The exception to this is expanded-nested nodes, in which a node is visible to the boundary of the outermost enclosing ancestor node.

The person responsible for designing a particular Composite-node will decide which services are to be visible externally by providing wires to the boundary.

This area may need further refinement as experience with applications accumulates. For example, how can it be specified that a node shall not be "cloned", i.e., have a Joining-bar attached, as in Figure 63? The qualification in the above formalism, "(at runtime)", exempts Joining-bars from this visibility restriction. That is, the Joining-bar is an issue during design and compilation.

Therefore, limits on visibility, with regard to nodes, are not fully developed as yet.

Expansion of resource objects

Figure 64 applies the same technique of Figures 60 and 61, in which the resources are removed from Composite-node 015 and placed in the expansion. This allows them to have more appropriate visibility limits.

Notice in Figure 64 that attention is given to the sequencing of execution in the form of the large Iterative-node "Waiting". A convenient convention with Iterative-nodes is that they be designed to sequence from inner ring to outer, which improves at-a-glance readability.

Apart from showing the correct dynamic/runtime behaviour, the exact details of resources also need to be shown. For nodes, the expansion concept is well developed, utilising a Joining-bar and Composite-node or Super-node.

Figure 64: Further localisation of data hiding.

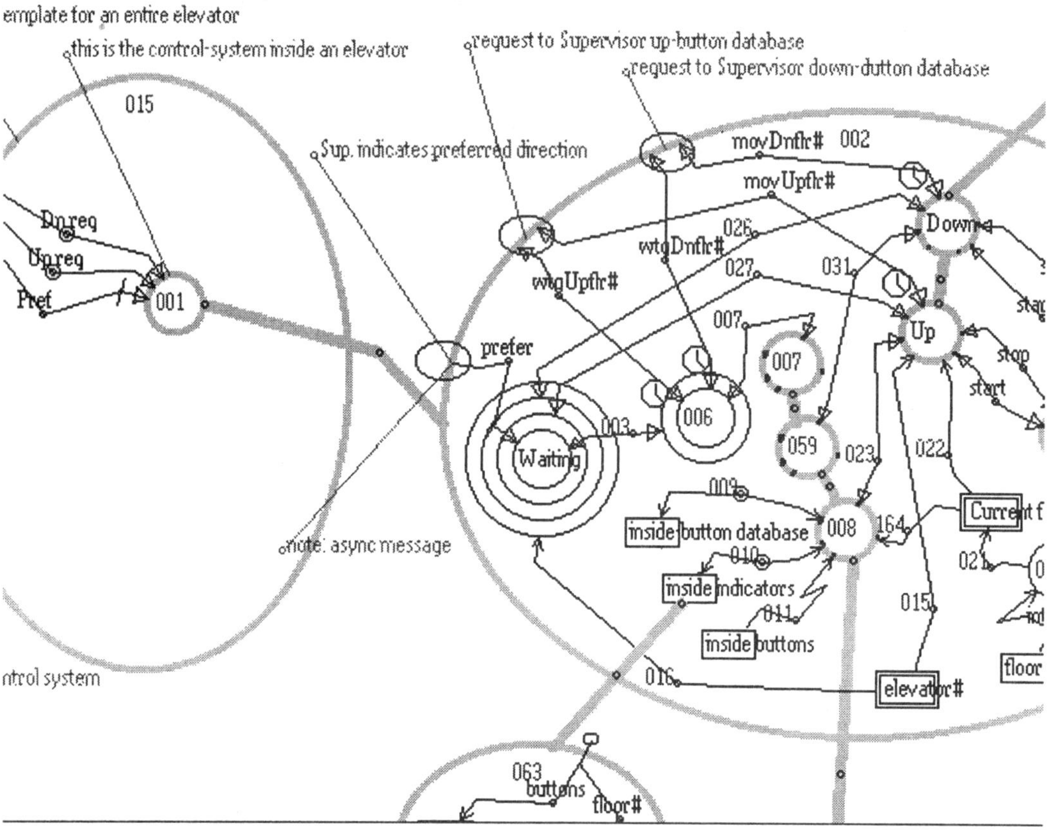

Figure 65 shows that the concept of expansion can also apply to resources. Node 063 is an expansion of "inside indicators".

Notice that the "current floor" global variable is read by node 012 (the expansion of 008) and forwarded to the display. The Reader may think that node 011 should directly display the current floor, which would be okay. At the time of analysis and early design, it seemed "nicer" to make one node responsible for all displays inside the elevator. Any design will involve identification of details like this, and numerous modifications.

Notice too, that node 060 does not need to read "current floor", as the incoming message supplies current-floor and mode (up/down/waiting).

The change is made in Figure 66.

Figure 65: Expansion of resources.

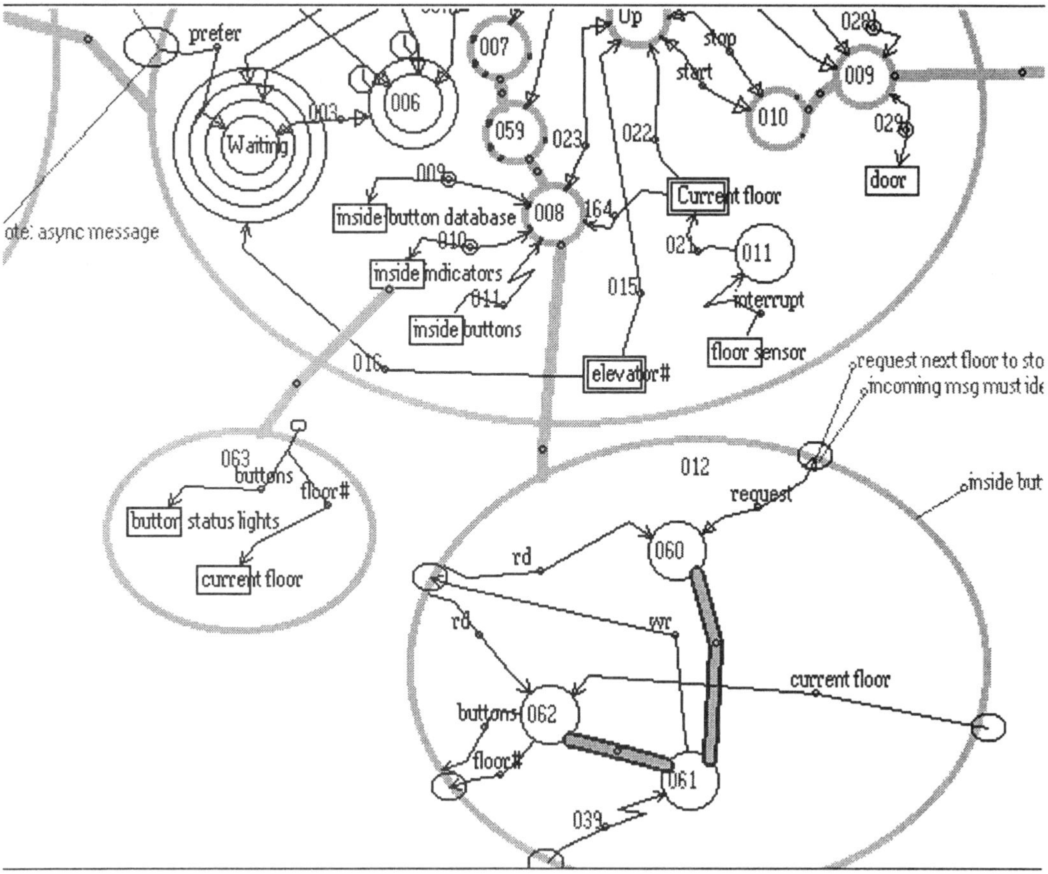

Interrupt handling

Notice the type of Joining-bar used inside node 012 (Figure 66). It is the "unrelated code and data, no-concurrency" type. This formalises the mutual exclusion requirement with accessing the database. Node 064 is an interrupt routine, entered every time a button is pressed, which then updates the button database. Notice that a button-press is not hardwired to a corresponding indicator, but the indicators are operated indirectly through node 062.

Node 062 previously read the "current floor" variable directly; now the information is being passed as a dataflow message ("flr#/mode"), which ensures correct execution sequencing of nodes 060, 061, and 062.

Figure 66: Small refinement in access to I/O.

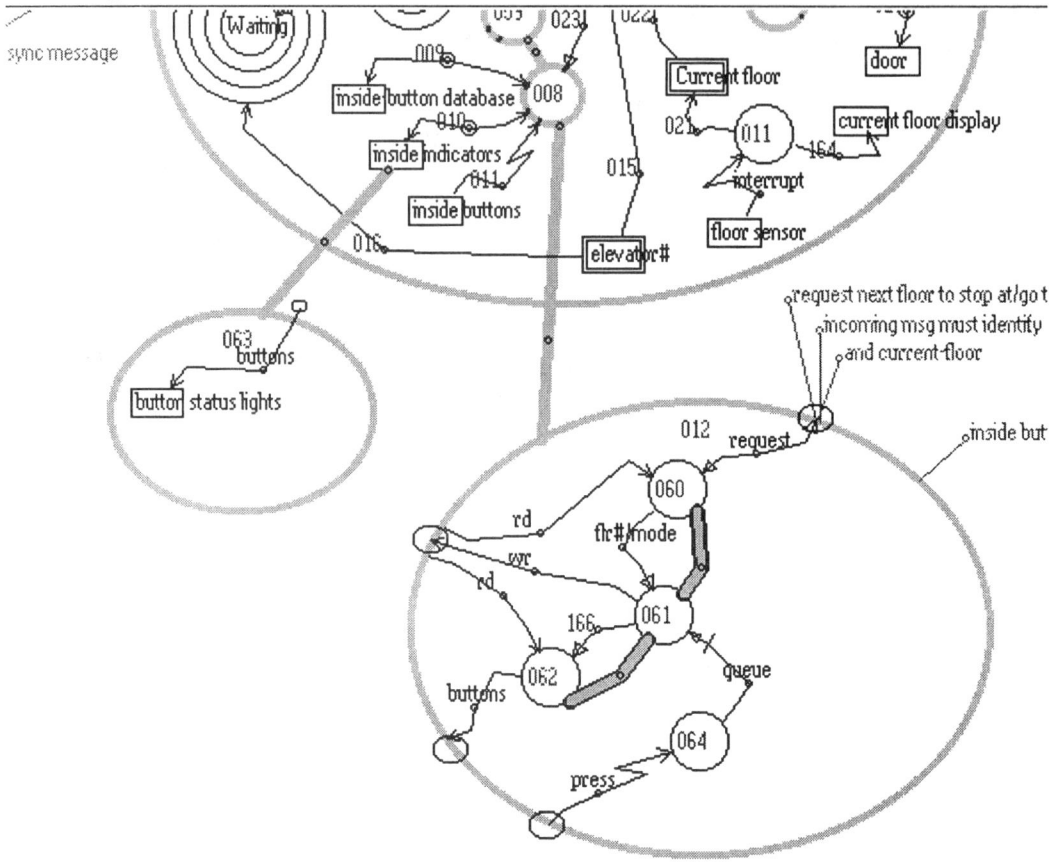

Notice that node 064, the interrupt routine, posts an asynchronous, n-deep queued message. Although with the simple button database, read and write operations will likely be atomic and not require special mutual-access protection, in general it is dangerous for an interrupt routine to write directly to the database. This code could be used as a template ("class") for other databases, so it is wise to construct it in a more formal manner. Formalising this:

- The operating system, or runtime executive, must be able to support an interrupt routine posting asynchronous messages to the message queue.

Node 061 reads which buttons have been pressed and updates the button database. Node 061 is fired whenever message "flr#/mode" arrives, and this information is used to clear button indicators, indirectly via the database. Obviously, if the elevator has reached a certain floor, that particular button indicator can be cleared, if set.

Resource persistence

Data/resource and code persistence is an important topic related to visibility, but different. Persistence is the duration that something exists; however, let me dredge up some old notes I made on C/C++ and GOOFEE node/object dichotomy, and I'll work my way back to this question of persistence.

When is a node not an object?

I went into this in Chapter 7; however, these earlier deliberations are relevant to the consideration of how data is mapped to C/C++.

A single node, with hidden data, is the same as a procedure, from the invocation point of view, because it receives parameters, all of which must arrive on the input wires to fire the node. This is analogous to a procedure call. The exit from the node is different from a procedure, however.

If a procedure can also have local hidden data, how can a node be considered as anything more than a procedure? How can it be considered as an object?

Apart from data hiding, the node in GOOFEE also can have inheritance and has the concept of class and instance, which classifies it as an object.

However, it is not an object in the usual sense, i.e., as Booch's cloud-shapes, because it effectively only provides one method. Also, the possible multiple output wires are definitely different from the single return path of a normal method.

The node is, however, an object, although a primitive one.

The conventional object provides one or more services that belong to that class or abstraction, i.e., multiple methods. In a sense, the node does go part-way toward this in the multiple exit wires.

To correctly map GOOFEE onto conventional objects, the Composite-node (also referred to as the Notional-node in some of my early writing) was introduced. It has been represented as an ellipse with a thick grey boundary line and is a logical grouping of any part of the diagram. Wires flow through the boundary without any impediment: i.e., conjunction of input tokens is not required, because it is not really a node. This is why it was originally referred to as a Notional-node.

However, the Composite-node does provide multiple methods, and can be treated like an ordinary node for the purposes of class/object distinction and inheritance. Refer to Figure 67.

Figure 67: Composite-node provides multiple services.

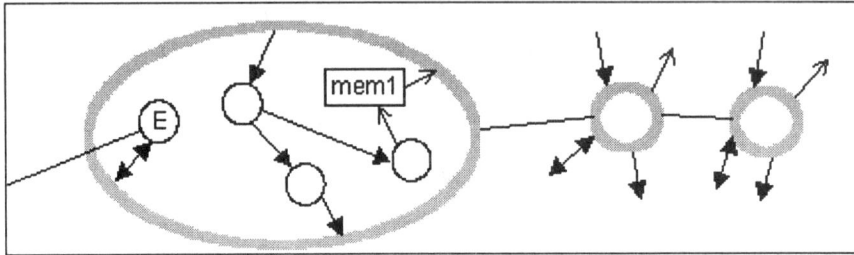

The Composite-node class defines which nodes and resources are visible outside the node, by virtue of wires to and from the boundary.

Note: In keeping with current work, "mem1" would have to be declared global to have wires going to more than one node. A normal resource connects to just one node and is only visible to that node. If declared global, it becomes visible inside the enclosing Composite-node. Global or hidden, mem1 in this old Figure violates all the rules.

Textual adornments

First, to reiterate the textual adornments that may be placed on a node and arc, see Figure 68.

Figure 68: Textual adornments.

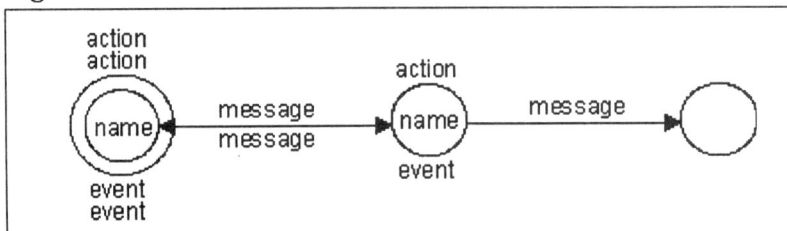

Note that the textual adornments of Figure 68 were devised during early formation of the GOOFEE model, and you will notice the lack of this formalism in the elevator case study.

The adornments of Figure 68 were conceived of with "fine grain" diagrams in mind. That is, GOOFEE diagrams would be drawn down to a level almost equivalent to per-code statements. These adornments would be appropriate for GOOFEE modeling of a state machine, which is possibly a little coarser grained.

However, the elevator control system has not been modeled down to quite this level of granularity, and it has been found sufficient to use less formal textual adornment. The operations, or data transforms, performed within each node of the elevator model, tend to be more complex than would be appropriate for the adornments of Figure 68.

However, Figure 68 still remains the formal standard for textual adornment for GOOFEE diagrams, with coarse-grain designs having a subset, such as only the "message" (outgoing above the wire, reply below) on a wire and "name" in a node.

Data scope

Figure 69 shows earlier work on equating GOOFEE data to C/C++ code, which in retrospect identifies a serious problem with data persistence. This is why I am weaving this path through history and back to persistence.

Figure 69: Scope of data in C.

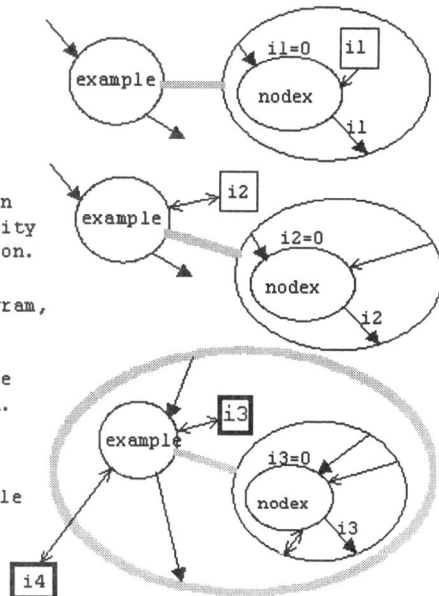

```
Automatic
   example() {      //i only exists for duration
   int i1=0;        //of execution of function,
   return i1;       //and only visible inside
   }                //function.

Static
   example() {      //variable exists for duration
   static int i2=0; //of program, however visibility
   return i2;       //is still only within function.
   }
   static int i3;   //although global to the program,
   example() {      //placing static here forces
   ...              //i3 to only be visible in
   }                //current file.  No other file
                    //can override this by extern.

extern
   extern int i4;   //this is redundant, as any
   example()        //global variable is accessible
                    //across files in C++.
```

Data "i1" was conceived as being automatic, while "i2" was static; however, the usage in the elevator case study has used all data and resources in rectangles as persistent, i.e., static.

However, it does appear that a distinction can be made between data inside a node and data inside a Composite-node. Data inside a node, including a Super-node, whether expressed only in code (coarse-grain diagram) or explicitly shown by a rectangle (as "i1"), is by default automatic.

However, the Composite-node, or Notional-node, although delimiting visibility of resources inside it, does not have to delimit their persistence. That is, a resource persists when execution is outside a Composite-node.

The main problem with this reasoning is whether a designer will be confused by the chameleon-like nature of the Composite-node. It defines the limit of visibility of resources, but not their persistence. On the other hand, a normal or Super-node (the Super-node is really the same as a normal node, just larger) limits both visibility and persistence.

Is there a more consistent way of representing both visibility and persistence?

Resource persistence rules

In the interest of simplicity and ease of understanding and usage by the designer, the node, Super-node, and Composite-node should have the same rules for resource visibility and persistence. Therefore, I will formalise some rules:

- A resource is *persistent* as long as execution is within the boundary that encompasses it.

- A resource is *visible* only to one node (and may only have wires to/from one node), unless declared global, when it is visible within the boundary that encloses it.

Referring back to Figure 64, "inside button database" resource is visible only to node 008 but is persistent within Composite-node 002. As the latter is the entire elevator control system, the database remains in existence as long as the elevator control system is running, which will be continuously.

What needs to be clarified is how exceptions are handled. Refer to Figure 70.

To further clarify, resource 004 (Figure 70) is visible and persistent as long as execution is anywhere inside node 002, including inside node 001.

Resource 001 is only visible when execution is inside node 001 but persists for as long as execution remains anywhere inside node 002. The simple solution to making any resource more persistent, without affecting visibility, is to do as is shown with Resource 002: drag it out.

Figure 70: Representing visibility and persistence.

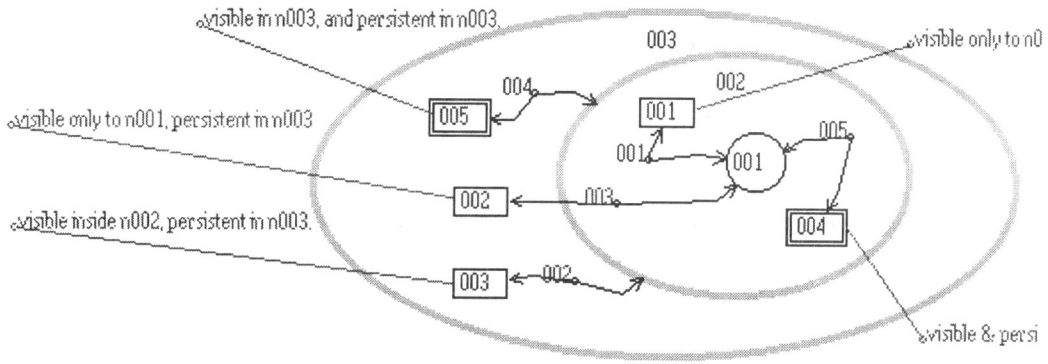

Any resource can be "dragged out". A normal resource will become more persistent as it is dragged out, while a global resource will become both more persistent and more visible.

This graphic manipulation of resources explicitly, in which they are very "visible" on the diagram outside the nodes in which they are encapsulated, may make an OO purist cringe; however, there is nothing actually "wrong" with the GOOFEE approach — it is just different and does not violate any OO principles.

Persistence of nodes

There is not much to say. GOOFEE allows persistence of nodes to be expressed with extreme clarity. In an embedded system, nodes are normally indefinitely persistent, but for applications in which they need to be managed, such as shunted off to disk when not in use, the GOOFEE principle is extremely simple:

- A node need only persist as long as the most persistent resource attached to it.

Comparison with other methodologies

This high level of flexibility for representing visibility and persistence cannot be matched by any other methodology. One of the key advantages of GOOFEE is the 2-dimensional representation that allows the at-a-glance representation of Figure 70.

The OOA/D methodologies deal with classes and objects, not specifically in terms of data/resources, so any reference to scope, visibility, and persistence is usually in relation to the former. The modeling of visibility of methods and attributes appears to be reasonably well covered in the established methodologies, although not all deal with visibility of objects themselves. The major weakness is the handling of persistence.

Using the keywords "scope", "visibility", and "persistence" as a basis for a search, is interesting by virtue of how infrequently these words are used. Major methodology books may contain only a few references to visibility and most have no mention at all of persistence. This can be quantified somewhat by an Internet search.

Table 6: Keyword search.

KEYWORD	Durham Uni. [1]	Indiana Uni. [2]	Object Agency [3]
Scope	0	0	0
Visibility	2	2	0
Persistence	1	1	1

Table 6 is a count of "appropriate hits" at these web sites. They are comprehensive surveys and comparisons of the major OOA/D methodologies, including (but not necessarily at all sites) Berard, Booch, Colbert, Coad/Yourdon, Embley/Kurtz, Martin/Odell, Rumbaugh, Shlaer/Mellor, and Wirfs/Brock:

1 Biggs, P. (1996) A Survey of Object-Oriented Methods. University of Durham. http://www.dur.ac.uk/~dcs3pjb/survey.html

2 author unknown (1994) Object Oriented Methodologies. http://www.indiana.edu/~sdg/projects/oodp/method.html

3 Object Agency (1993) A Comparison of Object-Oriented Development Methodologies. http://www.toa.com/pub/html/mcr.1html

Of course, the table does reflect the understanding of the people conducting the survey/comparison, as well as the capabilities of the methodologies themselves.

It is not that the OO languages and methodologies don't handle visibility, and to a much lesser extent persistence. It seems that object visibility and persistence are treated as incidental by the methodology authors, not as key factors. Visibility, used in the context of hiding of methods and attributes, may often not be explicitly mentioned because it is implied by the concept of encapsulation. Persistence is related to timing and dynamic performance, which is "tacked on" as an afterthought to many methodologies. The methodologies focus on static relationships, not dynamic (runtime) relationships, in the bulk of their documentation.

Conclusions

This chapter has shown that GOOFEE has the necessary mechanisms for hiding resources and code in accordance with the public, private, protected, and friends classifications, with some work still to be done with regard to code visibility. Therefore (in my opinion of course), GOOFEE is at least on a par with the popular methodologies such as Booch, OMT, and Coates/Yourdon.

A distinction is made between visibility and persistence of resources (and nodes), and it is shown that persistence can also be shown diagrammatically. The flexibility of expressing the relationships between resource—node—visibility—persistence is a very positive feature of GOOFEE.

The other main advantages claimed of GOOFEE tend to be subjective in nature. This is the overall readability, intuitiveness, and precision of the diagram. Both Yourdon and Gomaa (references given earlier in this chapter) have the elevator control system as a case study. Yourdon focuses more on OOA; less on OOD, but even that is very incomplete, making comparison difficult. Gomaa's treatment of the elevator case study reflects his expertise in real-time systems, and there are more specific interaction, interface, and timing details. Gomaa uses COBRA for analysis and CODARTS/DA for design. Both authors utilise the best principles of information hiding, though couched in different terminology.

Of the two, Gomaa's method most closely parallels the path of reasoning that was taken in the evolution of the GOOFEE-based solution and is thus the easiest to compare. In fact, much of Gomaa's early analysis could have been the basis for a GOOFEE design. GOOFEE could possibly utilise Gomaa's formalisms of the NRL method (pages 90 to 93 in his book). The GOOFEE elevator case study employs HIMs, DIMs, and SDMs, for example, without identifying them in such a formal manner.

A pragmatic point to add is that as GOOFEE has been developed for the 70% of engineers, scientists, and technologists who do not currently use a formal software analysis/design methodology, formalisms, in particular the rampant usage of acronyms, need to be minimised.

9
Modeling time

Preamble

The elevator control system case study is chosen as the focus as it has complex cardinality and information-hiding relationships, and the timing aspects are consequently complex.

This chapter asks if timing information can be portrayed to the level of detail that is required by a sophisticated real-time application, that has hard real-time constraints.

Then, it needs to be determined that a translation can be made to a scheduling table that is sufficiently expressive and unambiguous. The scheduling table developed in Chapter 5 and illustrated in Figures 38 to 40 are fine for small projects. However, complex projects may need a more "heavy duty" tabular scheduling specification.

A feature of the Scheduling table developed in this chapter is the expression of scheduling in terms of messages with fixed, "hardwired" source and destination nodes. The process is shown by which the diagram is analysed to arrive at such a table.

Having messages with hardwired source and destination greatly simplifies final implementation on a scheduler and implementation in non-OO code.

Node sequencing

Figure 71: Sequencing by use of the Iterative-node.

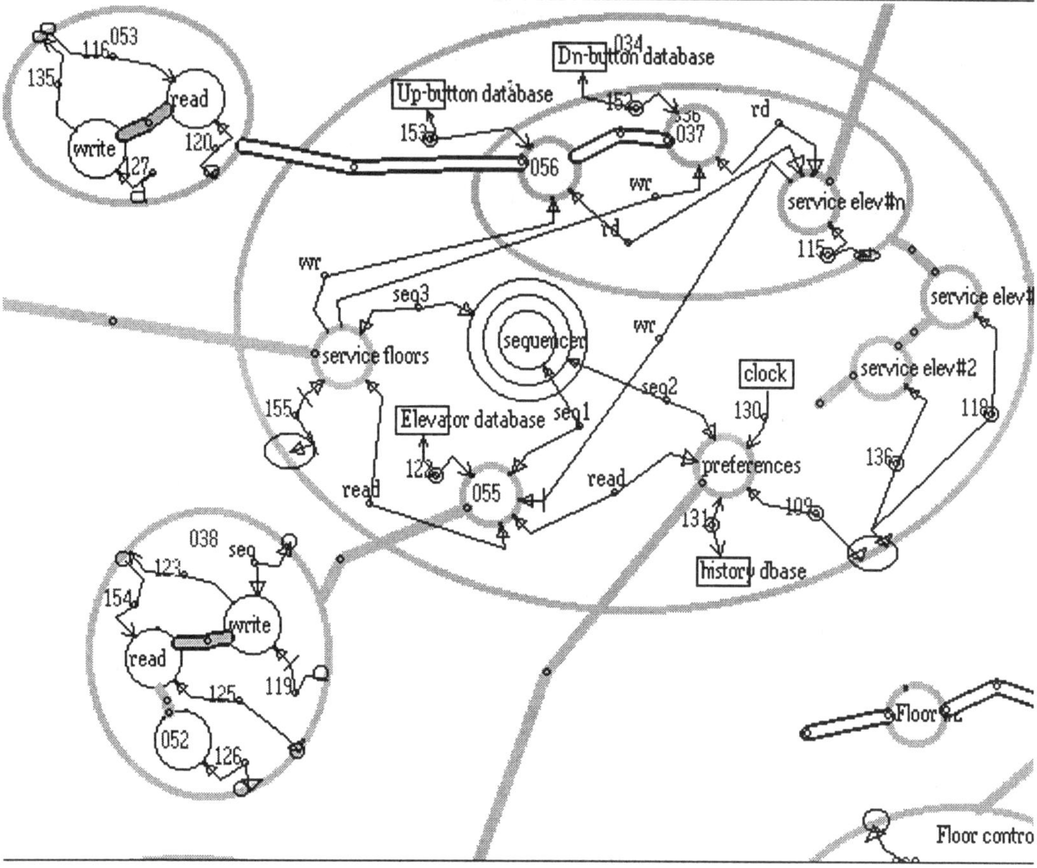

The Iterative-node is a very convenient mechanism to express sequential execution. In Figure 61, the execution order of "service floors", node 055, and "preferences" is not clear. For example, it would be reasonable for node 055 to execute before "service floors", so that "elevator database" is updated with the latest information before being read.

Figure 71 shows how this is achieved. The default convention for "sequencer" is that execution ordering is from inner to outer ring, so a synchronous dataflow message is posted first to node 055. However, this does NOT force node 055 to fire next; it simply places a message in the message buffer, and the runtime executive will see that node 055 is eligible.

Forcing execution of nodes with asynchronous inputs only

The problem with node 055 is that writes to its database from "service elev#n" are asynchronous messages, which the runtime executive buffers n-deep but doesn't use for scheduling.

The Composite-node "service floors" is in the same situation: asynchronous message inputs only. Wherever this situation is identified, it is a candidate for connection to the sequencer. A node requires as a minimum, one synchronous input node for it to be scheduled.

The above text develops the rationale for inclusion of "sequencer", however the overall time behaviour of the Supervisor processor, Composite-node 034, is not fully defined.

Note that an Iterative-node could be expanded, if desired. It is also possible that a Composite-node could be substituted; however, the Iterative-node conveys the significance of sequencing by virtue of its graphic symbol.

Servicing elevator requests

When an elevator sends a request for the next floor to stop at or go to, the message will arrive at the Supervisor's message buffer. The operating system can detect its presence and schedule the node it is addressed to. It is a synchronous message. For example, a remote input message addressed to "service elev#1" (wire 119) will result in that node firing. Internally, "service elev#1" is a shell that fires "service elev#n", and this is where actual code may not accurately reflect the diagram, though it still reflects the spirit of the diagram.

Skeleton code is developed in Chapter 6 that illustrates the principle of redirection. The empty shell "service elev#1" simply calls the appropriate node inside "service elev#n", passing necessary parameters via the stack.

It is clear in Figure 71 when all nodes become eligible to fire, but what is not clear is when the scheduler will actually fire them. The simplest scheduler will not be preemptive and will execute a node to completion, which will require the designer to make sure that nodes are small enough not to compromise timely servicing of waiting messages.

The most critical timing problem is the request from an elevator. Each elevator can send a request asynchronously, and each must obtain a reply within a certain time. Say an elevator is moving past floor n and posts a request. If the reply says to stop at floor n+1, it must arrive in time before the elevator has gone past floor n+1.

A more sophisticated scheduler will preempt a currently running node when it detects that another node is eligible to fire. The other node can be immediately scheduled as long as it is not restricted by a non-concurrency relationship (specified by a Joining-bar) and maybe in accordance with some priority scheme. This is of course far more complex than the non-preemptive route.

The challenge is that the GOOFEE diagram be able to show exactly WHEN each node fires, not just when it is ELIGIBLE. My usage of the word "when" needs to be carefully understood. It refers to when in the node firing sequence a particular node will fire, i.e., where it fits into the sequence, NOT the exact relative or absolute time of its firing. Node sequencing is dependent on dataflow messages, and this paper bases design on sequencing in response to those messages.

Anything beyond that, such as a node having to fire at some reference time, is considered a special case and not covered in this chapter.

Signature scheduling

The technique that I developed in parallel with GOOFEE is a dataflow operating system called TERSE, introduced in Chapter 5. A significant feature is that it enables the unambiguous and deterministic specification of the "when" of node sequencing. The specification is in the form of a Signature Scheduling table, with a refinement for efficient handling of remote (interprocessor) input messages coined as MESS scheduling.

Obviously there has to be a limit to placing annotations, textual adornments, and special symbols on a single GOOFEE diagram. To exactly specify sequencing now requires a separate table, one for each processor (or more correctly, a table for each diagram with independent cycle times and start/stop nodes).

The GOOFEE diagram of Figure 71 uses an absolute numbering scheme for nodes, wires, and resources, but when translated to a processor there would be local numbering. For the purpose of illustration, the scheduling table is designed here using the absolute numbering. Look ahead to Table 8; I have kept it compact by using numbering, but it is quite feasible to express all messages by textual aliases.

Figure 72: Showing numbering only.

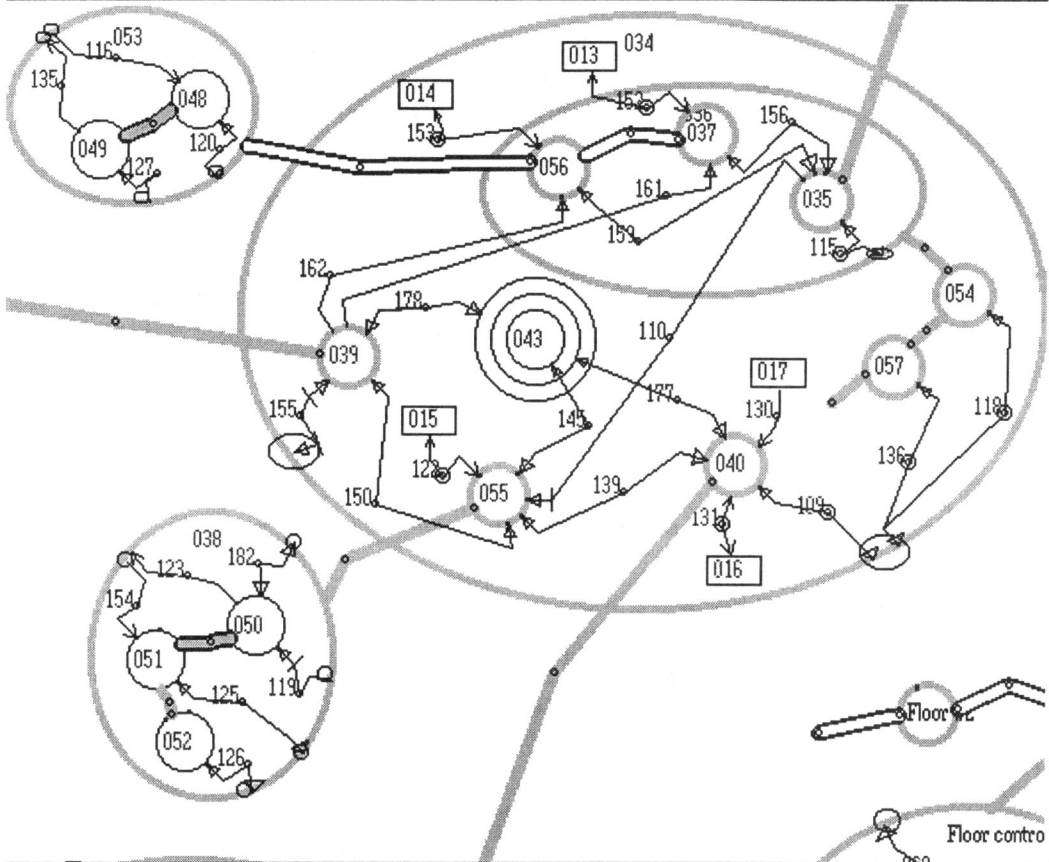

Table 7: Partial scheduling table.

SIGNATURE	NEXT NODE
>	N043
>W145>	N055
>W177>	N040
>W178>	N039
>W161>	N037
>W162>	N056

Table 7 is a starting point. Based upon use of a simple non-preemptive scheduler, it specifies which node will fire next when a certain message is present. The ">" delimiters indicate ordering in the message queue, with the left-most message being oldest.

Figure 73: Expansion of node 035.

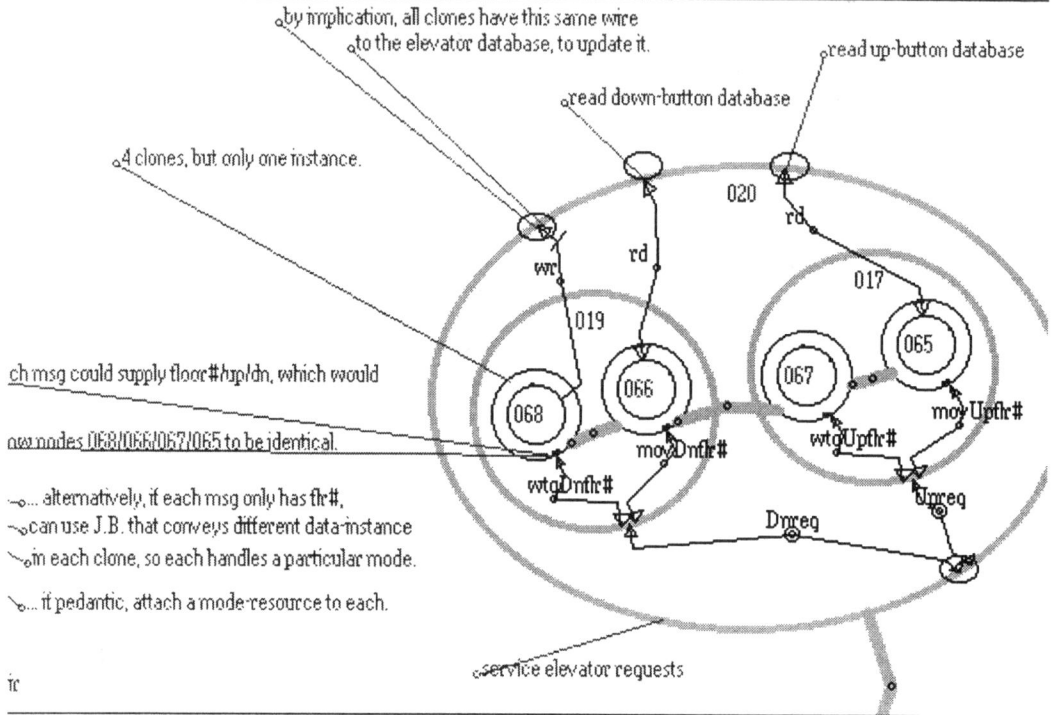

This is the original format for designing scheduling tables, as documented in Chapter 5. The argument below develops a new format, in which only node numbers are placed in the table. Table 7 shows wires with messages by the prefix "W" and node numbers with prefix "N"; however, I considered that as table complexity grows, the mixture of wire and node numbers might cause confusion. You are warned at this point to be aware that a transition will take place in the following text to a table based only on node numbers, which will NOT be prefixed with an "N".

Table 7 shows single messages in the buffer, in which case there is no doubt which node to fire next. What are not shown are the multiple messages and external input messages.

Figure 74: Expansion of node 035, with absolute numbering.

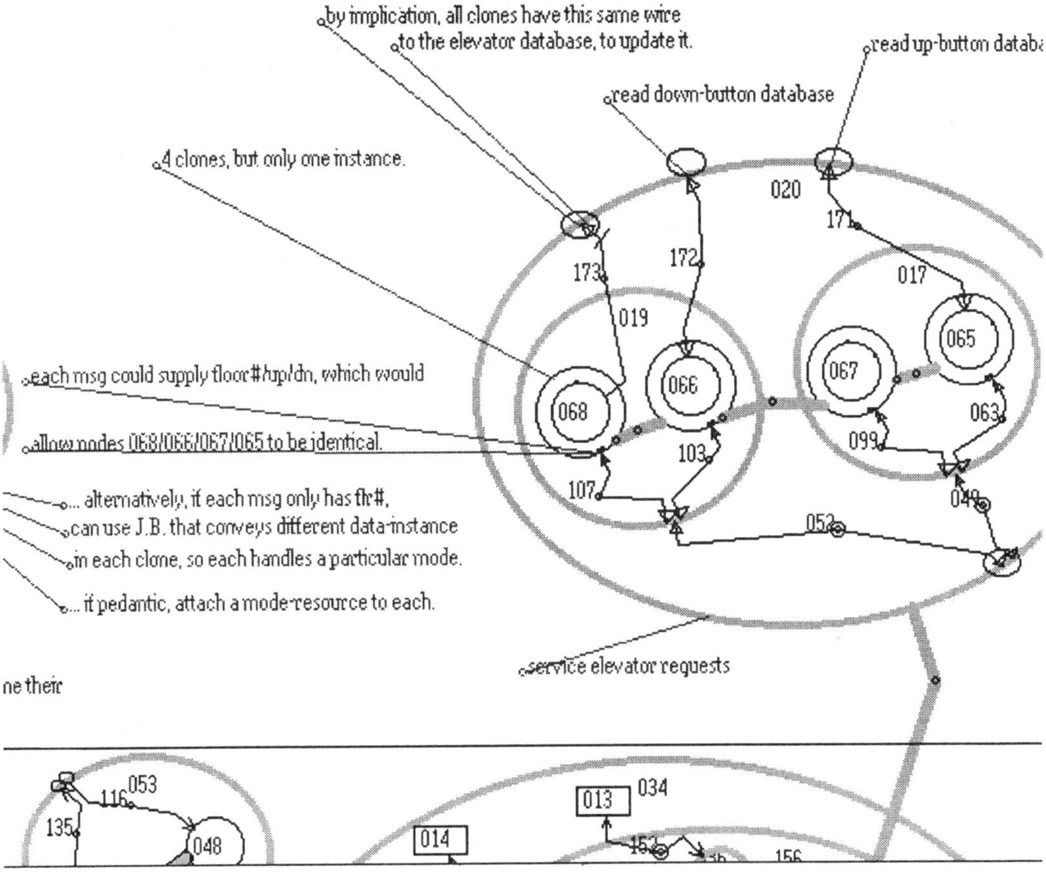

°by implication, all clones have this same wire
°to the elevator database, to update it.

°read down-button database

°read up-button databa

°4 clones, but only one instance.

020

171

173

172

017

019

065

°each msg could supply floor#/up/dn, which would

067

°allow nodes 068/066/067/065 to be identical.

068

066

063

103

099

°... alternatively, if each msg only has flr#,
°can use J.B. that conveys different data-instance
°in each clone, so each handles a particular mode.

107

049

°... if pedantic, attach a mode-resource to each.

052

ne their

°service elevator requests

116   053

034

135

013

048

014

015

156

It is not just whether the scheduler is preemptive or non-preemptive. The language used for coding is also a factor. For example, the relationship between "service elev#n", "service elev#1", "service elev#2", etc., would seem to indicate use of an object pointer, and it would seem that an OO language such as C++ is most appropriate. If an object such as "service elev#1" is to call the code in the template (class), i.e., the expansion of "service elev#n", it would seem appropriate to use a call, not the dataflow messaging as shown on the diagram, because there has to be a return to the caller. If a message contains its source, then a reply to the correct caller could be built into the OS.

Figure 75: Expansion of node 039.

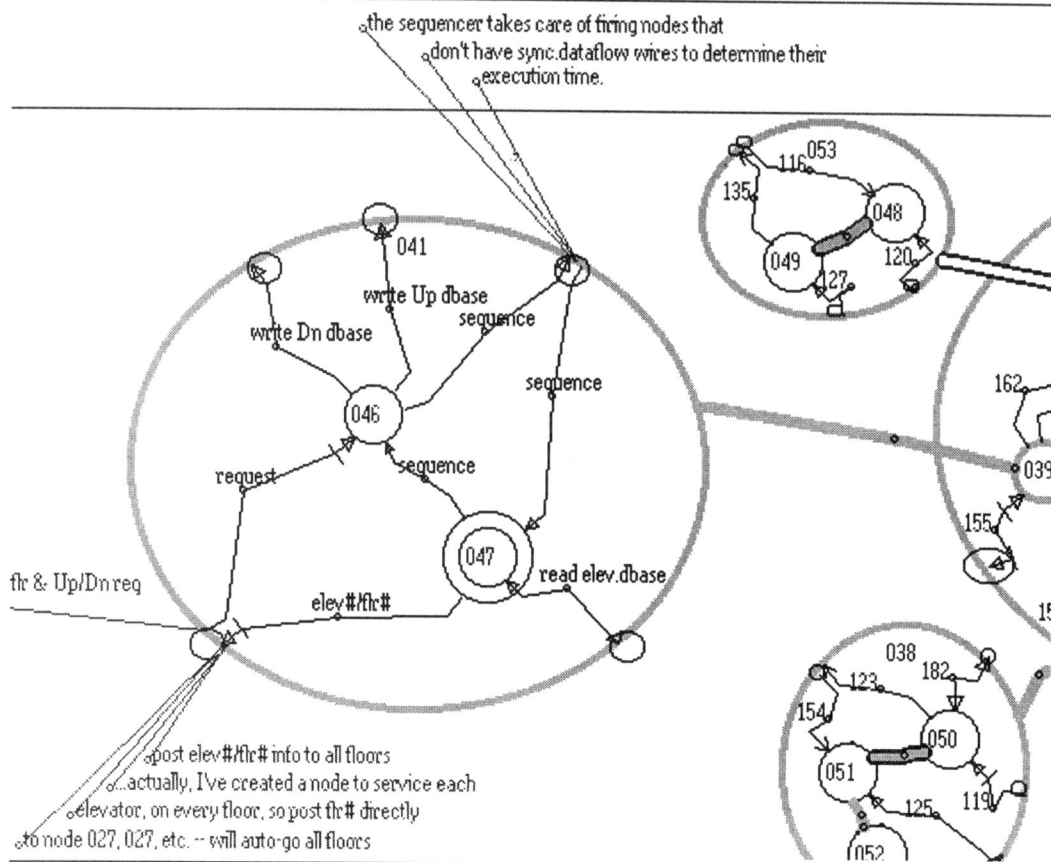

The implementation issues thus are:

1 Scheduler preemptive or non-preemptive

2 Scheduling algorithms

3 OO language or non-OO language

4 Method of calling templates (class) from a clone (object) (related to language)

5 Structure of dataflow messages

Construction of any kind of scheduling table cannot proceed until these are resolved.

Figure 76: Expansion of node 039, with absolute numbering.

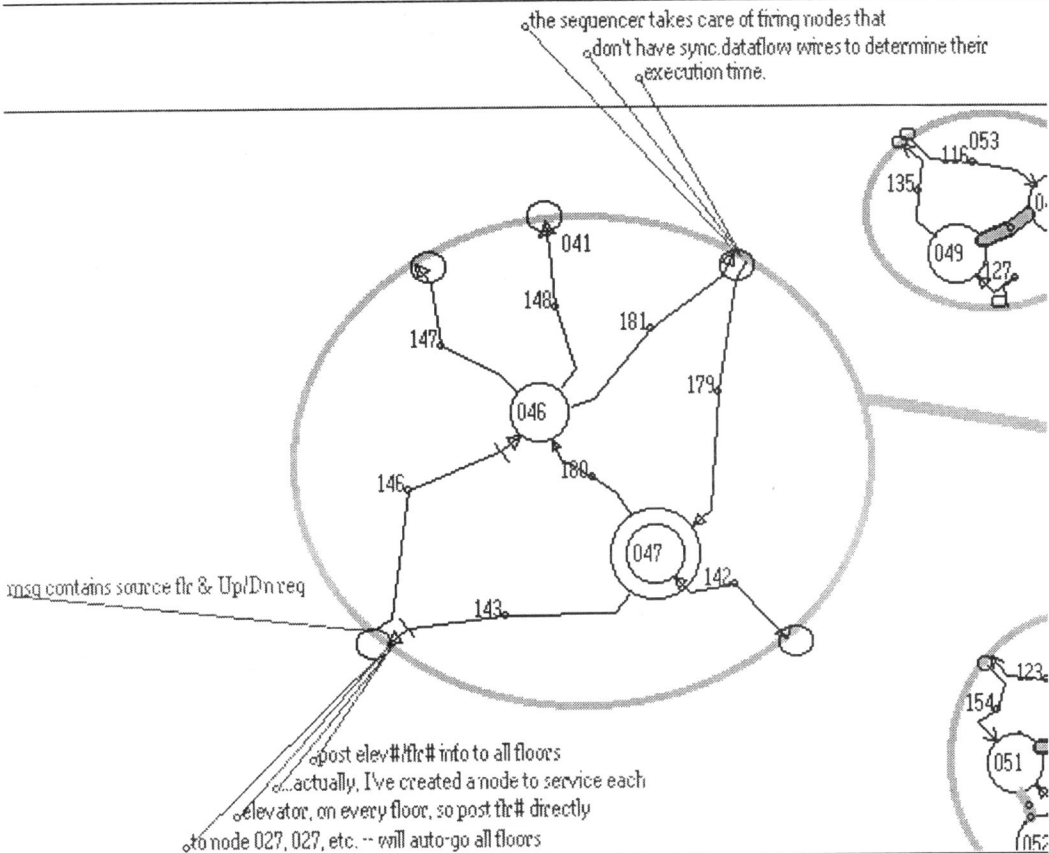

the sequencer takes care of firing nodes that
don't have sync.dataflow wires to determine their
execution time.

041

148

181

147

179

046

053

116

135

049

127

146

180

047

142

msg contains source flr & Up/Dn req

143

123

154

051

052

post elev#/flr# info to all floors
actually, I've created a node to service each
elevator, on every floor, so post flr# directly
to node 027, 027, etc. -- will auto-go all floors

Non-OO language full utilisation of dataflow scheduler

The heading for this section identifies a certain approach to implementation, in which the mechanism by which a clone accesses code in a template leverages off the dataflow scheduling mechanism.

Node 054 (Figure 72) is a clone of node 036 (number slightly hidden behind node 037), with a "union" Joining-bar (signifying only one instance of code and data). Looking inside node 036, it can be seen that node 035 is a clone of node 020 (Figure 73), again with a union Joining-bar. Similarly, nodes 056 and 037 are clones of 053, although in this case it is a "copied data, copied code, concurrency allowed" Joining-bar. Note that any Joining-bar filled with grey signifies no-concurrency.

Figure 77: Elevator control system, with absolute numbering.

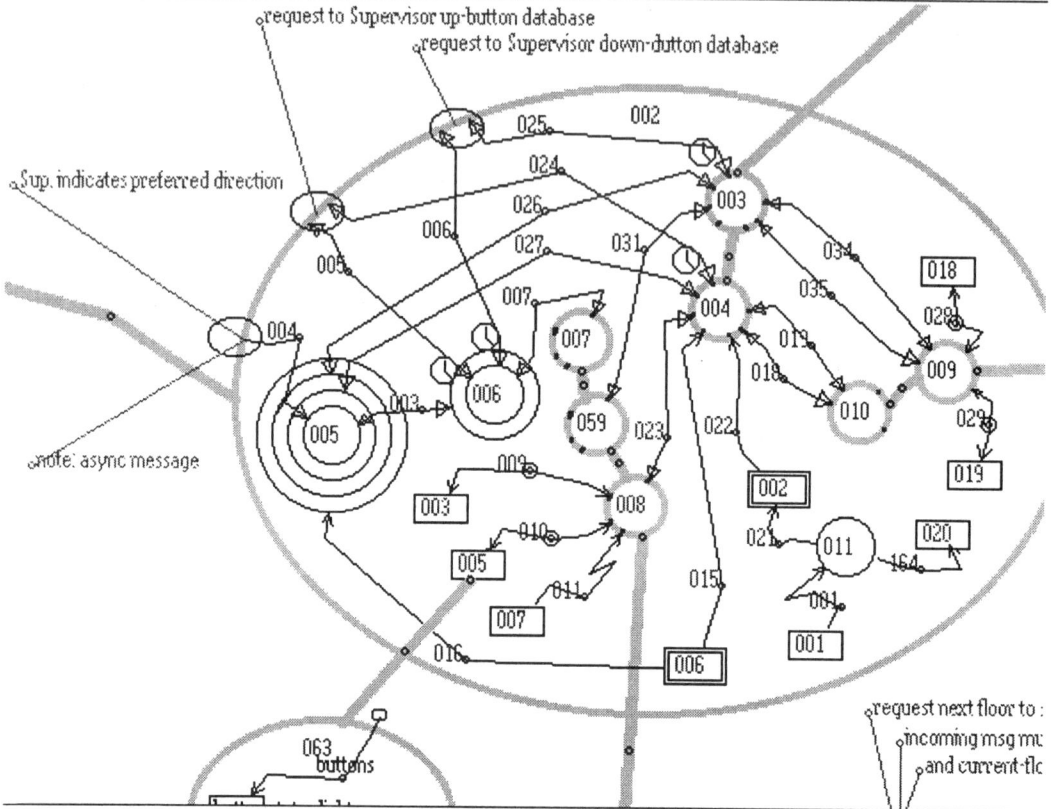

This approach to design is how GOOFEE was originally intended to be interpreted for coding purposes. All of the expansions of node 054 are **contained** in node 054 as clones. Everything is cloned, as per the union Joining-bar. For example, node 065 (Figure 74) is cloned and appears inside node 054 (Figure 72) — let it be designated as 054.065, but in the final design it will of course be assigned a local number. But what is inside 054.065?

Read the "." in 054.065 as loosely meaning "cloned from". That is, inside 054 there is a clone of 065. Read "054.065" as being an actual node. This is the symbolic name for a node that shows where it resides (054) and where it inherits from (065).

The content of 054.065 is defined by the Joining-bar. In this case, there is only one instance of the code/data, so there can only be one node 065. Node 054.065 has to be a shell, thunking to 065.

The point of confusion that arises here is that it appears that node 035 (Figure 72) must be cloned into 054, perhaps designated as 054.035. However, as this is a Composite-node, it does not have to be executed as an atomic node — messaging can go straight through to the actual destination. Strictly interpreted, node 065 (Figure 73) is cloned into 035, designated as 035.065, which when cloned again into 054 will need another designation 054.035.065. A message delivered to 054.035.065 would thunk to 035.065 and thunk again to 065.

There are some problems with implementing the strict interpretation given in the previous paragraph. The current section is dealing with messages that are hardwired between nodes, and pointers are not used. "Thunking" via 035.065 has a problem with a reply to the caller. It is better if the diagram can be "levelled" as much as possible. That is, every message will go directly between two clones, without intermediary "thunking".

The strict interpretation can be relaxed by application of common sense. An elevator will know that it wants to send a message to the clone of node 065 designated for servicing that particular elevator, i.e., 054.065. So only one thunk is required.

However, if the strict interpretation is rigidly applied, the correct situation is that 065 gets cloned into 035, becoming 035.065. Then a clone is made of that, into 054, giving a clone inside 054 of 054.035.065. This is a single clone and will be an actual instantiated clone in the implementation. It fits the requirement of a hardwired single destination for a message.

If speed is vital, thunking can be completely removed by making 054.065 a new complete instantiation of 065, which could be designated by an appropriate Joining-bar (copy code, copy data). Observe also that 054.065 reads the up button database, via a clone of 048. So, the reader might think why not clone 048 directly inside 054? Node 048 has to be cloned into 037 and 056 first, because they are connected to different databases, so what finally gets cloned into 054 will be node 054.037.048 and 054.056.048. The "strict interpretation" was required here.

The scenario now is that node 054 has inside it the following clones: 054.035.065, 054.035.066, 054.035.067, 054.035.068, 054.037.048, 054.056.048, 054.037.049, and 054.056.049. Here, the strict interpretations are applied, and the simplifications can easily be made later.

"Heavy duty" scheduling table

Messaging notation

With MESS scheduling, local (internal) synchronous messages take part in the signature calculation, but because remote input messages can arrive at any time, they do not take part. Instead, the OS selectively checks for the arrival of each remote input. This is context sensitive. For each state of the system, the OS will have a lookup table entry that gives a next-node based on calculated signature. There will also be a flags variable entry that designates which remote inputs to check. If one of those has arrived, its destination node is fired in preference to the normal next-node.

Before examining Table 8, review carefully the syntax developed for representing nodes. The designation "054.035.066" means a node that is a clone inside node 054 and inherits from node 066. Now look in the first column toward the bottom of Table 8 at the entry ">> 054.035.066". This signifies a message that (comes from node 003.070 and) has a destination at node 054.035.066. Note that I haven't specified the source of the remote i/p as I am restraining the design such that there shall be only one remote i/p wire to a node.

What is the point of this? Why use this notation? The reason is that it becomes very easy to translate the diagram to plain-vanilla non-OO code, without the use of object pointers and entirely by messages with fixed source/destination. So the message ">> 054.035.066" from clone 003.070 to clone 054.035.066 will also return to 003.070 if the message is the type with a reply. There will be another message in reply, designated 054.035.066 >> 003.070. Note that this message is not shown in Table 8, because it is an outgoing remote message that has nothing to do with local scheduling.

Notice that the entry in the table uses italics; " >> 054.*035*.066". The purpose of this is that although the strict interpretation is followed in every case, the italic is an embellishment showing a link that can be dropped. It indicates an optimisation to be made in implementation. That is, node 066 can be cloned directly into 054 as 054.066.

Table 8: Completion of the scheduling table.

LOCAL MESSAGE	LOCAL MESSAGE BUFFER (# shows order)
nothing >> 043	`1................................`
043 >> *040*.PR1	`.1...............................`
040.PRI >> 043	`..1..............................`
043 >> *055*.050	`...1.............................`
055.050 >> 043	`....1............................`
043 >> *039*.047	`.....1...........................`
039.046 >> 043	`......1..........................`
040.PR2 >> *055*.051	`.......1.........................`
055.051 >> *040*.PR2	`........1........................`
039.047 >> *055*.052	`.........1.......................`
055.052 >> *039*.047	`..........1......................`
047 >> 046	`..........1......................`
039.046 >> *056*.049	`...........1.....................`
039.046 >> *037*.049	`............1....................`
035.065 >> 037.048	`.............2.......2...........`
037.048 >> 035.065	`.............2.......2...........`
035.066 >> 056.048	`.............2.......2...........`
056.048 >> 035.066	`.............2.......2...........`
035.067 >> 037.048	`.............2.......2...........`
037.048 >> 035.067	`.............2.......2...........`
035.068 >> 056.048	`.............2.......2...........`
056.048 >> 035.068	`.............2.......2...........`
054-marker >> cleanup	`...............11111111.........1...`
057-marker >> cleanup	`....................11111111..1..`
REMOTE INPUT MESSAGE	TEST FOR ARRIVAL
>> 054.*035*.066	`XXXXXXXXXXXXX....................`
>> 054.*035*.065	`XXXXXXXXXXXXX....................`
>> 054.*035*.068	`XXXXXXXXXXXXX....................`
>> 054.*035*.067	`XXXXXXXXXXXXX....................`
>> 057.*035*.066	`XXXXXXXXXXXXX....................`
>> 057.*035*.065	`XXXXXXXXXXXXX....................`
>> 057.*035*.068	`XXXXXXXXXXXXX....................`
>> 057.*035*.067	`XXXXXXXXXXXXX....................`
WAIT	*enter timeout values vertically*
SIGNATURES	*enter signatures vertically*

Scheduling in the scheduling table

The right column of Table 8 is sub-divided into sub-columns. Each sub-column flags which messages are on the message buffer at that state of the system. The first row of the table identifies the case of no messages in the buffer, and identifies the starting node, 043.

Each sub-column has entries, that could be simple yes/no flags, signifying whether a message is in the buffer or not. Or the entries could be numerical, signifying ordering in the buffer, which is a requirement for TERSE where order is a factor in signature computation.

For each sub-column, there will be one or more entries shown bold, indicating which node will execute (i.e., the destination-node of that message) and which messages will be consumed.

This may not be clear, so study Figure 78.

Figure 78: Clarification of "heavy duty" scheduling table.

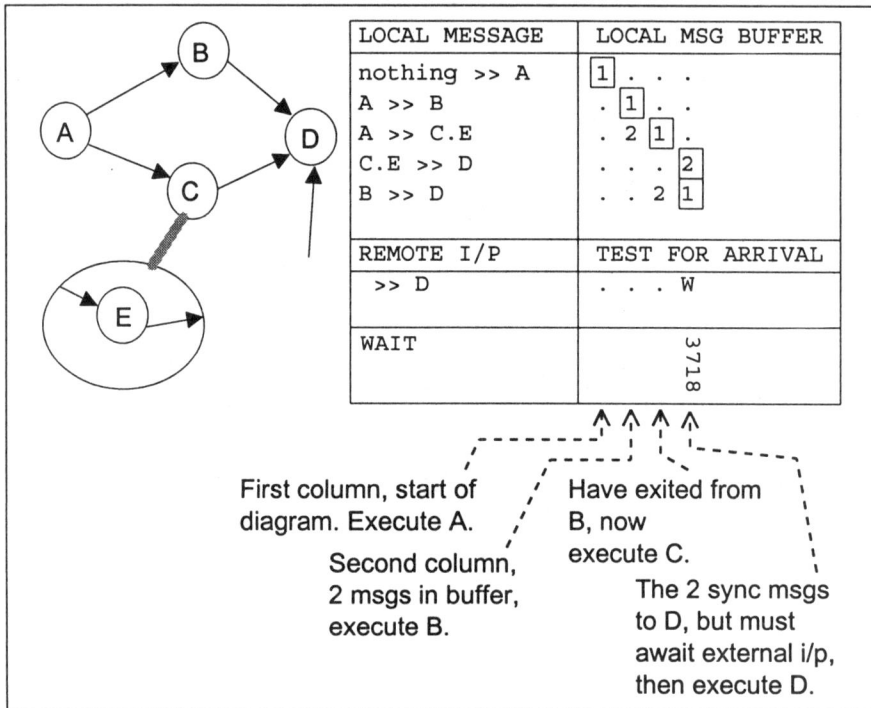

LOCAL MESSAGE	LOCAL MSG BUFFER
nothing >> A	1 . . . .
A >> B	. 1 . .
A >> C.E	. 2 1 .
C.E >> D	. . . 2
B >> D	. . 2 1

REMOTE I/P	TEST FOR ARRIVAL
>> D	. . . W

| WAIT | 3718 |

First column, start of diagram. Execute A.

Second column, 2 msgs in buffer, execute B.

Have exited from B, now execute C.

The 2 sync msgs to D, but must await external i/p, then execute D.

Each column in the right-half of the table in Figure 78 is a snapshot of messages on the buffer. The numbering indicates ordering, and you have to read this vertically. For example, the second column shows that after exiting from node A, there are two messages on the buffer, "A>>B" and "A>>C.E", with the latter on top (highest number).

You will observe in the next column that the number of "A>>C.E" decreases from 2 to 1, as "A>>B" got consumed.

I used bold numbers in Table 8 and little boxes in Figure 78 to indicate which node will execute next and which messages will be consumed. The final column shows by the boxes that both messages will be consumed

The final column shows that not only is a remote i/p checked for arrival, there is a wait for that i/p with a timeout.

Now back to Table 8. The Supervisor processor is conceived of as being normally sequential, with only one synchronous message in the buffer at any one time. This makes scheduling quite easy. For example, look at the row with "055.050 >> 043". There is one sub-column with a matching entry, it is the only entry in that sub-column, and it is bold. The bold shows that node 043 will be executed. In that same sub-column, if any other messages were flagged, it would mean that combination (or permutation, if ordering is a factor) would result in node 043 being executed.

The significance of the bottom part of Table 8 is that remote-input synchronous messages are tested for arrival if flagged in the sub-column. Again, it is possible to have numeric entries to assign priorities if the OS scheduler will support it. If a flagged entry has arrived, the appropriate node will execute instead of the node determined from the internal scheduling.

One of the main requirements is to enforce non-concurrency between nodes 054 and 057, and this is done by posting a message 057 marker or 054 marker when any clone inside 057 or 054 fires. While the markers are present in the message buffer, there will be no response to arrival of external messages. The remote messages will enter the message buffer but are not considered by the scheduler, as is shown by the un-flagged entries at the bottom-right of Table 8.

I have shown the markers to have a destination, labeled "cleanup", which will execute when only a marker is left in the buffer, to consume the marker.

The scheduling of Table 8 is very simple, and a simple non-preemptive scheduler will work, subject to certain qualifications. The OS should be able to buffer messages 1-deep for synchronous messages and n-deep for asynchronous messages. The main internal modules can be simple round-robin sequencing. This can be worked out for OSs other than TERSE.

Response time

The main problem with a simple non-preemptive non-time-sliced design is that of the response time. The OS schedules between nodes only, so if the longest node delay is "m", that will be how long a message must wait before being subject to scheduling. If a request arrives from an elevator, apart from the possible delay of "Tm", it will also have its own processing time, say "Tp". This involves looking up a button database and some computation. Then of course there is the OS overhead, the network overhead, and the overhead when the reply arrives back at the elevator processor. If the OS overhead is approximated to a single figure, "Ts", if there is a reply overhead at the elevator of "Te", and if there are "n" elevators, the total time for a reply to a request from an elevator is:

$Tt = Tm + (n * Tp) + (n * Ts) + Te + Tu$

The floor elevators may still be posting asynchronous messages to the Supervisor in response to people pressing up/down buttons outside the elevators. The Supervisor should be designed with a message buffer capable of queueing asynchronous incoming messages deep enough so that in a time "Tt" there will not be an overflow. This will depend on how many floors there are.

The simple scheduling of Table 8 doesn't service the asynchronous messages from the floors while an elevator request is being processed.

The factor "Tu" is the overhead servicing the messages of the floor processors. This is a clumped value, encompassing network traffic and delivery to the buffer in the Supervisor.

If it is found that "Tt" is too high, one option might be to reduce "Tm"; that is, break up the nodes into smaller ones. However, it may be easier just to select a faster processor.

Interrupt handling

Figure 79 shows two interrupts, wires 023 and 026. Wire 23 goes to node 12, which in turn posts a Notification to node 4. Wire 26 goes to node 11, which writes directly to the global variable "Floor".

Figure 79: Interrupt-handlers.

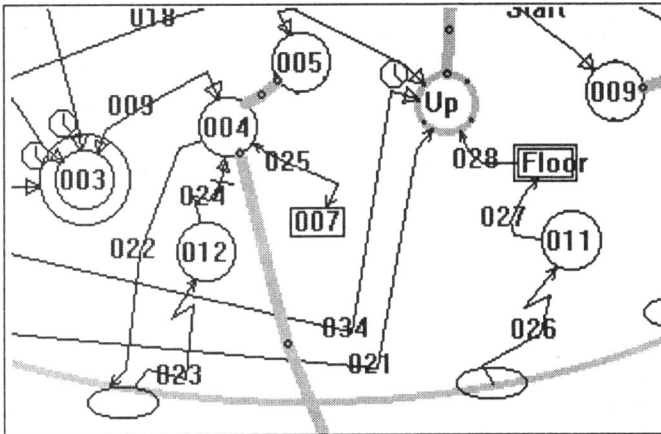

It is all very well drawing diagrams like this, but we need to think very carefully about the implications when we try to implement the designs.

With MESS scheduling, we considered how asynchronously arriving synchronous-dataflow messages can be accomodated. Normal dataflow messages are synchronous in the sense that they must all arrive at a node before it can fire, as opposed to the Notification, which may or may not have arrived when a node fires (and we therefore could refer to the Notification as being asynchronous).

However, a synchronous-dataflow message can arrive asynchronously, meaning that we don't necessarily know its exact arrival time, because it comes from some other processor.

Interrupts are really much the same as remote dataflow incoming messages, as they, too, arrive asynchronously. But an interrupt is NOT a dataflow message, it is an I/O wire that causes a direct interrupt to an interrupt-handler inside a node. That is, it hasn't got anything to do with the message-posting mechanism of TERSE.

Yet, if we could treat it like an incoming dataflow message, we could apply MESS scheduling to it.

Think about this a bit further — when an interrupt occurs, it must be serviced in a timely fashion, but it is usually then appropriate to make the outcome available in a more leisurely fashion to the rest of the diagram. Most sophisticated operating systems structure an interrupt-handler in two parts: one that runs in "interrupt mode", and one that runs in "user mode".

Thinking in terms of Figure 79, node 12 has these two facets. On the one hand, it has an interrupt service routine, that executes when the interrupt occurs. On the other hand, it posts a dataflow message to node 4. Well, it's a Notification, but it could theoretically be a normal synchronous dataflow message.

This two-part behaviour is not quite so straight-forward as it might at first seem. The first question is, how does node 12 post a dataflow message when it hasn't actually executed, at least as far as the TERSE scheduler is concerned. Remember, an interrupt service routine happens under-the-hood, transparent to normal code execution.

We could build a facility into the OS, a special function, that enables an interrupt service routine to insert a message into the message queue, in this case message 24. This is a common approach taken with many OSs and is easy to do with TERSE.

Another approach is for the interrupt service routine to generate a simulated remote-input dataflow message to node 12, thus causing TERSE to schedule the node.

Node 12 would need to have two blocks of internal code — the interrupt service routine and the "user mode" code that executes when the node is scheduled by TERSE. The latter code can post-process whatever is required and possibly post dataflow messages to other parts of the diagram.

In fact, to simulate an external incoming message is extremely easy with TERSE, because it is just a matter of setting a bit in the `extmsgwtg` variable.

This only works for nodes 1—7 though for TERSE51. If we used node 7, rather than node 12, then the interrupt service routine only has to set bit 7 of `extmsgwtg` and exit. Hey presto, whenever TERSE performs its next scheduling exercise, if the same bit in `extmsg` is set, then node 7 will be scheduled.

Have another look at Figure 79 — all that is conveyed by the diagram is that node 12 is entered by an interrupt, and an internal interrupt service routine is executed. However, there is nothing to indicate how message 24 gets generated. For synchronous dataflow, a node must be scheduled, then exit, and post its messages.

Perhaps you would understand anyway that the interrupt service routine has simulated the local message ... somehow.

Figure 80: Simulated external message.

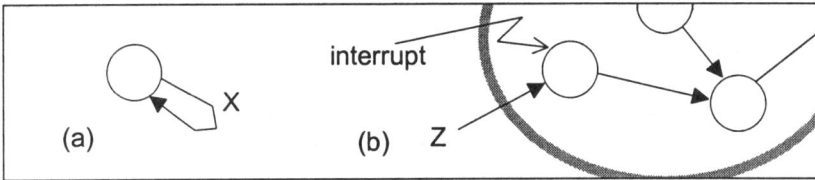

Figure 80(a) is very interesting. This node can never execute, because it can only post the dataflow message after it has executed, but it cannot be scheduled until it receives the message — "Catch 22"!

Note that such a loopback *is* allowed on inner rings of an Iterative-node but not on the outer ring.

Figure 80(a) is crying out to have some special significance attached to it. With the GOOFEE Diagrammer, if you place a new wire by simply clicking on a node boundary, then both ends of the wire will coincide, and you will get something that looks like wire Z, rather than wire X.

Figure 80(b) is a wire created by the above-mentioned method, and it looks like a wire that comes from "nowhere". We could use wire Z as a visual cue that the interrupt service routine in this node generates a simulated remote dataflow input message.

It can't have any other interpretation, because Figure 80(a) shows that it is not an allowable dataflow connection. Therefore, it can be assigned this special significance.

In conclusion, we can state that a dataflow wire that loops back on the outer-ring of a node is a special case, whether drawn as wire X or as wire Z, and is an exception to the principle of synchronous dataflow.

To further clarify, notice that I have drawn wire Z coming from outside the parent Composite-node. If the Composite-node represents the processor, then wire Z is showing that it is a simulated external input.

Timeout

You can see the little timeout symbols in Figure 79 — these are synchronous dataflow wires with reply and timeout.

However, what exactly do we want when we talk about timeout? Time is relative to something, that is, its magnitude is relative and so is its quantum intervals, or increments.

Looking at Figure 79, you can see that node 3 posts two messages from an inner-ring, then awaits replies. Notice that it also posts message 9, which has no timeout. The reason for the timeout on two wires, but not the other, is that we know that a timely reply will come back on wire 9, but in the elevator case study, those other two wires go off to another processor, and a timely reply is less certain.

A first level of thinking is that we could reason that we must wait a certain maximum time after posting the message. Thus, the timeout would be relative to when the message was posted.

However, what if node 3 itself is "running a bit late"? Maybe then there will be less slack time to play with, so we would want to decrease the time that node 3 will wait for the replies. In that case, we really want the timeout to be a value that is relative to some reference, perhaps the starting time of the local diagram.

Going even further, a distributed system could have a global time that is broadcast over the network.

What we have identified above is time relative to three different starting points.

Then there is the question of the granularity of time. Do we want to measure in microseconds, seconds, days? If our time is stored as an 8-bit value, our granularity is 1/256, and if we decide to measure in microseconds, we only get from 0 to 255 microseconds.

On the other hand, if we chose a granularity of seconds, we get 0 to 255 seconds, but in steps of 1 second.

An obvious solution to this problem is to use a bigger variable, say 32-bit. If a 32-bit variable has a granularity of 1 microsecond, it can count from 0 to $(2^{32}) - 1$, or 71.5827 minutes. Not bad, except that with small microcontrollers we don't have too much RAM to give away.

You might like to examine my x86 TERSE (Appendix E), in which I have used two bits of the time as "granularity bits". I have only implemented timeout relative to when a message is launched.

I wrote the code based on the scheduling table resident in the code segment, which will likely be in ROM. The timeouts are fixed; however, it would be quite simple to introduce runtime variation.

10

"Getting the job done"

Preamble

Chapters 7, 8 and 9, have been a journey of discovery; however, if your interest is mainly to "get the job done", I now finish with some pragmatic notes. In fact, you could have jumped directly from the end of Chapter 6 to here; the intervening chapters are of more academic interest, useful for the thinkers amongst us.

A fundamental problem is that we are often "blinkered" by what we think we should be doing. We think that we should be making use of OOP, and that we should go through certain steps in the analysis/design/ implementation process. Chapters 7 to 9 investigate GOOFEE within these established frameworks, that is, how GOOFEE can model various accepted concepts and structures.

If you have jumped here directly from Chapter 6, or skimmed lightly through the intervening chapters, this chapter will give you enough understanding to begin using GOOFEE.

However, there are some important points in Chapters 7 to 9 and I recommend future visits to those chapters, as required. There are many subtle problems that emerge during a project, and in many cases you will find the answers in those chapters.

Substituting pragmatism for ideology

Think back to my original ideas expressed in Chapters 1 and 2. These were an outcome of my intuition, a kind of gestalt that occurred. Much of the later analysis was academic meandering.

A problem with various abstractions developed in Chapters 7 to 9, such as the decomposition expressed in Figure 55, is how to translate to non-OO code. I tackled this in Chapter 9 and developed a "heavy duty" scheduling table shown in Table 8, in which the diagram has been "levelled" such that all messages are directly between source and destination nodes. However, the imposition of the various resource hiding, inheritance, relationship, and hierarchical concepts in the construction of the diagram actually obscures what we finally want to do.

The original intuitive approach involved a non-hierarchical design approach that is "I/O centric" (see Chapter 2). That is, design of a diagram starts by identification of all resources. These are drawn as nodes, and will have clones if multiple access is required, and they will all be at the top level, not nested indirectly inside some decomposition as is done in Figure 55. As the resources are all at the top level, all wires clearly show their source and destination.

Figure 81 illustrates the "pragmatic" approach. The rules to be applied here, are that you

- identify all nodes/clones that will be the ultimate destinations/sources of messages, and
- draw all wires directly between their actual destinations/ sources.

Elevator subsystem

Refer back to Figure 46 in Chapter 6, which shows my "first pass" at the design of an elevator control system. What is different from the figures of this chapter is that I have not been repetitive, and have avoided Composite-wires. That is,

- I have only drawn *one* motor, one floor display, etc., and
- I have left off the high-level Composite-wires.

Figure 81: "Pragmatic" elevator control system design.

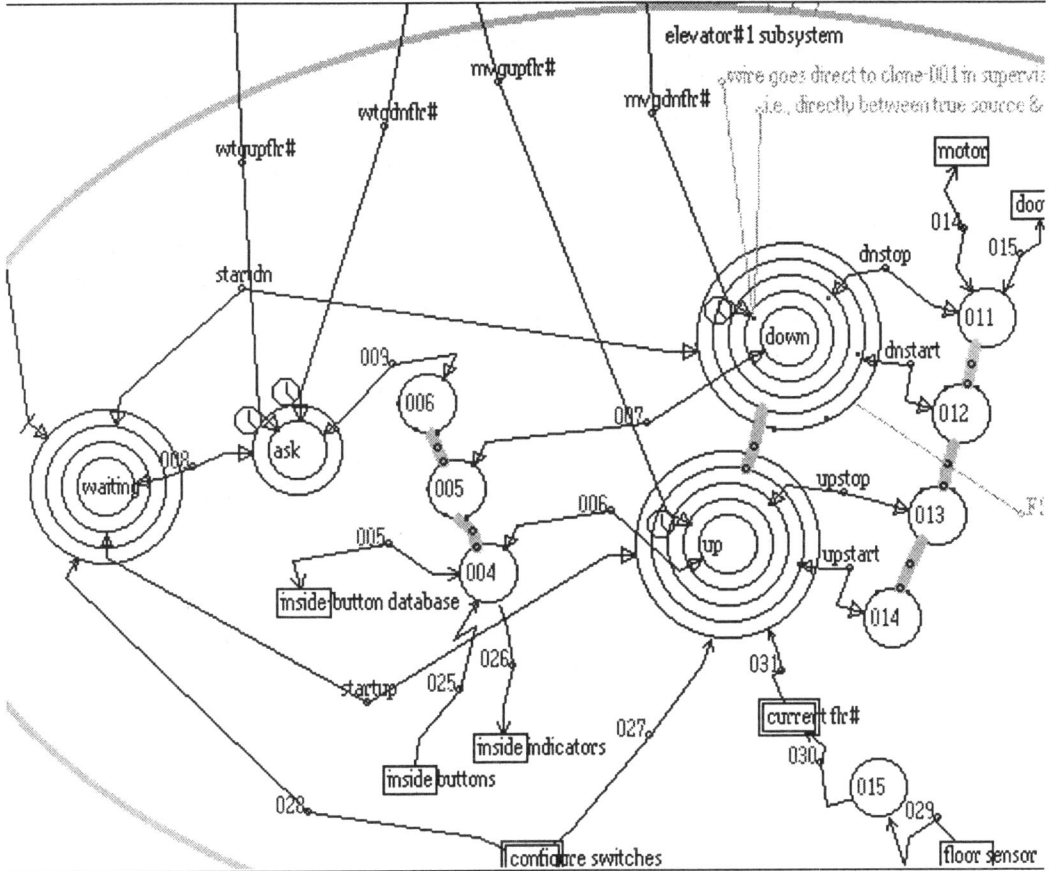

Compare Figure 47, my first pass at the elevator subsystem, with Figure 81. I have placed a Composite-node around the entire "elevator#1 subsystem", which groups that portion of diagram. I have enclosed everything inside the Composite-node, including all physical resources.

Now, notice that the messages to the Supervisor processor do not stop at the Composite-node boundary; they go directly to and from destinations and sources at the Supervisor.

Furthermore, note another refinement in the diagram of the elevator subsystem; replacement of "up" and "down" Composite-nodes with Iterative-nodes. The reason is simple; Iterative-nodes are a very clear representation of State Machines.

We can still have decomposition, for example "up" and "down" can be expanded to a Super-node with a diagram within; however, we try to initially design the diagram to identify all sources and destinations of messages and draw wires directly between them. The expansions of "up" and "down" are really below the messaging level and can be left for later.

In Figure 81, the wires that travel to and from the Supervisor cross the Composite-node boundary. However, during the development we are at liberty to draw them to the boundary at first, extending them later when the rest of the diagram is drawn.

Summarising the design guidelines, I

- identified the lowest-level of messaging, and constructed a "levelled" diagram inside the subsystem Composite-node,
- drew wires directly between sources and destinations, and
- standardised on the Iterative-node to represent a State Machine.

The diagram can be further decomposed, but it is understood that this is below the OS messaging level. We could formalise this as

- any normal node can be expanded as a Super-node, but
- the diagram in the Super-node is below the OS messaging level, and is a model of code inside the Super-node only.

These latter two formalisms should be treated as flexible — as desirable rather than essential. I am reluctant to set rules, as I'm a great believer in "gut feeling" design. Also, the kind of people that I am targeting are those 70% or so of designers of embedded systems that do not use much of a formal methodology and are likely to be put off by too many rules and complexity.

Figure 81 is very clear, and in the GOOFEE Diagrammer it is a simple matter to double-click on a node and invoke an editor to enter code. This is a fundamental reason why we need to avoid too much abstraction; we need nodes that can be double-clicked for coding purposes. Earlier work, in Chapters 7 to 9, resulted in "virtual nodes", identified in Table 8, that are source/destination of wires but aren't shown on the diagram. Some of the ideas developed in these chapters may be ok if OO languages can be used, but the situation becomes awkward if only assembler or C is available.

Please note that the "pragmatic design" is on the Companion Disk as ELEVATR8.GOO, while the solution developed in Chapters 7 to 9 is ELEVATR7.GOO.

Figure 82: Floor subsystem.

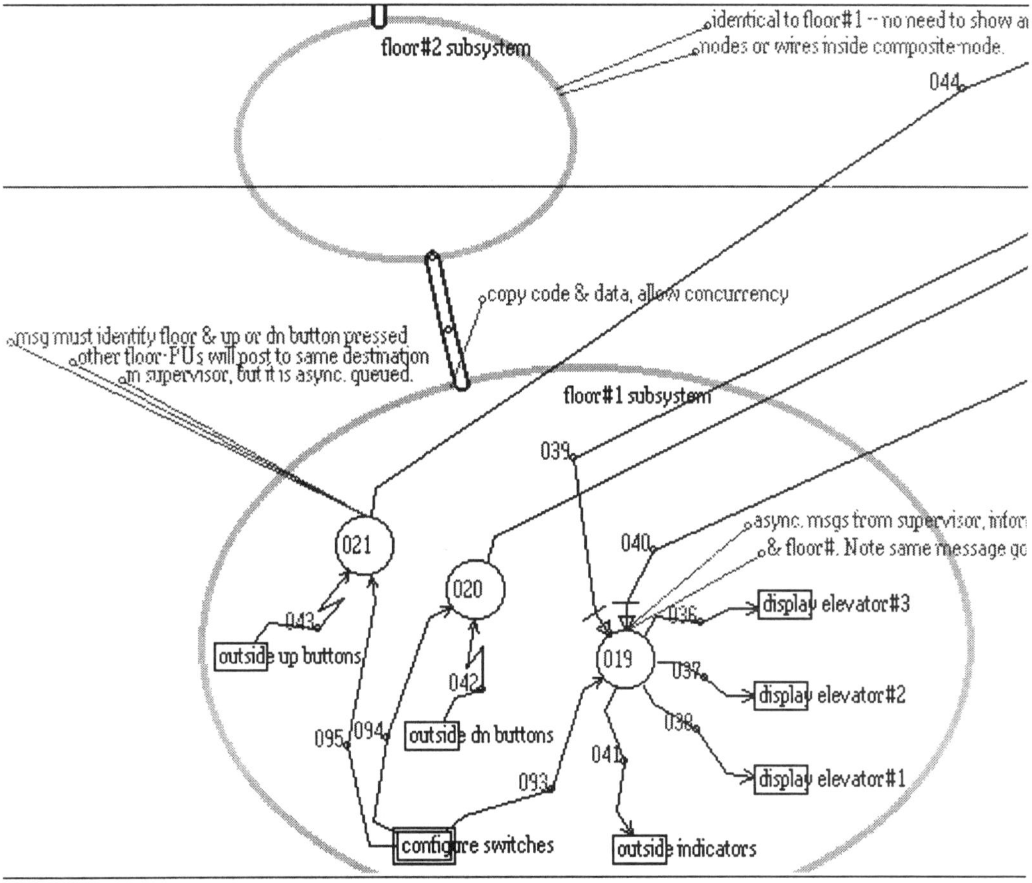

Floor subsystem

Figure 82 is the floor subsystem, but note that I have deliberately left something off, as a little exercise. You can see three nodes inside the subsystem, nodes 019, 020, and 021, but note that they do not have any synchronous inputs. Therefore, how will the nodes be executed? Think about this.

What I have drawn in Figure 82 is exactly what I want, without any fancy abstractions, and it is very easy to understand. Node 019 receives asynchronous messages from the Supervisor, and each message contains an elevator number and its current floor number. Node 019 simply updates the floor displays outside each elevator and the up/down button indicators.

The asynchronous inputs will queue until node 019 is executed, so you will need to add a sequencing node, and if you got the hint from Figure 81, an Iterative-node will do the trick.

Nodes 020 and 021 post asynchronous messages (Notifications) back to the Supervisor processor. Each message has to contain the floor number. I have split the up requests from the down requests, as that suits the way the Supervisor is organised, which in turn suits the operations of the elevators themselves. Therefore, although there is a comment in Figure 82 that the message indicates up or down button pressed, this is not a field in the message, as it is implied by the very existence of the message. Very simple, yes? But, what about the other floors?

Figure 82 shows "floor#2 subsystem", and that's all there is to it!

The type of Joining-bar chosen is copy of code and data/resources, with concurrency allowed. This means that each floor processor is identical, but it is most important to note that this "identicalness" extends to all external wires. Therefore, the asynchronous messages posted to node 019 in "floor #1 subsystem" will also go to node 019 in "floor#2 subsystem". The reverse is also true; messages posted from nodes 020 and 021, from any floor subsystem, will go to the same destination in the Supervisor — which is why they have to be asynchronous queued messages.

If any floor subsystems can post asynchronous messages to the Supervisor, that's fine; technically, that situation is easy to handle with an OS like

TERSE. The slight difficulty is the reverse, where the Supervisor posts asynchronous messages to all floors, by implication. Each Floor subsystem will have a different processor number, or address, in the local area network, which would require the source-node in the Supervisor to explicitly post duplicate messages, one to each floor. Yes, that can be done, but if absolute simplicity is the goal, why can't each floor processor be given the same network address? Strange as that might seem, it would work.

Ok, so it is obvious I think, but the answer to the question about what is missing from Figure 82, is a three-ring Iterative-node, to schedule nodes 019, 020, and 021. Synchronous wires will be required from the Iterative-node to nodes 019, 020, and 021.

Study the differences between Figures 46 and 82. Notice that in Figure 82 I have identified everything belonging to the subsystem and avoided repetition. Study Figures 48 and 82. Within the subsystem I have drawn a levelled diagram, avoiding indirection.

Figure 83: Zoomed-out view.

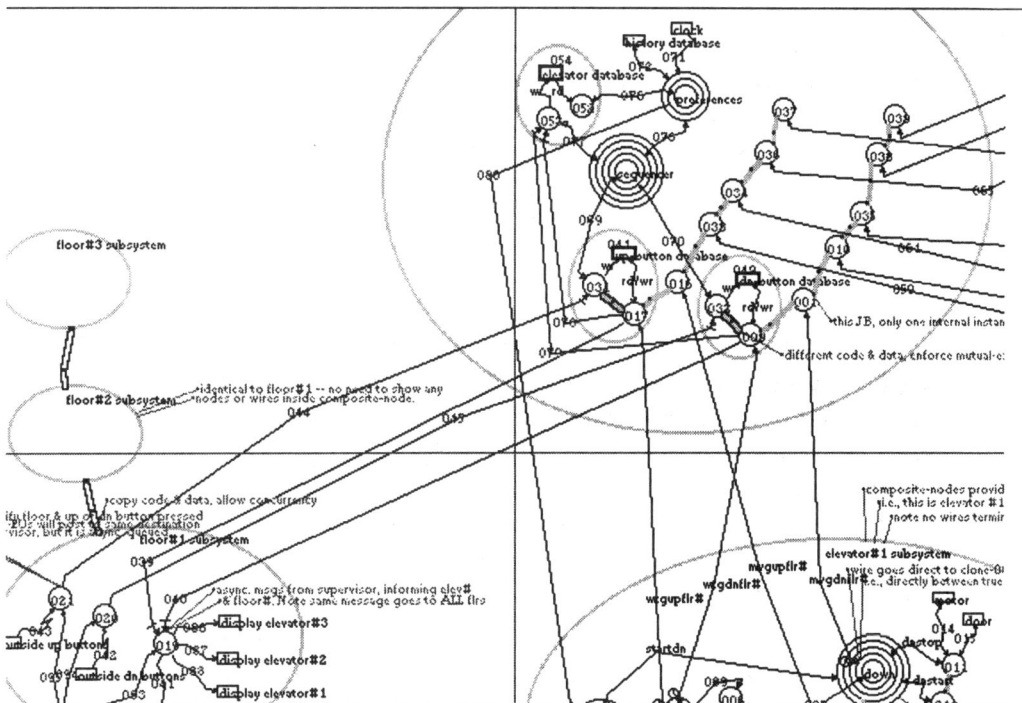

Supervisor subsystem

Figure 83 is an expanded view, to show how the wires from elevators and floors connect to the Supervisor.

You might like to compare the simplicity of the Supervisor with the hierarchical construction developed in Chapters 7 to 9. Wires from/to elevators and floors go directly to clones in the Supervisor. Each clone is very easy to code, because it has fixed sources/destinations for all wires in/out.

Notice (well, it would have been immediately obvious) the long strings of clones. This is what I mean by "non-hierarchical", or "levelled" expansion, as distinct from the hierarchical, or indirect, expansion in Figures 71 and 73. Communication with the floor subsystems is very easy, and you can see that only four nodes are required. The long string of clones is required for communication with the various elevators; in this case study it is three elevators.

The improvement in clarity — how clearly it conveys the intention of the designer — of Figure 83 compared with Figures 71 and 73 is obvious.

Before focusing on the Supervisor itself, consider the messaging between Supervisor and the elevators, as shown in Figure 84.

There is of course an obvious difference between the messaging Supervisor—floors and Supervisor—elevators, because each elevator processor must communicate independently with the Supervisor. Therefore, as every path of communication must be shown by an actual wire, in keeping with our pragmatic approach, a lot of wires must be drawn.

The result, though, is extreme clarity on how this system works. You can clearly see that each elevator processor communicates with clones in the Supervisor, thus sharing access to the up/down button databases.

"Elevator #2 subsystem" cannot simply be an empty Composite-node, but do note the Joining-bar is copy data/resources and code, allow concurrency, which is no surprise. We need a simple way to show which nodes inside "elevator#2 subsystem" have different external wiring, and I have done this by drawing only those nodes that are different.

I have shown only the labels for the nodes, not their absolute assigned numbers, because that is not important here. "Elevator#2" is an identical copy of "elevator#1", with same internal node numbering, except the

"Configuration" switches would be set to identify the elevator number and to give the processor its unique network address.

Figure 84: Communication between Supervisor and elevators.

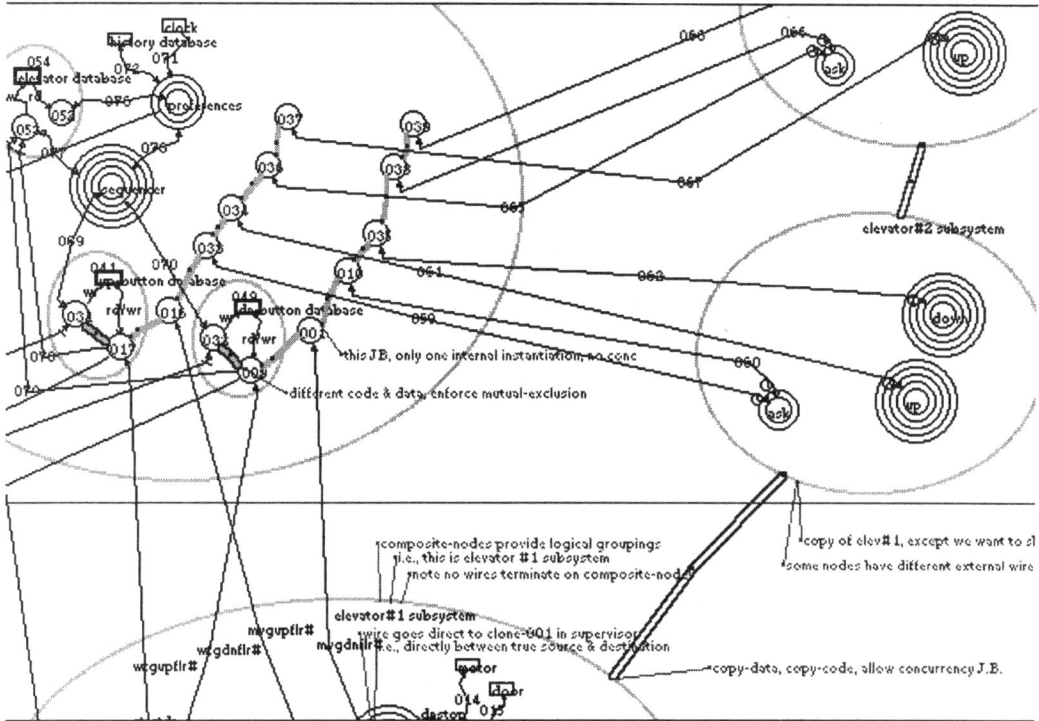

An elevator can make a request to the Supervisor, and you can see in Figure 84 that they are synchronous messages, with reply and timeout.

An operating system, such as TERSE, will receive these messages, and queue them one-deep only. If MESS scheduling is used, which is available in current versions of TERSE, it is a very simple matter for TERSE to detect that a message is waiting and to schedule the node.

Figure 85 shows the Supervisor.

In Figure 85, look at the up/down button databases. The floor processors post asynchronous messages to nodes 031 and 032 to update the databases, and this had to be separate from the elevator accesses to the databases; yet, mutual exclusion must be enforced. Actually, current versions of TERSE do not preempt nodes in the same virtual processor, so it is not a problem, but for correctness I have drawn a "different code/data, enforce mutual exclusion" Joining-bar between nodes 032 and 089, and between 031 and 017.

Figure 85: Supervisor subsystem.

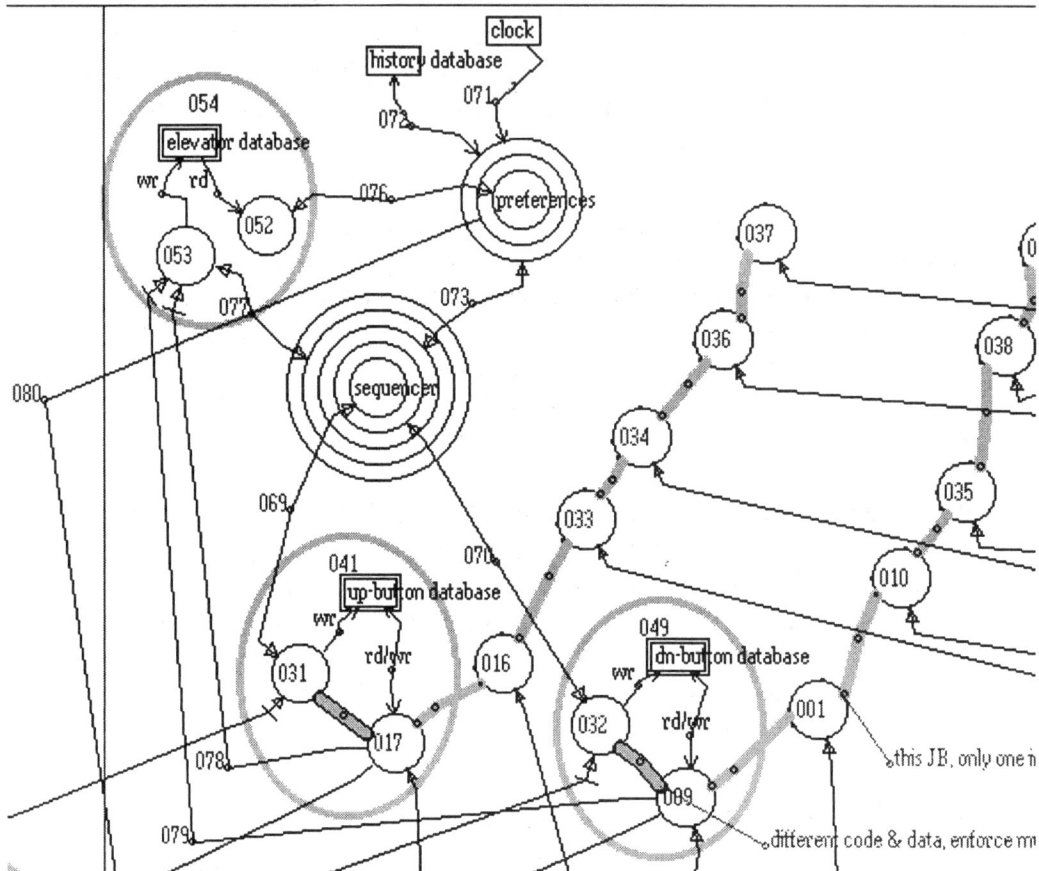

The databases are global only within the enclosing Composite-node, so data hiding is still enforced.

One little, but important, point here. In the case of the "dn-button database", you may wonder if node 032 could be done away with and the incoming asynchronous wire fed straight to node 089. The answer to that is no, it won't work.

The fundamental problem is that by implication, the incoming asynchronous wire would go to all the clones as well and would queue at each one. Therefore, we have to have a separate node, node 032, that is not cloned.

However, notice that because node 032 only has an asynchronous input, it will require a synchronous input to schedule it: hence the wire from the sequencer.

There are other management functions in the Supervisor, with a couple of databases. The "preferences" node, for example, can post asynchronous messages to the elevators, giving specific elevators preferred directions or preferred floors to stop at.

Consider how you would implement scheduling for the various nodes in the Supervisor. TERSE easily handles the remote synchronous input requests from the elevators, whereas the other nodes are scheduled by the sequencer. If using a non-preemptive TERSE, you will of course need to calculate the execution times of the nodes, to make sure that any request from an elevator will be serviced in a timely manner. If you determine that nodes 031 and 032, for example, take too much time, the solution is simple; split them into more than one node.

What if an elevator request is *not* serviced in time? The system can easily be made to degrade gracefully. If a request arrives at node 001 for example, but the Supervisor doesn't service it "in time", the elevator, having sent a timeout message, can simply be made to resend the message — default behaviour of x86 TERSE is to set the _TIMEOUT flag and reexecute the waiting node. Because synchronous messages only queue one-deep, the previous simply gets overwritten.

Methodical abstraction

If you want to "tidy up" the diagrams of this chapter, one way is to introduce the Composite-wire between subsystems. This is all right, as long as sources and destinations of wires remain obvious. If you need to further expand some nodes, this can be done, and you might find it useful to apply my suggested constraint that all Super-node expansion is below the OS messaging level.

Figures 81 to 85 show a diagram constructed with a minimum of abstraction, and the operation of the elevator control system is "crystal clear". However, that does not negate the value of higher abstractions. Analysis/design could have started by drawing single high-level

Composite-nodes, as shown in Figure 86. High-level Supervisor and floor nodes are shown, and this is very much in keeping with methodology developed through most of this book.

Figure 86: Higher abstractions.

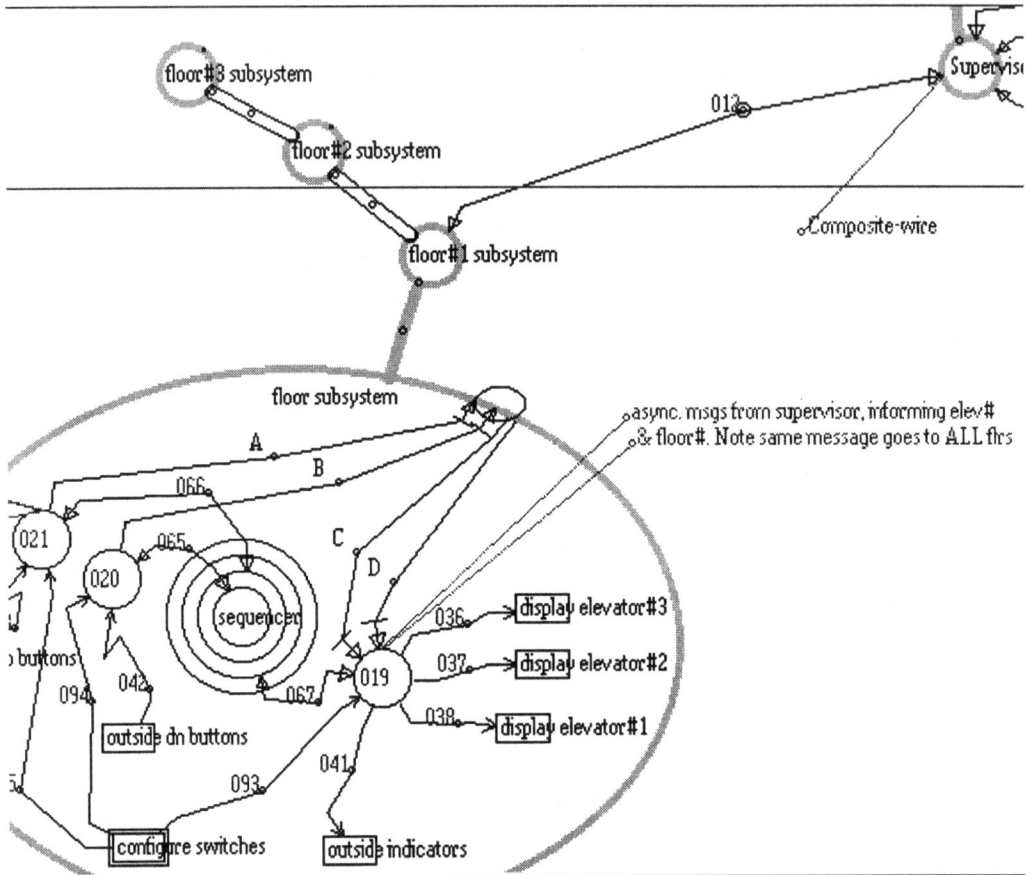

In Figure 86, the floor subsystem is still levelled within the expansion, and you can still easily trace wires via the Composite-wires. For example, wires A, B, C, and D go via Composite-wire 012 and will be unbundled within the expansion of the Supervisor subsystem.

If you are pedantic about structure, and/or you think that analysis/design methodology should abstract in this way, then Figure 86 is fine. It is equivalent to Figures 82 and 83, and if you find the latter figures clearer, again fine.

Figure 86 certainly seems more structured, and you may think that stringing wires directly from anywhere to anywhere as has been done in Figures 81 to 85 is wrong. However, again we are being blinkered in our vision, and we need to make the paradigm shift to GOOFEE's two-dimensional view of the world. Use whatever of these approaches looks easiest to you.

Conclusions

The publisher has to rip the manuscript off me, otherwise I'll just keep on researching and writing. Where is the end point? GOOFEE and TERSE are not mature products; they are new. You will find them extremely useful already, with enormous potential to be enhanced in a number of directions.

It is great for one person to "come up" with good ideas; however, it takes many people to make those ideas successful. If you feel inspired by the concepts, please participate as a hobbyist or in a commercial capacity. I will be happy to acknowledge any significant developments from anyone. The main condition applied to anyone further developing TERSE and GOOFEE is that I be acknowledged in any published works as the original developer, and this book be acknowledged.

The main areas with great potential are:
- Rules for translation to C++
- Incorporation of enhanced timing information on the diagram
- Automatic signature code generation
- Automatic scheduling table generation
- Automated time analysis
- Network-enhanced versions of TERSE (e.g., CAN)
- Virtual-machine enhanced TERSE (e.g., running on top of other OSs)
- Refinement of the GOOFEE symbols
- Further development of analysis/design methodology of GOOFEE

I am typing this just before the book goes to print, and there are major developments that I will place on-line or on the disk. I have been able to use GOOFEE to model procedural and OO languages right down to a line-by-line basis, making automatic code generation a snap. Figure 87 is a code fragment of a Java program. Note that I have redefined some of the sub-nodes, and the Figure shows their different appearance.

Figure 87: Line-by-line modeling of an OOL.

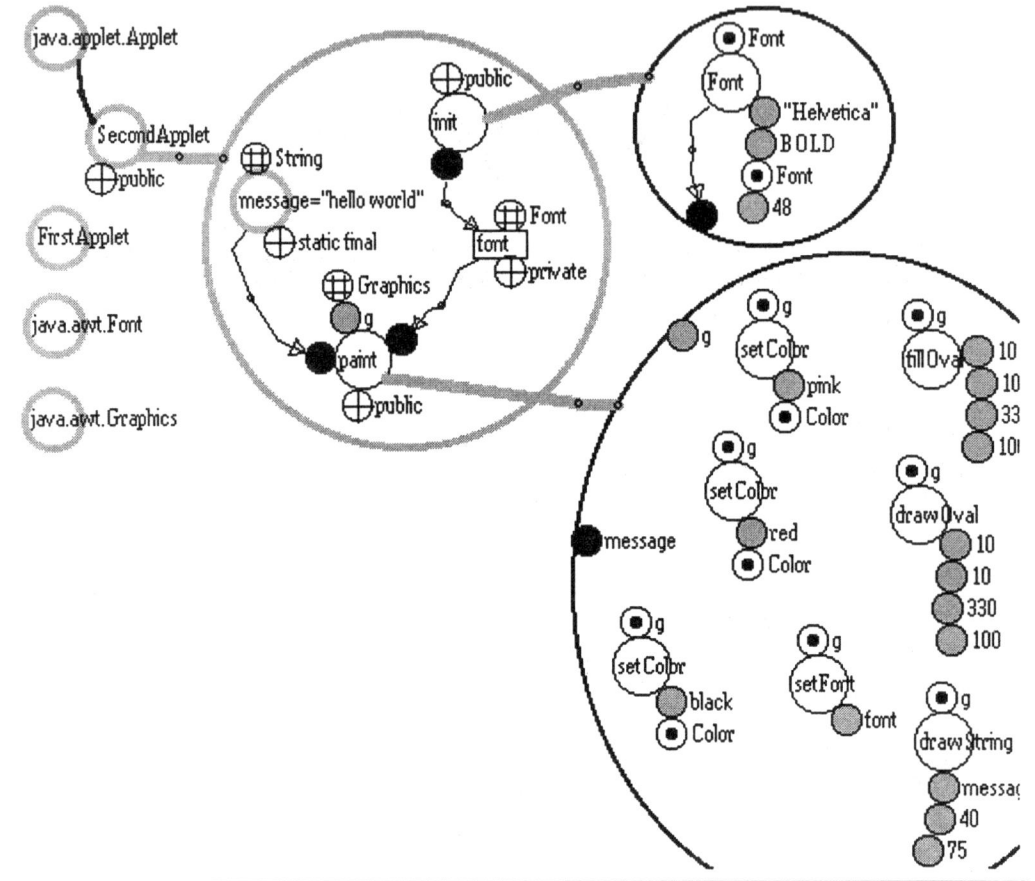

The Appendices contain the practical stuff: my various versions of TERSE, using C, constructing a network, and virtual machines. Software, including my superb GOOFEE Diagrammer CASE tool, is on the Companion Disk.

I will endeavour to post new material to my home pages, such as application notes/technical reports, particularly the exciting GOOFEE enhancements.

Have fun!

A

The 8051 microcontroller

If you are coming from the Motorola 68HC11 family, the first thing you have to come to terms with is the *Harvard architecture*. Actually, it's a sort of modified Harvard architecture, as the strict definition is that there are separate buses for data and code — this is the case inside the CPU, but the external bus is quasi-common.

Having data and code on separate buses means that they are also in separate memory, and perhaps unfortunately, if you like simplicity, two sets of instructions are required. If you know anything about the Intel x86 family, i.e., the 8086, '286, '386, '486, etc., you will be aware that a similar situation prevails there, except it applies to input/output. The x86 family has a separate I/O address map and so needs special instructions, namely IN and OUT, to access this map.

When you first see the 8051 instruction set, it looks darn confusing, but there is a neat little summary that came with one of my evaluation boards (the Philips DS750), and I am moved to reproduce it here, in Table A.1.

The Legend for Table A.1 is:

```
Rn  ::= 0,,7          There are 8 registers, named R0, R1, R2, etc.
Dir ::= 0h,,0FFh      Direct addressing mode, only 8-bit address.
Ri  ::= R0, R1        Some instructions limited to these 2 registers.
rel ::= +127, -128    Relative addressing mode.
```

Data addressing

People familiar with the 68HC11 only will be surprised to learn that the 8051 has not just eight registers, but four banks of eight. These banks are switchable, so that R0—R7 can refer to any bank. Inside the CPU is up to 256 bytes of RAM, and this is the place where data is kept. It is also why the direct addressing mode only has 8 bits.

In fact, *all* data is kept in this data address map, including the registers and all I/O ports and configuration registers.

The program code is in ROM, normally, and it is important to be clear that the code is in a separate address map to the data. For example:

```
MOV A, 20h        ;moves the contents of address 20h to A.
MOV A, R7         ;moves the contents of register 7 to A.
MOV A, @R1        ;indirect. Moves contents pointed to by R1.
MOV A, #56        ;immediate. Moves value 56 into A.
```

Address 20h and register 7 are both in the data address map, i.e., the on-chip RAM. In fact, the registers R0—R7 are in one of four banks in the RAM, located from absolute address zero. The default is that R0 is at address zero, so the instruction MOV A, 0 is exactly the same as MOV A, R0!!

A mental picture of this RAM area, is as follows:

ADDRESS	CONTENT OF DATA ADDRESS MAP
00—1Fh	Four banks of registers, R0—R7.
20h—2Fh	Bit-addressable RAM.
30h—7Fh	Byte-addressable RAM.
80h—FFh	Special Function Registers (SFRs).

Table A.1: Summary of 8051 instruction set.

	Instruction	Destination	Source
Moves	MOV	A	#, Rn, Dir, @Ri
	MOV	Rn, @Ri	#, A, Dir
	MOV	Dir	#, A, Rn, Dir,
	MOV	DPTR	# (16 bits)
	MOVX	A	DPTR, @Ri
	MOVX	DPTR, @Ri	A
	MOVC	A	@A+DPTR, @A+PC
Logical	ANL, ORL, XRL	A	#, Rn, Dir, @Ri
	ANL, ORL, XRL	Dir	A, #
	RL, RLC, RR, RRC	A	
Arithme-tic	ADD, ADDC, SUBB	A	#, Rn, Dir, @Ri
	INC, DEC	A, Rn, Dir,	
	INC	DPTR	
	MUL, DIV	AB	
Jumps, calls	ACALL, AJMP	addr11	
	LCALL, LJMP	addr16	
	RET, RETI		
	SJMP	rel	
	JMP	@A+DPTR	
Condition branch	JZ, JNZ	rel	
	CJNE	A,dir,rel	
	CJNE	A,#,rel	
	CJNE	Rn,#,rel	
	CJNE	@Ri,#,rel	
	DJNZ	Rn,rel	
	DJNZ	Dir,rel	
Bit ops	ANL, ORL	C	bit, /bit
	MOV	C, bit	bit, C
	CLR, CPL, SETB	C, bit	
Bit jumps	JC, JNC	rel	
	JB, JNB, JBC	bit, rel	
Misc.	PUSH	++(SP)	Dir
	POP	Dir	(SP)−
	XCH	A	Rn, Dir, @Ri
	XCHD	A	@Ri
	SWAP	A	A (nibbles)
	DA	A	A (decimal adj.)
	CLR, CPL	A	
	NOP		

Bit addressing

One very nice feature of the 8051 is that it is a "boolean processor", i.e., can address and manipulate individual bits. Examination of Table A.1 will show a set of bit instructions. For bit instructions, the Carry flag, C, is used as the equivalent of the Accumulator register. Notice the reference to "A", in Table A.1 — this is a general purpose register called the Accumulator. There is also a B register.

Everything — A, B, C, I/O ports, configuration registers — resides in the address range 80h—FFh, and registers in this area are called *SFRs*.

So the A register is actually at some absolute address in the SFR region. In fact, it is at address E0h, and can be accessed by reference to its actual address. Some of the SFRs are also bit addressable, as shown:

```
MOV   A, #77        ;move immediate, 77 into accumulator-A.
MOV   E0h, #77      ;...same
MOV   C,Acc.1       ;Bit-addressing. Acc-A, bit-1, into Carry.
MOV   C,E0h.1       ;...same
```

Constant addressing

Well, if you have followed me so far, we are almost there! One more major issue to resolve — since all data access is to the separate data memory map, what if you have data stored inside your code? If the code is stored in ROM, then such data can only be constants, but still, how do you get at it?

To facilitate this, a Data PoinTeR is used, DPTR, which is a *16-bit* register, as code can be up to 64Kb. Examine Table A.1, and you will see these instructions:

```
MOV   DPTR, #600        ;immediate. Move value 600 into DPTR.
MOV   A, #0
MOVC A, @A+DPTR         ;indirect. A+DPTR points to source.
```

In this example, the content of address 600 will be fetched into A (thus destroying the offset that was previously placed in A).

This should be all you need to read the example code given in the Companion Disk. There's a lot more to it, of course, but sufficient detail is provided here — you don't have to understand all of the instructions in Table A.1 immediately.

One clarification I must make right now — the RAM is *not* limited to 256 bytes, as you can have up to 64Kb off-chip. The MOVX instruction is used for addressing external RAM. Note that it utilises the DPTR — the Harvard architecture breaks down outside the chip.

The 8051 family has about 30% of the 8-bit microcontroller market and is made by many semiconductor manufacturers. There are also more variants than any other family, and it is this richness that is its main attraction. Although I have referred to "external" memory, please note that this is an historical term, and many variants place "external" RAM and ROM on-chip.

B

Uniprocessor TERSE source listing

I propose a file naming scheme for TERSE, as follows:

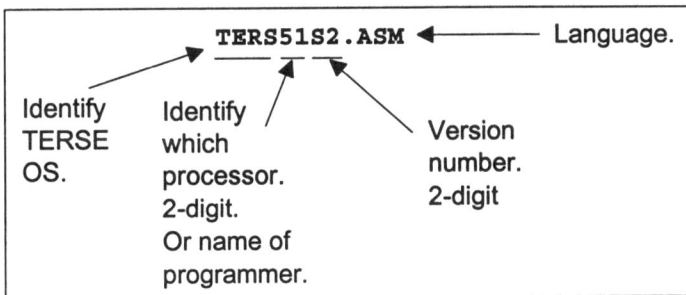

This Appendix contains the source file for the TERSE uniprocessor version 2, for the 8051, written in assembly language. Other versions are available online, at:

`http://scorpion.cowan.edu.au/science/terse/index.html`

The assembly language source file can be assembled by the freeware version of the Metalink assembler, available from various sources, including the above Internet site.

Source, uniprocessor TERSE51

```
;TERS51S2.ASM
;This version is for the 8051 family.
;This is the single-processor cut-down version 2.
$MOD51            ;config. info for Metalink assembler.

DSEG
      ORG 2Dh
flags:      DS    1 ;flags.1,2,3,4=1, msg on terminal-1,-2,-3,-4.
pdata1:     DS    1
data1:      DS    5    ;reserve 5 bytes.
pdata2:     DS    1
data2:      DS    5    ;reserve 5 bytes.
pdata3:     DS    1
data3:      DS    5    ;reserve 5 bytes.(end is addr 3Fh)


;....................................................
CSEG
START:      ajmp start1      ;reset entry point.

        ;leave space for isrs....
        ORG 32h
emptyst     EQU 07
numentries EQU 5
signatures: DB 255, 0,08,22,152
nodenum:    DB 0,   1, 2, 3,  4
nodeptr:                  ;these occupy 2 bytes each.
        ajmp node0
        ajmp node1
        ajmp node2
        ajmp node3
        ajmp node4

;.....               msgs will always be two bytes...
POSTMSG MACRO node,term,notif,datavalue
    IF ((node >= 0) AND (node <= 31))
    IF ((term > 0) AND (term <= 4))
    IF ((notif = 0) OR (notif = 1))
    mov   b,datavalue
    push  b
    mov   b,#(node + ((term-1)*32) + (notif*128))
    push  b
    ENDIF
    ENDIF
    ENDIF
POSTMSG ENDM
;note that TERM is stored one-less. EX: TERM-1 is stored as 00.
;Headerformat: bit7=notif, 5-6=term, 0-4=node.
```

```
NORMALEXIT MACRO      ;use this for normal operation.
     ajmp nodereturn
NORMALEXIT ENDM

FASTEXIT  MACRO nextnode   ;bypasses signature
     mov  r5,#nextnode         ;calc. and lookup, if
     ajmp gonode              ;you know the next node.
FASTEXIT  ENDM
;....................................................
;*****MAIN LOOP*******
start1:                     ;program entry point 1.
     mov  pdata1,#data1   ;initalise pointers, to
     mov  pdata2,#data2   ;/ buffers empty.
     mov  pdata3,#data3   ;/
     ajmp start2

nodereturn:
start2:                     ;program entry point 2.
     mov  r2,#0           ;initially, signature=0.
;calculate the signature....
     mov  r0,sp           ;save initial sp.
loop3:
     cjne r0,#emptyst,loop2
     ajmp sigout
loop2:
     mov  a,@r0                 ;get 1st byte of msg.
     mov  r1,a                  ;save it for calcsig.
     dec  r0                    ;go past Header.
     dec  r0                    ;bypass the data.
     jb   acc.7,loop3           ;ignore notifications.
calcsig:
;entered with r1=msg-header, r2=accumulated signature
     mov  a,r2
     jnb  acc.7,sig1     ;jump if bit a.7 is clear.
     xrl  a,#00100001b   ;tapping points.
sig1:
     xrl  a,r1
     rl   a
     mov  r2,a
     ajmp loop3
sigout:

;if comes out of above, with sig=0, diagram will
; restart, as must be complete...
lookup:
;signature in r2, use lookup table to get address of node...
     mov  r0,#numentries
     mov  dptr,#signatures
loop1:
```

```
        mov    a,r0
        dec    a
        movc   a,@a+dptr       ;start at end of array.
        xrl    a,r2            ;compare signatures
        jz     gotonode        ;signature found.
no2:    djnz   r0,loop1
        ;...sig. not found....
        inc    r0      ;make r0=1. (r0= lookup-index + 1).
sigfnd:

gotonode:
        mov    dptr,#nodenum   ;get node number.
        mov    a,r0            ;       /
        dec    a               ;       /
        movc   a,@a+dptr       ;       /
        mov    r5,a            ;       / -->r5
gonode:
        anl    flags,#11100001b    ;bits 1-4 set by extractmsgs...
        ajmp   extractmsgs      ;extracts all msgs for this
                                ; node.(comes back
main1:                          ; here)(preserves r5)
        mov    dptr,#nodeptr
        mov    a,r5
        rl     a               ;*2 --each entry is 2 bytes.
        jmp    @a+dptr          ;jump to next node to execute.
                               ;r5 = node-number.(0--> ).
;*****END MAIN LOOP*****
;.............................................

extractmsgs:
;entered with r5=node-number (0-->31, node-0=0, etc)
;extracts all msgs for this node-->r1,r2,... first-bank of
;registers, where r1 is terminal-1, etc.  Dumps msg-header.
        mov    r0,sp
rex1:   cjne   r0,#emptyst,ex2
        ajmp   main1            ;*get out*>>>>>>>>
ex2:    mov    a,@r0            ;get msg header.
        anl    a,#1Fh           ;extract node.
        cjne   a,05,ex3         ;test if required node.
        mov    a,@r0            ;yes.
        dec    r0
        anl    a,#60h           ;extract term
        cjne   a,#0,nxt1        ;test if term1
        mov    01,@r0
        setb   flags.1
        ajmp   ex4
nxt1:   cjne   a,#20h,nxt2      ;test if term2
        mov    02,@r0
        setb   flags.2
```

```
        ajmp   ex4
nxt2: cjne   a,#40h,nxt3              ;test if term3
        mov    03,@r0
        setb   flags.3
        ajmp   ex4
nxt3: mov    04,@r0     ;term4
        setb   flags.4
ex4:  pop    acc                ;move top msg down to fill gap.
        pop    b                  ;(note that this technique
        mov    @r0,b              ; modifies the ordering of
        inc    r0                 ; of msgs in the queue,
        mov    @r0,a              ; which needs to be taken
ex3:  dec    r0                 ; into account when
        dec    r0                 ;calculating the signatures.
        ajmp   rex1

;$$$$$$$$$$$$$$$$$$$$$$$$$$$$$$$$$$$$$$$$$$$$$$$$$$$$$$$$$$$$
;a node is entered with r5 (address 05) = node
;number (first register-bank selected, as rest used
;by stack, so r1 is addr.01,etc).
;msgs are in terminal-order, in addresses 01,02,03,04.
;Bit-addressable "flags" has bits set if msg present
;-- example, msg in term1 (addr.01, or r1),then flags.1 is set.

;. . . . . . . . . . . . . . . .
node0:                   ;node-0 is the error-handler
  NORMALEXIT

;. . . . . . . . . . . . . . . . . . . . . . . . . . . . . . . . . . . . . . . . . . . .
node1:
  POSTMSG 2,1,0,#34h ;node-2,term-1,not-notif,immediate-data.
  POSTMSG 3,1,0,#00h ;node3,term1,notnotif,immediate-data.
  NORMALEXIT
;. . . . . . . . . . . . . . . . . . . . . . . . . . . . . . . . . . . . . . . . . . . .
node3:

  POSTMSG 4,2,0,32h ;node4,term2,notnotif,direct-data.
  NORMALEXIT
;. . . . . . . . . . . . . . . . . . . . . . . . . . . . . . . . . . . . . . . . . . . .
node2:
      jnb    flags.2,n22
      ;...notification is in r1
n22:

  POSTMSG 4,1,0,#00h ;node4,term1,0,immediate-data.
  NORMALEXIT
;. . . . . . . . . . . . . . . . . . . . . . . . . . . . . . . . . . . . . . . . . . . .
node4:
  POSTMSG 2,2,1,#11    ;notification, back to node-2,term-2.
```

```
NORMALEXIT
;%%%%%%%%%%%%%%%%%%%%%%%%%%%%%%%%%%%%%%%%%%%%%%%%%%%%%
      END

COPYRIGHT & LIABILITY NOTICE
****************************
```

Source, 8-bit signature calculator

```
.MODEL SMALL
.STACK
.DATA
        DB    10 DUP(0)
asciitbl DB    7 DUP(0)
        DB    "$","$"
intromsg DB    0Ah,0Dh
 DB "Type-in active-set of messages, crtl-z to clear\
                        , crtl-x to quit",0Ah,0Dh
 DB "This version generates 8-bit signatures for\
                        TERS51S2.",0Ah,0Dh
intr2 DB "Do not enter remote-output, nor\
                Notification messages.",0Ah,0Dh
intro3 DB "FOR TERSE51: Node range = 1 - 32. \
                Terminal range = 1 - 4."0Ah,0Dh
     DB "FOR TERSE51: Signature-calc starts from\
                        latest msg on stack."
        DB 0Ah,0Dh,0Ah,0Dh,"$"
destnode DB "Destination-node: $"
destterm DB " Destination-terminal: $"
sigtxt   DB "  SIGNATURE:$"
newline  DB 0Dh,0Ah,"$"

signature DB 0             ;8-bit signature
input    DB 0             ;binary input
header   DB 0             ;used for sig-calc

.CODE
start:
    mov ax,@DATA
```

```
        mov ds,ax
start2:
;intro message...
        mov ah,9
        lea dx,intromsg
        int 21h
start3:
;Ask for destination node....
        mov ah,9
        lea dx,destnode
        int 21h
        call getinput          ;comes back with "input", in
        mov  al,input          ; binary...
        and  al,00011111b
        mov  header,al


;ask for destination terminal...
        mov  ah,9
        lea  dx,destterm
        int  21h
        call getinput
        mov  al,input
        dec  al          ;as terminal no. stored as 0 - 3.
        and  al,011b
        shl  al,1
        shl  al,1         ;modified hdr. term is bits 5-6.
        shl  al,1          ;(notif is bit-7)
        shl  al,1
        shl  al,1
        or   header,al


;calculate the signature....
        mov  al,signature
        test al,80h
        jz   sig1
        xor  al,00100001b
sig1:
        xor  al,header
        shl  al,1
        mov  signature,al


;convert it to ascii....
        mov  al,signature
        mov  ah,0
        mov  dx,0
        call bin2dec
        mov  BYTE PTR asciitbl+7,"$"  ;...hex o/p stuffs this up.


;display result...
```

```
            mov ah,9
            lea dx,sigtxt
            int 21h
            mov ah,9
            lea dx,asciitbl
            int 21h
              ;also display signature in hex...
              mov bl,signature
              mov bh,0
              mov cl,4
              rol bx,cl
              mov ax,bx
              and ax,000Fh
                cmp al,9
                jbe xx
                add al,7
xx:             add al,30h
              mov asciitbl+1," "    ;al
              rol bx,cl
              mov ax,bx
              and ax,000Fh
                cmp al,9
                jbe yy
                add al,7
yy:             add al,30h
              mov asciitbl+2," "    ;al
              rol bx,cl
              mov ax,bx
              and ax,000Fh
                cmp al,9
                jbe zz
                add al,7
zz:             add al,30h
              mov asciitbl+3,al
              rol bx,cl
              mov ax,bx
              and ax,000Fh
                cmp al,9
                jbe mm
                add al,7
mm:             add al,30h
              mov asciitbl+4,al
              mov BYTE PTR asciitbl+5,"h"
              mov BYTE PTR asciitbl+6,0Ah
              mov BYTE PTR asciitbl+7,0Dh
              mov BYTE PTR asciitbl+8,"$"
              mov ah,9
              lea dx,asciitbl
              int 21h
```

```
        jmp start3
getout:
        mov ax,4C00h
        int 21h

getinput:
        mov input,0
getinput2:
        mov ah,0
        int 16h
        cmp ax,2C1Ah       ;crtl-z
        jne notcrtlz
        mov signature,0
        mov ah,9
        lea dx,newline
        int 21h
        pop ax             ;dump return address
        jmp start2
notcrtlz:
        cmp ax,2D18h       ;crtl-x
        jne notcrtlx
        mov ah,9
        lea dx,newline
        int 21h
        jmp getout
notcrtlx:
;test if outside range 0-9...
        cmp al,30h
        jb  below0
        cmp al,39h
        ja  above9
inrange:
;echo it to screen...
        mov  ah,0Eh
        push ax
        mov  bx,02
        int  10h
        pop  ax
        and al,0Fh         ;convert to binary
        mov ah,input
        and ah,0Fh         ;see if 2nd char already there
        jnz second
        mov input,al       ;save in lo-nibble.
        jmp getinput2
second:
        mov cl,4
        shl input,cl
        mov ah,input
        or  al,ah          ;combine them
```

```
        mov input,al    ;save. ...value is in bcd format.
below0:     ;any char outside range, terminates entry
above9:                 ;          /
;convert input to binary....
        mov al,input
        and al,0F0h
        mov cl,4
        ror al,cl
        mov dl,10
        mul dl          ;result --> ax
        mov bl,input
        and bl,0Fh
        add al,bl       ;now have binary value.
        mov input,al    ;          /
        ret
;.....................................................
bin2dec PROC        ;requires binary number in dx:ax...
        lea di,asciitbl
        mov bx,di
        add di,6   ;8
ssss:
        mov cx,10
        div cx
        add dl,30h
sssss:
        mov [di],dl
        dec di
        mov dx,0
        cmp ax,0
        jne ssss
        mov dl," "
        cmp bx,di
        jbe sssss
        ret
bin2dec ENDP

        END  start
```

C
Using Dunfield C with TERSE

I chose *Dunfield C* for the first example of a C interface, because it is very cost effective. The company, *Dunfield Development Systems*, are on the Internet, at

```
http://www.dunfield.com/
```

The Dunfield Developer's Kit includes a C compiler, assembler, monitor/debugger, and Integrated Development Environment. Optional extras include *Emily52*, an excellent simulator, and *Monica52*, an enhanced debugger.

The tools are designed mostly to work with the type of hardware in which you have a serial cable from PC to microcontroller board and an on-board monitor (which can be downloaded from PC to board). This would have to be the least expensive way to develop applications.

Integrated Development Environment

With Dunfield C, you will need to edit a configuration file and a couple of library files to use TERSE — for example, 8051.IDE, RUNLIB2.ASM and 8051RLPT.ASM.

The first one, 8051.IDE, is the configuration file for the Integrated Development Environment, DDSIDE.EXE.

8051.IDE **configuration file**

```
file   *.C
temp   0 0
tab    4
rem Remove following line if have MONOCHROME video system
color WH|BL WH|MG BL|GR WH|RD BK|WH RD|CY BK|WH BL|WH
rem Provide "hotkey" access to main menu itemsfrom editor
key !C|$~F8C !T|$~F8T !O|$~F8O !F|$~F8F !K|$~F8K !A|$~F8\
                              A !B|$~F8B !L|$~F8L
target   1 9600 0 1
simulate c:\emily52\EMILY52.COM
debug    c:\emily52\MONICA52.COM
option
       pick    0 Memory model |Tiny$'0'A| Small$'1'A|\
                       Compact$'2'A |Medium$'3'A|Large$'4'A
       switch    0    C-source comments |-c
       switch    0    Fold literals     |-f
       switch    0    Optimizer debug   |-d
       switch    0    Full ASM listing  |-f -s L=$f.LST|-t
       switch    0    Case sensitive ASM|-c
       switch    0    2K addressing     |-a
       switch    1    Intel output      |-i
       end
setup $0
step Preprocess|CC|   $H\MCP.COM $I $O l=$H -q$' -l'1
step Compile|ASM| $H\MCC51.COM $I $O -q m=$A $1 $2$' -l'0
step Optimize|ASM|    $H\MCO51.COM $I $O -q $3
step -Macro|ASM|      $H\MACRO.COM $I >$O
step Link|ASM| $H\SLINK.COM $I $O -q\
                      l=\8051\TTERSC51\LIB51 i=$0.LIB
step Assemble|HEX|    $H\ASM51.COM $I $4 $5 $6 $7 C=$O
```

I copied the original 8051.IDE to my working directory and modified it as shown in bold letters. I chose the "tiny" memory model, turned off case sensitivity, and changed from Motorola to Intel HEX file output format. I turned on the C compiler preprocessing by removing the "-" prefix in front of the word "Preprocess", and did the same for "Optimize".

As I modified some library files, I created a new LIB51 directory and referenced it in the Link step.

Note that, much to my surprise, when I tried to edit 8051.IDE with my Microsoft Programmer's Workbench (PWB) editor, DDSIDE had problems with reading the file. I never chased that one down, but from then on, I did all editing of 8051.IDE using DDSIDE itself.

Library files

Because I chose the "tiny" model, which is for systems with 128 bytes of internal RAM only and all code and constants in ROM, the main file requiring editing is 8051RLPT.ASM. This is a special prefix file as you can see from TINY.LIB.

8051RLPT.ASM **library file**

```
* DDS MICRO-C 8031/51 Startup Code & Runtime library
* TINY model
* Copyright 1991-1995 Dave Dunfield
* All rights reserved.
*
* System Memory map
    ORG  $0800       ROM Starts here
*Fixed memory locations for alternate access CPU\
* register bank.
*If you are NOT using BANK 0, these equates must be
* adjusted.
?R0  EQU  0          Used for "POP" from stack
?R1  EQU  ?R0+1      Used to load index indirectly
?R2  EQU  ?R0+2      " "        " "        " "    " "
?R3  EQU  ?R0+3      Used by some runtime lib functions
?R4  EQU  ?R0+4
?R5  EQU  ?R0+5
?R6  EQU  ?R0+6
?R7  EQU  ?R0+7
*
* Startup code entry point
*
* If you are NOT using interrupts, can reclaim 50 bytes
* of code space by removing the following TWO lines.
    AJMP *+$0032         Skip interrupt vectors
    DS   $0032-2     Reserve space for interrupt vectors
*
    MOV  SP,#?stk-1 Set up initial stack
;**CHANGED**     LCALL main        Execute program
  ajmp start0 ;**CHANGED BY B.KAULER***<<<<<<<<<<<<<<<<<
  ;**Reason is, we want to enter TERSE with empty stack**

*EXIT to MON51 by calling the 'timer1' interrupt vector.
*This causes MON51 to think that a single-step operation
*has just completed, and therefore it saves the user
*registers, and performs a context switch back to the
*monitor.
exit LCALL $001B      Call Timer-1 interrupt
    SJMP exit         Incase he go's again
```

```
$SE:1
*#map1 Segment 1, initialized variables
$SE:2
*#map2 Segment 2, internal "register" variables
   ORG 02Dh ;**CHANGE**    <<<<<<<<<<<<<<<<<<<<<<<<<<<<<
;**CHANGE** ORG $0008    Internal ram ALWAYS starts here
* S/N:
```

I have highlighted places in the above listing that you might need to change, as well as places I have changed. First, notice that the origin of code is set to 0800h — this is to allow a monitor on the target board that occupies the first 2048 bytes (800h). If you were downloading to a target without monitor, you could change this to zero.

A little further on is the comment that space is reserved for interrupt handlers — this is where you can place jumps to interrupt service routines if your program requires them.

Further on again is my first modification — I changed the LCALL to AJMP to the start of execution of my TERSE program, because I do not want anything on the stack initially.

Finally, I changed the position of the variables from 08, to 2Dh — this is because I want the stack to be from 08 to 2Ch for very small microcontroller systems that may only have 64 bytes of RAM. However, this meant that I had to modify another file, RUNLIB2.ASM, to shift the stack.

The default behaviour is that the stack starts from the end of the variables, which assumes that some space is left, and of course the default is that the variables start at 08. You may like to change this to suit your requirements, but do be careful of the flags variable, because it must be bit-addressable. I have placed it as the first declared variable, and by starting variables at 2Dh, I ensured flags is in the bit-addressable memory range of 20h—2Fh.

RUNLIB2.ASM **library file**

```
* DDS MICRO-C/51 runtime library support files for TINY models
*
* Load a byte from external memory into TEMP register
?extb MOV   R3,A       Save A
      CLR   A          Zero offset
      MOVC  A,[A+DPTR]  Get the byte
      XCH   A,R3        Restore A, save result
      RET
```

```
* Load a word of external memory into TEMP register
?extwMOV   R4,A        Save A
     CLR   A           Zero offset
     MOVC  A,[A+DPTR]   Get the low order byte
     MOV   R3,A        Save result LOW
     MOV   A,#1        Offset to HIGH
     MOVC  A,[A+DPTR]   Get the high order byte
     XCH   A,R4        Restore A, save result HIGH
     RET
* Load a word of external memory into INDEX register
?extiMOV   R2,A        Save A
     CLR   A           Zero offset
     MOVC  A,[A+DPTR]   Get the low order byte
     MOV   R1,A        Save result LOW
     MOV   A,#1        Offset to HIGH
     MOVC  A,[A+DPTR]   Get the high order byte
     XCH   A,R2        Restore A, Save result HIGH
     RET
$FS:
* Define the stack (at the end of segment 2)
?stk    EQU   08   ;**CHANGE BY B.KAULER** <<<<<<<<<<<<<<<<
; ?stk     EQU   * Stack goes at top of user variables
* S/N:
```

The above listing shows how I changed the starting address of the stack. Note that the 8051 stack grows to higher addresses. Placing it in the range 08—2Eh is very constrictive and will need considerable care, if you intend to program in C. However, unlike ordinary C programming, TERSE programming does not nest the stack so deeply, due to the tendency for each function to be a node in the TERSE flow diagram — the transition between nodes uses the stack for message passing, but there is no nesting beyond that of messages waiting to be delivered.

TERSE — C interface

The listing below is the "F" uniprocessor version of TERSE, named TERS51SF.C, which is basically the same as the assembly language version TERS51SF.ASM, except that it has interfacing for C programmers. You can use the same principles for any other version of TERSE.

Whatever C you use, this file can probably be adapted without much trouble. I have kept it as one large file that you may want to break up, maybe into include files or as separate files to be linked.

TERS51SF.C **uniprocessor TERSE**

```
/*TERS51SF.C--Tiny Embedded Real-time Software Environ.*/
/*This version is for the 8051 family.*/
/*This is the single-processor version, for Dunfield-C*/
/*LIB51\8051RLPT.ASM, LIB51\RUNLIB2.ASM, and 8051.IDE*/
/*, have been modified.*/


#include <8051REG.H>
#include <8051IO.H>
#include <8051ADC.H>
#include <8051BIT.H>
extern register unsigned char R1,R2,R3,R4;


#define emptyst  ?stk-1 /*?stk is defined by RUNLIB2.ASM*/
#define TERM1flag flags&0x02
#define TERM2flag flags&0x04
#define TERM3flag flags&0x08
#define TERM4flag flags&0x10


#define POSTMSG(node,term,notif,datavalue) asm {\
     mov   b,datavalue\
     push  b\
     mov   b,#(node*8+((term-1)*2)+notif)\
     push  b\
 }
/*note that TERM is stored 1-less. EX: TERM-1 is stored*/
/* as 00*/


#define EXITNODE asm {\
 ajmp nodereturn \
 }

/*-----------PROGRAMMER TO MODIFY-------------------*/
#define numentries 5
char signatures[numentries]={255,0,64,176,200};
char nodenum[numentries]=   {0,  1,  2,  3,  4};
/*--------------------------------------------------*/


register unsigned char flags; /*must be bit-addressable*/
#define sizedata 5
/*-----------USABLE BY PROGRAMMER-------------------*/
register unsigned char pdata1;        /*pointer to data1*/
register unsigned char data1[sizedata];/*general-purpos*/
register unsigned char pdata2;        /*pointer to data2*/
register unsigned char data2[sizedata];/*general-purpos*/
/*--------------------------------------------------*/


/*----------PROGRAMMER'S GLOBAL VARIABLES-----------*/
```

```
register unsigned char x;
/*------------------------------------------------------*/
```

What I have done in the above listing is shift the equates, constant, and variable data declarations of TERSE "up" to the C-code level.

Notice that I have defined the registers R1, R2, R3, and R4 as external, so that they can be accessed from the C-code level. Other common registers are defined in the include file, 8051REG.H. R1—R4 are where the message data is when a node is fired.

The macro is interesting. In moving it from assembly language, I have used the ability of the #define to perform just like a macro, including the passing of parameters. However, Dunfield C has a limitation, in that there are no conditional compilation directives, so I could not put in the range checking that was in the original assembly version.

Constructing the Signature table was easy, and by defining the entries as char, ensures they go into ROM — but for your C and memory-model, check if anything else is needed to clarify this. Signatures is only 8-bit, not 16-bit, because the smaller size is adequate for small single-processor systems.

To fill up a processor with 64 bytes of RAM, I have defined only two data buffers, data1 and data2, that are 5 bytes each, making 12 bytes total. I defined the pointers as ordinary unsigned char, because Dunfield C makes all pointers 16 bits. That leaves 6 bytes available.

TERS51SF.C continued: Main() function

```
main()
{
nodeptr:                    /*these occupy 2(or 3) bytes each.*/
     goto node0;            /*1st node in table error-handler.*/
     goto node1;            /*this must be in ascending order*/
     goto node2;                      /*of node number.*/
     goto node3;
     goto node4;
/*....................................................*/
/******MAIN LOOP*******/
start0:                     /*entry point*/
start1:                     /*program entry point 1.*/
```

I put the jump table right at the beginning of the code. In the assembly language version, the jump table was AJMPs, but Dunfield C substitutes

LJMPs for the `goto` statement, unless a switch is set to force everything to AJMPs.

If LJMPs, each entry will occupy 3 bytes, which must be taken care of in the part of TERSE responsible for calculating the jump address.

TERS51SF.C continued: embedded TERSE

```
asm
{
mov  pdata1,#data1  ;initalise pointers, to buffers
mov  pdata2,#data2  ;/ empty.
ajmp start2

gotonode:
            mov    dptr,#nodenum      ;get node number.
            mov    a,r0               ;        /
            dec    a                  ;        /
            movc   a,@+dptr           ;        /
            mov    r0,a               ;        / -->r0
gonode: anl    flags,#11000000b   ;bits 1-4 set by
                                  ; extractmsgs...
            ajmp extractmsgs       ;extracts all msgs for
                          ;this node.(comes back here)
main1:
        mov    dptr,#?AB3   ;*IMPORTANT DUNFIELD-C SUBSTITUTES
                          ; nodeptr*
        mov    a,r0  ;*ANY CHANGES, CHECK .LST FILE, ?AB3 OK**
;     rl     a            ;*2 --each entry is 2 bytes.
;Unless AJMPs are forced on Dunfield-C, each entry is 3
; bytes...
        add a,r0
        add a,r0
        jmp    @+dptr              ;jump to next node to execute.
                                 ;r0 = node-number.(0--> ).
nodereturn:

start2:
        ;program entry point 2.
        mov    r2,#0              ;initially, make signature = zero.

;calculate the signature...
        mov    r0,sp              ;save initial sp.
loop3:      mov    a,r0
        cjne   a,#emptyst,loop2
        ajmp   sigout             ;   /  (v1.14)
loop2:      mov a,@r0              ;get 1st byte of msg.
        mov    r1,a               ;save it for calcsig.
        dec    r0                 ;go past Header.
```

```
        dec    r0                  ;bypass the data.
not9:   mov a,r1                   ;get Header again.
        jb   acc.0,loop3           ;ignore notifications.
get5:ajmp   calcsig               ;...compute signature,
                                    ; accumulate in r2...
main3:
        ajmp   loop3
sigout:

;if comes out of above, with sig=0, diagram will restart,
; as must be complete...
lookup:
;signature in r2, use lookup table to get address of node...
        mov    r0,#numentries
        mov    dptr,#signatures
loop1:  mov    a,r0
        dec    a
        movc   a,@a+dptr           ;start at end of array.
        xrl    a,r2                ;compare signatures
        jz     sigfnd
no2:    djnz   r0,loop1
        ;...sig. not found....
        inc    r0           ;make r0=1. (r0= lookup-index + 1).
sigfnd:
        ajmp   gotonode             ;r0 = lookup-index + 1
;....
;*****END MAIN LOOP*****
;.............................................
calcsig:
;entered with r1=msg-header, r2=accumulated signature
        mov    a,r2
        jnb    acc.7,sig1           ;jump if bit a.7 is clear.
        xrl    a,#00100001b         ;tapping points.
sig1:xrl    a,r1
        rl     a
        mov    r2,a
        ajmp   main3  ;ret
;.............................................
extractmsgs:
;entered with r0=node-number (0 --> 31, node-0 = 0, etc)
;extracts all msgs for this node-->r1,r2,... (bank-0)
;where r1 is terminal-1, etc. Dumps msg-header.
;array must be rotated exactly once around....
        mov    a,sp ;a complication-- must exit with array
        clr    c     ; in same order on stack, as at entry.
        subb a,#emptyst         ;/
        mov    r5,a            ;/(r5 is used as loop count)
rot2:
        mov    a,sp                ;top of array (=top of stack).
```

```
        clr    c
        subb   a,#emptyst          ;size of array
        jnz    zip1                ;array is empty.
        ajmp   rot6
zip1:
        clr    ie.7                ;disable all interrupts.
        pop    acc                 ;get top of array.
        inc    sp                  ;...but leave sp as-is.
        setb   ie.7                ;enable all interrupts.
        anl    a,#0F8h             ;extract node-number.
rot4:   rr     a                   ;node-number hard-over on rhs.
        rr     a                   ;            /
        rr     a                   ;            /
        xrl    a,r0                ;is msg for this node?
        jnz    rot3                ;no.
          pop    acc               ;get top of array, again.
          anl    a,#06h            ;get destination-terminal-field.
          cjne   a,#00,nxt1 ;is it terminal-1?(stored as 00)
          pop    01                ;pop data-byte to r1.
            setb flags.1           ;flag a msg on terminal-1.
          ajmp extr1
nxt1:     cjne   a,#01,nxt2        ;is it term-2?
          pop    02                ;pop data-byte to r2.
            setb flags.2           ;flag a msg on terminal-2.
          ajmp extr1
nxt2:     cjne   a,#10,nxt3        ;is it term-3?
          pop    03                ;pop data-byte to r3.
            setb flags.3           ;flag a msg on terminal-3.
          ajmp extr1
nxt3:     pop    04                ;term-4 --> pop data-byte to r4.
            setb flags.4           ;flag a msg on terminal-4.
          ajmp extr1               ;/
rot3:
;>>>>>>>>>>>>>>>>>>>>>>>>>>>>>>>>>>>>>>>>>>>>>>>>>>>>>>>>>>>>>>
rotatestack:
                    ;rotates the stack up *two* bytes.
        mov    07,r0               ;save.
        clr    flags.6
tat1:
          mov    a,sp              ;get size of array.
          clr    c                 ;         /
          subb   a,#emptyst        ;        /
          mov    r6,a              ;       /
          mov    r0,#emptyst
rot1:   inc    r0
        xch a,@r0    ;(indirect addressing mustuse r0 or r1)
        djnz r6,rot1           ;r6=size of array.
          mov    r0,#emptyst ;rotate the top element down to
            inc    r0                ;the bottom.
```

```
        mov   @r0,a               ;         /
      jb flags.6,tat2  ;need to do above operation twice.
      setb  flags.6              ;         /
      ajmp  tat1                 ;         /
tat2: clr   flags.6              ;         /
      mov   r0,07                ;restore.
;>>>>>>>>>>>>>>>>>>>>>>>>>>>>>>>>>>>>>>>>>>>>>>>>>>>>>>>>>>>>>>
extr1:
      dec   r5         ;r5 must cnt down in steps of 2.
      djnz  r5,rot2    ;master loop, array circulate
                       ; exactly once.
rot6:
      ajmp  main1  ;ret
 }
```

That's the entire source for TERSE, though when you try this for yourself, be sure to use the latest versions of TERSE, because they may have some refinements.

Notice the "}" at the end of the above listing, which brings us out of the in-line assembly and back to C code.

There are a couple of idiosyncrasies about the Dunfield assembler. You cannot have a comment on the same line as a code label, unless there is also an instruction on that line. Therefore, you will see places where I have moved the comment onto the next line. Another peculiarity is that expressions cannot have spaces in them, and you may have to use parentheses to enforce correct evaluation of expressions, because there is no precedence to the operators. These notes do of course apply to the versions I purchased late in 1995, and later versions will have improvements.

Notice the code label ?AB3. This actually refers to nodeptr at the start of the jump table, but Dunfield C substitutes all C code labels with a new label always beginning with "?". I found out that it was ?AB3 from the .LST file.

TERS51SF.C continued: C-level coding of nodes

```
/*.............................................*/
node0:
 EXITNODE
/*.............................................*/
node1:

 POSTMSG(2,1,0,#34)   /*node2,term1,no-notif.,imm.-data.*/
 POSTMSG(3,1,0,#00)  /*node3,term1,notnotif,immediate-data.*/
 EXITNODE
```

```
/*..................................................*/
node3:
 POSTMSG(4,2,0,32)    /*node4,term2,notnotif,direct-data.*/
 EXITNODE
/*..................................................*/
node2:
     if(TERM2flag) {  /*TERM2flag is a true/false macro*/
     /*a Notification has arrived... in register R1*/
     x=R1;
     }
 POSTMSG(4,1,0,#00)   /*node4,term1,0,immediate-data.*/
 EXITNODE
/*..................................................*/
node4:
 POSTMSG(2,2,1,#11)   /*notification, back to node-2,term-2.*/
 EXITNODE
/*..................................................*/

}
```

With this simple uniprocessor version of TERSE, there are no remote messages to worry about, so all messages are only 2 bytes, a header and data byte. Therefore, `POSTMSG` has been modified, such that there is no need to specify a destination PU.

Although node 0 is still designated as the error-handler, it is not handled in any special way by TERSE — you simply post a message to it, like any other node.

Also, as the signature is only 8 bits, to construct the Signature table, you have to use the 8-bit program, `SIGCAL8.EXE`, that runs under DOS on a PC (see Appendix B).

D

Distributed TERSE with MESS scheduling

The following listing is a distributed version of TERSE with MESS scheduling written for the 8051 and requiring only the in-built UART and an external RS-485 driver/receiver chip.

This is a lean and mean version of only about 350 bytes but really packs a punch. Although under the hood there is one master processor, from the messaging level it is peer-to-peer. It is designed for distributed systems in which the network is reliable, such as inside the same chassis, because it doesn't do any error detection or recovery on transmissions between processors. It does, however, have a synchronisation facility for when power fails and returns on one processor.

At the time of writing, I am planning to write a version of TERSE that uses a network chip or one of the microcontrollers with on-chip network hardware; however, I have been restricted by lack of funds (apart from the ever-existing lack of time!). It will come though. Some other people have expressed an interest in doing some work in this direction.

Figure D.1 shows that a complete network node is extremely simple, only requiring two chips — in this example, the Atmel 2051 microcontroller and the 75176 RS-485 driver/receiver.

Figure D.1: A complete network node.

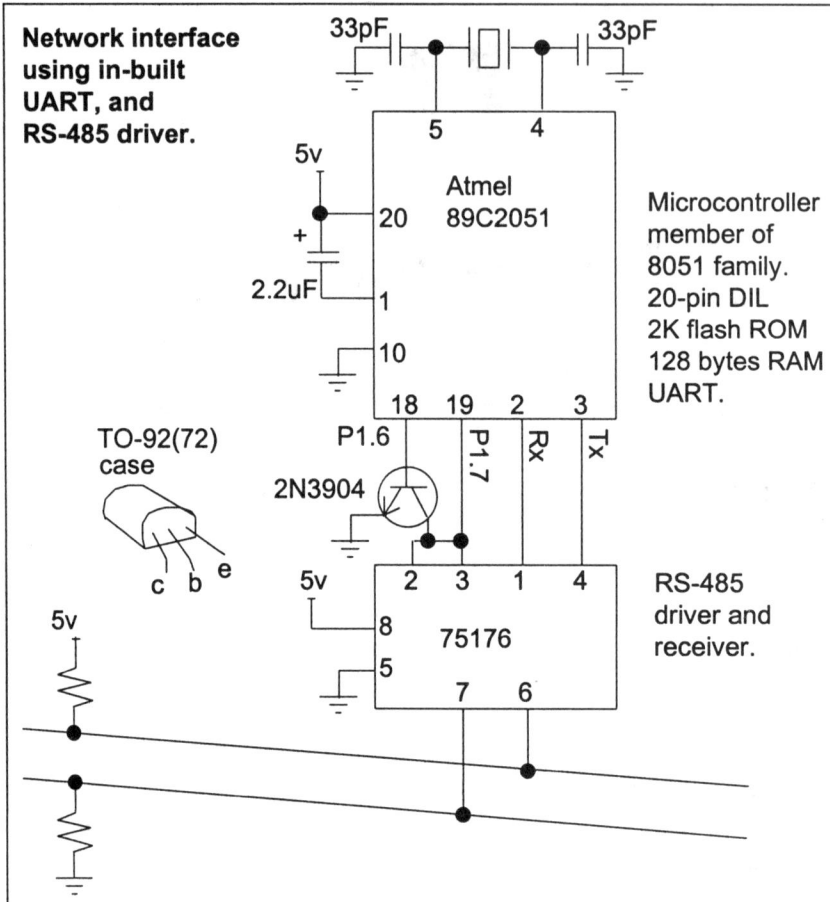

Network interface using in-built UART, and RS-485 driver.

Atmel 89C2051

Microcontroller member of 8051 family. 20-pin DIL 2K flash ROM 128 bytes RAM UART.

TO-92(72) case

2N3904

RS-485 driver and receiver.

75176

TERS5130.ASM distributed TERSE

```
; VERSION 3.0 1996 (c) Barry Kauler.
;Uses MESS scheduling.
;Please check Web site for latest version (see end this file).

;TERS5130.ASM
;Token-passing network, 16 processors max.
;uses in-built UART. Can use RS-485 line drivers, single
;twisted pair.  Designed for open-ended, terminated each end,
;transmission line.
;NOTES ON THIS VERSION:
;Remote i/p msgs only have 4-bit pu-field, 3-bit node,
```

```
; 1-bit token/notif,
;so can only go to terminal 1, and node 0 -- 7.
;This TERSE uses 4th reg.bank -- nodes can use 1st - 3rd
; banks.

;......EQUATES YOU MAY HAVE TO MODIFY.............
$MOD51                  ;config. info for Metalink assembler.
THISPU     EQU 1        ;range is 1 - 16.(stored as 0-15)
D1SIZE     EQU 4        ;buffer1 size.
DSIZE      EQU 4        ;size of other buffers.
;.....................................................


DSEG
    ORG 18h
sp2in:      DS  1       ;ptr to top circ.buf (this is also R0,
                        ; 4th reg.bank)
sp2out:     DS  1       ;ptr to end circ.buff.(r1    "  )
databyte:   DS  1       ;(r2)msgisr puts incoming msg here,
                        ; temporarily.
header:     DS  1       ;(r3) /
databyte2:  DS  1       ;(r4)outgoing msg here, temp.
header2:    DS  1       ;(r5) /
timercnt:   DS  1       ;PU1: used by timer0isr to set
                        ; token-posting rate.
tokencnt:   DS  1       ;PU1: used by msgisr to construct tokens.


    ORG 20h
flags:      DS  1       ;flags.1,2,3,4 = 1, msg on
                        ; terminal-1, -2, -3, -4.
flagsB:     DS  1       ;flags.0,.4-.7 used by msgisr, to
                        ; sync networking.
flagsC:     DS  1       ;error flags.
extmsgwtg:  DS  1       ;flags set if ext.msg has
                        ; arrived.(see extmsg) ###
temp1:      DS  1        ;used by msgisr. ###
timeoutcnt: DS  1       ;<<<USER CAN CHOOSE HOW TO INCR.
                        ; THIS<<<
pdata1:     DS  1
data1:      DS  D1SIZE  ;Allows messages to queue, for
                        ; terminal1.
pdata2:     DS  1
data2:      DS  DSIZE   ;memory management -- see book.
pdata3:     DS  1
data3:      DS  DSIZE   ;  /
pdata4:     DS  1
data4:      DS  DSIZE   ;  /
;......
;***PUT APPLICATION VARIABLES IN HERE***<<<<<<<<<<<<<<<<<<
;....
```

```
EMPTYST        EQU $-1   ;stack starts from end of internal
                         ; variables.


;......EQUATES YOU MAY HAVE TO MODIFY.............
SP2TOP         EQU 7Fh   ;circular buffer, for i/p msgs.
SP2BOTTOM      EQU 6Bh   ;  / allow it to hold 20
                         ; msgs.(6C--7F buffer)
fENABLETX      EQU p1.7  ;enable to rs-485 driver chip
                         ; (1=enabled).
fPROTECT       EQU  p1.6 ;prevents fENABLETX from
                         ; momentary tx'ing.
TIMERSETTING   EQU 2     ;no. entries to timer0isr before
                         ; fTOKENOUT set.
;.............................................


;..............FLAGS..............
fTOKENHERE     EQU flagsB.7 ;set when THISPU owns token.
f2NDBYTEIN     EQU flagsB.6 ;set when 2nd i/p byte pending,
                            ; clrd when arrived.
fPOSTREMOTE    EQU flagsB.5 ;set from request by
                            ;POSTREMOTE, clrd on completion
f2NDBYTEOUT    EQU flagsB.4 ;set to request 2nd byte Tx,
                            ; clrd when posted.
f2NDBYTEGONE   EQU flagsB.3 ;set when 2nd byte posted, clrd
                            ; when gone.
fTOKENOUT      EQU flagsB.2 ;req. by Timer0 post token,
                            ; clrd when posted(PU1)
fTOKENGONE     EQU flagsB.1 ;set when token posted, clrd
                            ; when gone (PU1 only)
fSYNCHRONIZED  EQU flagsB.0 ;clrd on reset, set after all
                            ; initialisation.
fPOSTTIME      EQU flags.7  ;set for request post
                            ; globaltime, clrd when done.
fIGNORE1       EQU flags.6  ;set; ignore next incoming
                            ; byte.
fIGNORE2       EQU flags.5  ;set; ignore next incoming
                            ; byte.
fTERM4           EQU flags.4  ;set if msg on terminal4.
fTERM3           EQU flags.3  ;set if msg on terminal3.
fTERM2           EQU flags.2  ;set if msg on terminal2.
fTERM1           EQU flags.1  ;set if msg on terminal1.

fSIGFAIL       EQU flagsC.7 ;set if sig.table lookup
                            ; failed.
fTIMEOUT       EQU flagsC.6 ;set if timeout.


;.............................................

;......SYSTEM CODES................
```

```
;POSTREMOTE to node=0, notif=1, is global sytem msg.
;(but, note, THISPU originates msg and will not receive
; it).
;POSTLOCAL can also post system msgs to node 0, but they
; dont get intercepted by system: (urgent response inside
; msgisr)
;The following codes go into the databyte:
KILLTOKEN    EQU 01    ;use global msg only, to all pus.
                       ; kills token.
RESET        EQU 02    ;reset program.
GLOBALTIME   EQU 03    ;CURRENTLY USED FOR START-UP SYNC


;.................................................
CSEG
start:
      clr   fENABLETX      ;turn off rs-485 driver.
      clr   fPROTECT       ;power-on network protection
                           ; mechanism.
      ajmp start1          ;reset entry point.
;....
      ORG  0Bh    ;timer0. entered every 256*12/clk (clk in
                  ; Hz) sec.
      xch  a,timercnt ;save old acc., load timercnt.
      jnz  run1
      IF (THISPU = 1)
        setb fTOKENOUT        ;want to post token.
        setb scon.1          ;cause Tx interrupt.
      ENDIF
      mov  a,#TIMERSETTING ;reload.
run1: dec  a            ;NOTE: should get reloaded every time
                        ; a token arrives.
      xch  a,timercnt ;restore old acc.
      reti
;....
      ORG  23h
      ajmp msgisr    ;serial interface.
      ORG  32h


WAIT EQU 80h                ;bit7 = 1
;have a different signature table for PU3, as it has a
; remote i/p msg...
 IF (THISPU EQ 3)
signatures: DB 255, 0,08,     22,152  ;starting node has
                                      ; signature=zero.
nodenum:   DB 0,  1, 2, WAIT+126,4 ;wait on node3 for
                                   ; 126 timeunits.
extmsg:    DB 0,  0, 0,    08,    0 ;set bit3, means wait
                                    ; on node3.
 ELSE
```

```
signatures: DB 255, 0,08,22,152  ;starting node has
                                  ; signature=zero.
nodenum:    DB 0,   1, 2, 3,   4
extmsg:     DB 0,   0, 0, 0,   0
 ENDIF
numentries EQU nodenum - signatures
nodeptr:                 ;these occupy 2 bytes each.
     ajmp node0     ;1st node in table is
                    ; error-handler(always node-0).
     ajmp node1     ;this must be in ascending order
     ajmp node2          ;of node number.
     ajmp node3          ;
     ajmp node4
;.....                   ;msgs will always be two bytes...
POSTLOCAL MACRO node,term,notif,datavalue
     IF ((node >= 0) AND (node <= 31))
     IF ((term >= 1) AND (term <= 4))
     IF ((notif = 0) OR (notif = 1))
     mov   b,datavalue
     push  b
     mov   b,#(node + ((term-1)*32) + (notif*128))
     push  b
     ENDIF
     ENDIF
     ENDIF
POSTLOCAL ENDM
;note that TERM is stored one-less. EX: TERM 1 is stored
; as 00.
;Headerformat: bit7=notif, 5--6=term-1, 0--4=node.

NORMALEXIT MACRO             ;use this one for normal
                            ; operation.
     ajmp nodereturn
NORMALEXIT ENDM

FASTEXIT  MACRO nextnode    ;bypasses signature calc. &
                           ; lookup,
     mov   r5,#nextnode    ; if you know the next node.
     ajmp gonode
FASTEXIT   ENDM

SUPERFASTEXIT MACRO nextnode    ;bypasses everything, incl
                               ; msg delivery
     mov   r5,#nextnode    ;mechanism. Need to deliver
                           ; msgs directly
     ajmp main1            ;to r1-r4 and fTERM1-4.
SUPERFASTEXIT ENDM

POSTREMOTE MACRO pu,node,notification,datavalue
```

```
      IF ((node >= 0) AND (node <= 7))
      IF ((pu >= 1) AND (pu <= 16))
      IF ((notification = 0) OR (notification = 1))
      jb    fPOSTREMOTE,$  ;wait until previous msg has
                            ; been posted.
    mov header2,#(node + ((pu-1)*8) + (notification*128))
      mov   databyte2,datavalue
      setb  fPOSTREMOTE               ;flag intention to msgisr.
      ENDIF             ;(dont set scon.1 now, as will
                        ; happen
      ENDIF             ;when token arrives or in
                        ; extractmsgs)
      ENDIF
POSTREMOTE ENDM
;Header: bit7=notification, bit3--6=pu-1, bits0--2=node.
;Delivery will be to terminal 1 of destination pu/node.
;We reserve Node=0 & notification=0 to identify a token.
;Notification=1 and node=0, is a global system msg.
;(remote system msgs are acted upon immediately inside
; TERSE
; -- see system: procedure -- and are best for global
; error handling).



;. . . . . . . . . . . . . . . . . . . . . . . . . . . . . . . . . . . .
;*****MAIN LOOP*******
start1:                 ;program entry point 1.
      mov   sp2in,#SP2BOTTOM;initialise circ.buff(r0,
                            ; 4th reg.bank)
      mov   sp2out,#SP2BOTTOM   ;   / (r1)
      mov   sp,#EMPTYST     ;initialise 1st stack.
      mov   pdata1,#data1   ;initalise pointers, to buffers
                            ; empty.
      mov   pdata2,#data2   ;/
      mov   pdata3,#data3   ;/
      mov   pdata4,#data4   ;/
      mov   scon,#90h       ;setup serial interface. Mode-2.
      setb  ie.4            ;    / allow serial interrupts
      clr   scon.0          ;/ clr Rx interrupt flag
      setb  ip.4            ;/ select high-priority
      ;anl  pcon,#          ;/select baud rate for
                            ; mode-2(default clk/64).
      mov   flags,#00
      mov   flagsB,#00
      IF (THISPU EQ 1)      ;tokens will start at pu1
        setb fTOKENHERE     ;  /
        setb fSYNCHRONIZED  ;used to sync to network
                            ; messaging.
      ENDIF                 ;  /
```

```
;NOTE that timer0 could be activated for any pus, not
; just PU1...
    IF (THISPU EQ 1)
        mov  timercnt,#(TIMERSETTING - 1)    ;setup timer0.
        mov  th0,#0         ;   /reload value.
        mov  tmod,#02       ; / timer0 mode 2 (8-bit
                            ; auto-reload).
        setb tcon.4         ; / starts timer0.
        setb ie.1           ; /allow timer0 interrupts.
    ENDIF
        setb ie.7               ;global interrupts allow.


nodereturn:     ;<<<<<<<<<< Nodes return to here <<<<<
        anl  psw,#0E7h          ;make sure we are on
                                ; register-bank-0.


start2:                 ;program entry point 2.
        mov  r2,#0      ;initially, make signature = zero.
;calculate the signature....
        mov  r0,sp              ;save initial sp.
loop3:      cjne  r0,#EMPTYST,loop2
        ajmp  sigout
loop2: mov a,@r0                ;get 1st byte of msg.
        mov  r1,a               ;save it for calcsig.
        dec  r0                 ;go past Header.
        dec  r0                 ;bypass the data.
        jb  acc.7,loop3         ;ignore notifications.
calcsig:
;entered with r1=msg-header, r2=accumulated signature
; (starts =0)
        mov a,r2
        jnb acc.7,sig1          ;jump if bit a.7 is clear.
        xrl a,#00100001b        ;tapping points.
sig1:   xrl a,r1
        rl  a
        mov r2,a
        ajmp  loop3
sigout:


;if comes out of above, with sig=0, diagram will restart,
; as must be complete...
lookup:
;signature in r2, use lookup table to get address of
; node...
        mov  r0,#numentries
        mov  dptr,#signatures
loop1: mov  a,r0
        dec  a
        movc  a,@a+dptr             ;start at end of array.
```

```
        xrl    a,r2                ;compare signatures
        jz     gotonode            ;signature found.
no2:    djnz   r0,loop1
        ;...sig. not found....
        inc    r0          ;make r0=1. (r0= lookup-index + 1).
        setb   fSIGFAIL         ;...go to error handler, node0.

sigfnd:     mov timeoutcnt,#0    ;timeout when WAITing on a
                                 ; remote msg.
look4:              ;need to respond to possible expected
                      ; ext.Norm.i/p msgs...
        mov  dptr,#extmsg;get extmsg flags.
        mov  a,r0       ;/
        dec  a          ;/
        movc a,@a+dptr  ;/ appropriate ext.msgs
                         ; expected.
        ;extmsgwtg has actual-arrival flags...
        anl  a,extmsgwtg ;find conjunctions.
        jz      gotonode ;no appropriate ext.msgs
                         ; arrived.
        mov  r5,#1
        jnb     acc.1,look4b    ;if a flag is set, then
                                ; the ext.Norm
        clr  extmsgwtg.1
        ajmp gonode
look4b: inc  r5                 ;msg for that node has
                                ; arrived, and
        jnb     acc.2,look4c    ;the internal signature is
                                ; okay
        clr  extmsgwtg.2
        ajmp gonode
look4c:     inc  r5             ;so this node must run now
        jnb     acc.3,look4d    ;(and not the node in
                                ; nodenum)
        clr  extmsgwtg.3
        ajmp gonode
look4d:     inc  r5
        jnb     acc.4,look4e
        clr  extmsgwtg.4
        ajmp gonode
look4e:     inc  r5
        jnb     acc.5,look4f
        clr  extmsgwtg.5
        ajmp gonode
look4f:     inc  r5
        jnb     acc.6,look4g
        clr  extmsgwtg.6
        ajmp gonode
look4g:     inc  r5
```

```
            jnb     acc.7,gotonode   ;nothing expected has
                                     ; arrived.
            clr   extmsgwtg.7
            ajmp gonode
;...
gotonode:
      mov   dptr,#nodenum       ;get node number.
      mov   a,r0               ;         /
      dec   a                  ;         /
      movc  a,@a+dptr          ;      /
            ;need to respond to WAIT (do nothing)          **
            jnb  acc.7,look3 ;no wait
            anl  a,#7Fh          ;get timeout allowed.(bits0--6)
            cjne a,timeoutcnt,look4     ;<<<< USER
                                        ;IMPLEMENTATION <<<<
            mov  r5,#0           ;go to error-handler.
            setb fTIMEOUT        ;/
            ajmp main1           ;/(r0 references table entry)
look3:      mov   r5,a          ;         / -->r5
gonode:     anl    flags,#11100001b     ;bits 1-4 set by
                                        ; extractmsgs...
ext1:ajmp  extractmsgs      ;extracts all msgs for this
                            ; node.(comes back
main1:                              ; here)(preserves r5)
      mov    dptr,#nodeptr
      mov    a,r5
      rl     a                     ;*2 --each entry is 2 bytes.
      jmp    @a+dptr               ;jump to next node to
                                   ; execute.>>>>>>>>
                                   ;r5 = node-number.(0--> ).
;....
;*****END MAIN LOOP*****
;.............................................

extractmsgs:
;move notifications from circ.buff. to stack...
      orl    psw,#18h    ;select 4th reg.bank.
sub1:mov    a,r1      ;(r1 is sp2out)
      cjne   a,sp2in,sub3
      ajmp   sub4
sub3:cjne  a,#SP2TOP,sub2
      mov    r1,#SP2BOTTOM
sub2:inc    r1
      mov    a,@r1            ;extract databyte.
      push   acc
      inc    r1
      mov    a,@r1            ;extract header.
      push   acc
      ajmp   sub1
```

```
sub4: anl    psw,#0E7h  ;select 1st reg.bank.

nonotifs:
;entered with r5=node-number (0 --> 31, node-0 = 0, etc)
;extracts all msgs for this node-->r1,r2,... first-bank
; of registers, where r1 is terminal-1, etc.  Dumps
; msg-header.
      mov    r0,sp
rex1: cjne   r0,#EMPTYST,ex2
      ajmp   main1            ;*get out*>>>>>>>>
ex2:  mov    a,@r0            ;get msg header.
      anl    a,#1Fh           ;extract node.
      cjne   a,05,ex3         ;test if required node.
        mov a,@r0             ;yes.
        dec r0
        anl a,#60h            ;extract term
        cjne   a,#0,nxt1      ;test if term1
        jnb  flags.1,tile1    ;jmp if no earlier msgs here.
          push 01             ;temp save.
          mov  r1,pdata1
          cjne r1,#data1+D1SIZE,tile2
          ajmp tile3          ;dump the msg, as buffer full.
tile2:          mov  a,@r0
          mov  @r1,a          ;place msg databyte in data1.
          inc  pdata1
tile3:          pop  01       ;restore.
          ajmp ex4
tile1:          mov  01,@r0
          setb fTERM1
          ajmp ex4
nxt1:   cjne   a,#20h,nxt2    ;test if term2
          mov  02,@r0
          setb fTERM2
          ajmp ex4
nxt2:   cjne   a,#40h,nxt3    ;test if term3
          mov  03,@r0
          setb fTERM3
          ajmp ex4
nxt3:   mov  04,@r0           ;term4
          setb fTERM4
ex4:
      pop    acc              ;move top msg down to fill gap.
      pop    b
      mov    @r0,b
      inc    r0
      mov    @r0,a
ex3:  dec    r0
      dec    r0
      ajmp   rex1
```

```
;.................................................
system:
;can handle urgent system messages at this point.
;the message is in header:databyte, and default here is
;that it will be delivered to 2nd stack then Node-0 in
;the normal way...
        cjne r2,#GLOBALTIME,chk0      ;(r2 is databyte)
                ;do nothing...
                ajmp endisr          ;do not deliver msg locally.
chk0:       cjne r2,#KILLTOKEN,chk1 ;global kill. token got
                                     ;stuck,so try kill.
            clr   fTOKENHERE
            clr   fENABLETX
            ajmp endisr        ;do not deliver msg locally.
stupidplace: reti             ;part of weird reset below.
chk1:       cjne r2,#RESET,chk2      ;reset processor.
rst1:       clr   ie.7
            acall stupidplace        ;weird technique to
                                     ; reset processor!
            ajmp  start       ; / restart program.
chk2:
        ;....**OPTIONAL MORE CODE HERE**.....
    ajmp go1                  ;for optional local delivery.
;.................................................

msgisr:
;incoming msgs are always delivered to term1, nodes1--7.
    push acc    ;save acc.
    push psw
    mov  psw,#18h   ;select 4th reg.bank.
    jnb  scon.0,txh ;give Rx first go.

;.............RX HANDLING.............
msg1:
    clr  scon.0             ;Rx interrupt processing.....
    IF (THISPU <> 1)
      jnb fSYNCHRONIZED,rx3    ;jmp if local-pu not
                              ;time-synchronised to pu1.
    ENDIF
    jb  f2NDBYTEIN,rx2     ;jmp if this is 2nd byte of
                           ; msg.
    ;fall-thru is to receive 1st byte of msg or
    ; token....
;.....
rx4: mov a,sbuf       ;receive 1st byte of remote i/p msg.
     anl a,#87h              ;test for token, to any pu.
     jnz rx5                 ;jmp if not a token.
;....
;arrived byte is a token....
```

```
          IF (THISPU <> 1)
            mov    a,sbuf
            cjne a,#((THISPU-1)*8),endisr ;test for token
                                          ; addressed THISPU.
            setb fTOKENHERE   ;(pu1 should NEVER get this!!)
            setb scon.1     ;see if anything to post.
          ENDIF
            ajmp endisr ;...does it immediately, via Tx-int.
;....
rx5: ;arrived byte is 1st of a message, so process it.
     mov   header,sbuf
     setb f2NDBYTEIN ;flag that first byte arrived, 2nd
                     ; pending.
     ajmp endisr     ;will reenter to rx2 when 2nd byte
                     ; arrives...
;....
rx2:                 ;will only come here if 2nd byte has
                     ; arrived.
     clr   f2NDBYTEIN
     mov   databyte,sbuf    ;receive 2nd byte of remote i/p
                            ; msg.
     mov   a,header
     anl   a,#07h           ;extract dest. node.
     jz    system    ;>>>>>URGENT HANDLING SYSTEM
                     ; MSGS>>>>>
     mov   a,header
     anl   a,#078h          ;extract dest. pu.
     cjne a,#((THISPU-1)*8),endisr   ;jmp if addressed to
                                     ; another pu.
go1:                 ;deliver msg to circular buffer.
     cjne  r0,#SP2TOP,ok1 ;(r0 is sp2in)add msg to
                          ; circ.buffer.
     mov   r0,#SP2BOTTOM   ;/(Note, we are not checking
ok1: inc   r0        ;   /  for overrun)
     mov   @r0,databyte   ;    /databyte(r2)-->circ.buf
     inc   r0        ;   /

;if a sync-msg (not notif), need to set flag in
; extmsgwtg...                                      ###
     mov a,r3  ;(header)                            ###
     jb   acc.7,go3f    ;jump if a notification.    ###
go3d: anl  a,#07    ;extract dest.node.             ###
     mov  temp1,a    ;convert node to a flag.       ###
     mov  a,#1        ;/                            ###
go3e: rl   a          ;/                            ###
     djnz temp1,go3e  ;/                            ###
     orl  extmsgwtg,a  ;/   save flag.              ###

     mov  a,r3     ;(header)
```

```
go3f: anl  a,#087h      ;clr the pu-field (makes term-1=0)
      setb acc.7     ;make into a Notification, regardless.
                     ;Delivery is to terminal 1.
      mov  @r0,a    ;   /header(r3)-->circ.buf

      ajmp endisr
;.....
    IF (THISPU <> 1)
rx3:                    ;await system GLOBALTIME msg.
      jb  f2NDBYTEIN,rx2   ;possible for fSYNC set in middle
of msg.
      mov  a,sbuf          ;header
      cjne a,#80h,endisr  ;jmp if not broadcast system msg
                          ; from PU1.
      jnb  scon.0,$       ;wait for databyte (system code).
      clr  scon.0
      mov  a,sbuf
      cjne a,#GLOBALTIME,endisr
      setb fSYNCHRONIZED   ;tells application that time
                           ; set ok.
      ajmp endisr         ;do not deliver msg locally.
    ENDIF
;......
endisr:
      pop  psw
      pop  acc
        reti

;...........TX HANDLING...........
txh:
    clr      scon.1  ;clr transmit flag, prevent reentry.
      jb  fTOKENHERE,txj
      IF (THISPU EQ 1)
        jb  fTOKENGONE,tx0b    ;token has gone.(PU1 only)
        jb  fTOKENOUT,tx1      ;jmp if token to be posted." "
      ENDIF
      ajmp endisr
txj: jb     f2NDBYTEGONE,tx0  ;jmp if 2nd-byte gone
      jb  f2NDBYTEOUT,tx2   ;jmp if 2nd-byte user post from
                            ; this pu(after .3)
      jb     fPOSTREMOTE,tx3 ;jmp if user want post
                             ; from this pu(must be after.4)
      ;nothing to post, then fall-thru is...
;......
tx0: clr  fTOKENHERE
      clr  fPOSTREMOTE    ;only clrd when all finished.
      clr  f2NDBYTEGONE   ;(next POSTREMOTE can
                          ;proceed...but await nxt token)
tx0b: clr  fTOKENGONE      ;token has been posted (PU1 only).
```

```
        clr  fENABLETX          ;turn-off rs-485 driver.
        ajmp endisr
;.......
tx3: ;post msg from local user application....
          setb fENABLETX        ;turn-on rs-485 driver chip.
        mov  sbuf,r5            ;(header2)
        setb f2NDBYTEOUT        ;flag 1st byte is now txing.
        ajmp endisr            ;will reenter and go to tx2...
;.....
tx2: ;post 2nd byte of msg...
        mov  sbuf,r4            ;(databyte2)
        clr  f2NDBYTEOUT       ;
        setb f2NDBYTEGONE      ;flag 2nd byte is now txing.
        ajmp endisr        ;will reenter and go to tx1 then tx0...
;.....
     IF (THISPU EQ 1)
tx1:                           ;post a token.
        clr  fTOKENOUT
        mov  a,tokencnt
        add  a,#8              ;this increments dest.pu of token.
        mov  tokencnt,a
        anl  a,#78h            ;convert to a token.
        jnz  tx1b             ;jmp if token not addressed to pu1.
          jnb  fPOSTTIME,tx1c;jmp if no request to post
                                ; globaltime.
        setb fENABLETX
  mov  sbuf,#(0 + (0*8) + (1*128)) ;global system msg.
        jnb  scon.1,$         ;wait until gone.
        clr  scon.1
        mov  sbuf,#GLOBALTIME        ;system-code.
        jnb  scon.1,$             ;wait until gone.
        clr  scon.1
        clr  fPOSTTIME
        clr  fENABLETX
  clr  fTOKENOUT ;precaution, next token-post overwrite.
        ajmp endisr   ;don't post any local outgoing msgs.
tx1c: setb fTOKENHERE
      setb scon.1     ;see if anything to post from thispu.
      ajmp endisr
tx1b: setb fENABLETX
      mov  sbuf,a     ;post token.
      setb fTOKENGONE ;
      ajmp endisr     ;...will reenter to tx0.
     ENDIF
;..........................................................

;Circular buffer:       |_____|
;        SP2TOP = 7F> |        | upper limit
;                       |        |
```

```
;                        |_____|
;sp2in (r0, 4th bank)>|        |    sp2in is the head of the
;                        |        |    circular buffer.
;                        |_____|
;sp2out(r1, 4th bank)>|        |    sp2out is the tail(one
;                        |_____|    below actually).
;     SP2BOTTOM = 6B>  |        |    one below lower limit.
```

```
;TOKEN-PASSING NETWORK
;It's not really, token-passing, as I've changed it with
;the latest version, to a very rigid TDM (time division
;multiplexing), in which PU1 posts the tokens to each
;processor, including itself (internally) on a
;round-robin basis.  The complete token cycle is:
; (256*12*TIMERSETTING*16)/clock
;where clock is in Hz, and result of above formula is in
;seconds.
;If we make TIMERSETTING=1, then cycletime=4.4mSec.
;This is the worst-case time that any processor will have
;to wait to post a message.  If you want faster than
;this, you can modify the timer0 preload register, TH0.
;Note that if a processor has a cycletime <=4.4mSec and
;only posts one message per cycle, it won't have any
;delay if it self-syncs to the token.
;The above formula presumes 16 processors, and works even
;if there are less, but it is more efficient to cut-down
;the round-robin token firing to the exact number of
;processors.  If there are 4 processors, token cycle time
;becomes 4.4/4 = 1.1mSec.
;(this is recommended, in preference to altering TH0).

;GLOBALTIME
;The global-time mechanism is real simple, and effective.
;.... coming soon.
;Already in this version:
;I was concerned about a PU going off/on-line at odd
;times...
;now, when a PU comes on-line, it awaits the GLOBALTIME
;system message, before receiving any other messages.
;This mechanism also prevents pickup of partial-msgs when
;coming on-line.

;MODIFIED EXTRACTMSGS
;Introduced with version-G.
;For speed, when a message is delivered to a node, it is
;extracted from the stack-frame, and the gap is filled by
;popping the top message off the stack and moving it to
;the gap. This means that the ordering of messages in the
```

```
;stack-frame is not purely historical, and this
;complicates signature calculation.
;It is, however, faster than filling the gap by shifting
;all msgs above the gap, down.

;$$$$$$$$$$$$$$$$$$$$$$$$$$$$$$$$$$$$$$$$$$$$$$$$$$$$$$$$$$$$$$$
;a node is entered with r5 (address 05) = node number.
;(first register-bank selected, as rest used by stack, so
;r1 is addr.01,etc)
;msgs are in terminal-order, in addresses 01,02,03,04.
;bit-addressable "flags" has bits set if msg present
; -- example, msg in term1 (addr.01, or r1), then flags.1
; is set.

;................
node0:               ;node-0 is the error-handler

        NORMALEXIT

;.................................................
node1:
;Presume that this is the first node, when signature =0.
    IF (THISPU EQ 1)
       setb  fPOSTTIME ;request to post globaltime to all PUs.
    ELSE
       jnb  fSYNCHRONIZED,$ ;optional wait (only maybe wait here
  ENDIF                ;on 1st iteration of application cycle)

;Note: any PU other than 1, can resync to globaltime
;simply by clearing fSYNCHRONIZED:
;    clr  fSYNCHRONIZED
;    jnb  fSYNCHRONIZED,$  ;this wait is optional.

;.....
;this tests msg-passing around the network....
    IF (THISPU EQ 1)
       cpl p3.7            ;LED
       POSTREMOTE 2,1,1,acc    ;pu2,n1,notif,data.
       POSTREMOTE 3,3,0,acc    ;pu3,n3,not_notif,data.
    ENDIF
    IF (THISPU EQ 2)
       jnb  fTERM1,z11 ;(all remote i/p msgs are to term1).
       cpl p3.7          ;LED *flash notifs coming from pu1*
z11:
    ENDIF
;....

  POSTLOCAL 2,1,0,#34h ;node-2,term-1,not-notif.,immediate-data.
  POSTLOCAL 3,1,0,#00h ;node3,term1,notnotif,immediate-data.
```

```
        NORMALEXIT
;..............................................
node3:

 IF (THISPU EQ 1)
     mov b,0FFh               ;delay
dn3b:mov a,0FFh               ;/
dn3: djnz acc,dn3             ;/
     djnz b,dn3b              ;/
 ENDIF
 IF (THISPU EQ 3)
    jnb     fTERM1,z31    ;test if msg coming from pu1/node1.
    cpl     p3.7              ;LED *flash to confirm arrival*
z31:
 ENDIF

 POSTLOCAL 4,2,0,32h    ;node4,term2,notnotif,direct-data.
 NORMALEXIT
;..............................................
node2:
     jnb  fTERM2,z22    ;node4 posts notif. back to here.
     mov  a,r2          ;Notification is in r2.
z22:

;     mov b,0FFh
;dn2b:     mov a,0FFh
;dn2:djnz acc,dn2
;     djnz b,dn2b

     POSTLOCAL 4,1,0,#00h ;node4,term1,0,immediate-data.
     NORMALEXIT
;..............................................
node4:

    mov b,0FFh                ;delay
dn4b:mov a,0FFh               ;/
dn4: djnz acc,dn4             ;/
    djnz b,dn4b               ;/

; POSTREMOTE THISPU,1,1,#00 ;test loop-back. pu1,n1,notif,data.
;;(posting to itself means totally ignored, except if a
;; global system msg -- node=0/notif=1)

 POSTLOCAL 2,2,1,#11 ;notification, back to node-2,term-2.
     NORMALEXIT
;...............
;%%%%%%%%%%%%%%%%%%%%%%%%%%%%%%%%%%%%%%%%%%%%%%%%%%%%%%
     END
```

E

x86 TERSE

The port of TERSE to the x86 processor family was a very exciting project. My target market is applications that require more processing power than the 8-bit 8051, but not as much as a 486 or Pentium. The '86 slots very nicely in here, and Intel have the '186 microcontroller version. There are many chip manufacturers making versions of the '186, and I discovered that Advanced Micro Devices (AMD) makes a very nice range, that execute as fast as a '386, and one of them even has 32Kb of RAM on-chip. No manufacturer has made a '186/188 variant with on-chip ROM, I suppose because the target market for this class of chip typically requires more ROM than is economical to place on-chip.

I have the low-cost AMD SD186EM Evaluation Board (the picture above has the AM186ER processor), which is virtually a complete PC in a few chips optimised for embedded usage. My board has 256Kb SRAM, 256Kb Flash memory, and all the hardware and software tools to download from a PC. We all know the potential advantages of using the x86 architecture in terms of our existing investment in development tools, their relatively low cost, and our familiarity with this environment. I'm thrilled with this AMD board, but I'm not a salesperson for them, so enough of a publicity plug — for more information, look at their Web site:

`http://www.amd.com/html/products/epd/epd.html`

TERSE is superb for distributed processor systems; however, "virtual processors" can exist on the same physical processor. The x86 version 3.1 of TERSE, which is actually the first version for this processor, is uniprocessor but supports multiple virtual processors.

The beauty of this is that they execute independently, which does of course require time slicing. All synchronisation between virtual processors is taken care of automatically by the synchronous messaging fundamental to TERSE. Mutual exclusion, wherever required, is also taken care of by placing access to resources via clone nodes in the same virtual processor. A node in any one virtual processor must always execute to completion before another node in that same virtual processor can execute.

TERS8631 is conceptually very simple. If you don't want to use the Signature scheduling, then don't — it is still an excellent RTOS with only the virtual processors and message delivery mechanisms. However, do note that it is designed for "static" applications, in which you will not be dynamically creating and destroying tasks. Therefore, the task management is primitive, and requires direct alteration of the operating system itself.

Time slicing between virtual processors is simple round-robin, although it is easy to give any one processor more time by allocating it more than one time slice in the complete cycle. This is static prioritising, but it would be easy to add some refinements, not in this first version, for dynamic adjustment of allocation. For example, a simple function can be added to allow any virtual-processor to yield or give up its current time slice allocation. Also, a function can delay the next time slice. I expect that refinements will be posted on my Web pages.

You can write the application code for the nodes in Small-C. I have slightly hacked the superb Small-C developed by Rick Grehan of *Byte* magazine. I would also like to acknowledge others who developed the compiler prior to Rick; J. E. Hendrix, Ron Cain, and L. E. Payne.

Source listing

The listing starts here. It is well commented, but I have interjected extra comments in 11-point Times Roman font.

```
;TERS8631.ASM, for x86 embedded.
;Written for MASM v6.1.
;VERSION 3.1, Oct. 1996 (first version for this processor).
;Uses MESS scheduling.
;Now has timesliced multitasking of virtual processors.
;Works with small-C.

;Message structure:
;BIT:        7 6 5 4 3 2 1 0
;ADDR n+3:   0 s p p p p p p    header high (msg3)
;ADDR n+2:   t t t n n n n n    header low  (msg2)
;ADDR n+1:   d d d d d d d d    data   high (msg1)
;ADDR n:     d d d d d d d d    data   low  (msg0)

;Legend:                                         value:
;s = 0 sync message, = 1 async message           (0 -- 1)
;p =0 empty slot,=111111b rem.i/p msg, else is dest.-pu(1--62)
;t = destination terminal, less 1.               (0 -- 7)
;n = destination node.                            (0 -- 31)
```

The message is now 32 bits in size, with a 16-bit data field, which is appropriate for a 16-bit processor. Notice that we can have up to 62 virtual processors, 8 input terminals at a node, and 32 nodes per virtual processor.

```
;......EQUATES YOU MAY HAVE TO MODIFY.............
SPEEDUP     EQU 55    ;how many times we are speeding-up int8.
CIRCBUFSIZE EQU 128   ;size of circ. buff.(1 for each virt-PU).
STACKSIZE   EQU 512   ;each virt-PU has its own stack also.
TIMESLICE   EQU 20    ;#msec timeslice (for SPEEDUP=55).
```

Because I wrote this code to run on a PC, I utilised the background INT8 55 millisecond timer, except that I have speeded it up to 1 millisecond. The SPEEDUP equate determines this. Then, I have allocated the time slice as 20 milliseconds, by the TIMESLICE equate. Note that although I have modified INT8, the PC still works as normal; however — I do have to put in a disclaimer here — do this at your own risk!

Note that bit 7 of msg3 is clear. If set, the message is a different format, which I call a *Signature transform*. However this is a new idea I'm working on and is not implemented in this version.

```
;...........EQUATES USED BY TERSE..........................
SYNC        EQU  0      ;used in POSTMESSAGE.
ASYNC       EQU  1      ;/
FALSE       EQU  0
TRUE        EQU  1
;.........................................................


;.........MACROS USED BY TERSE...........................

;note, uses ax,bx,es...
POSTMESSAGE MACRO pum,nodem,termm,asyncm,datawordm
     LOCAL msg1,msg2
  IF ((pum LE 0) OR (pum GT 61)) ;assemble-time limit testing.
    EXITM                                    ;/
   ELSEIF ((nodem LT 0) OR (nodem GT 31))    ;/
    EXITM                                    ;/
   ELSEIF ((termm LT 1) OR (termm GT 8))     ;/
    EXITM                                    ;/
   ELSEIF ((asyncm LT 0) OR (asyncm GT 1))   ;/
    EXITM                                    ;/
   ELSEIF pum EQ THISPU            ;true, then local msg.
     mov  bx,pcircout
     cmp  bx,OFFSET PBOTTOM        ;tail-end of circ.buffer.
     jne  msg1
     mov  bx,OFFSET PTOP   ;(note that PTOP is lowest address).
msg1: mov  ax,datawordm
     mov  WORD PTR [bx],ax         ;msg0,msg1
     inc  bx
     inc  bx
     mov  BYTE PTR [bx],(nodem + ((termm - 1) * 32)) ;msg2
     inc  bx
     mov  BYTE PTR [bx],(pum + (asyncm*64))        ;msg3
     inc  bx
     mov  pcircout,bx              ;new tail-end.
   ELSE                ;false, so remote o/p msg.
msg1:
     mov  ax,SEG dataISR           ;get ds of destination PU.
     mov  es,ax            ;/
     mov  bx,OFFSET es:dsPU            ;/
     mov  ax,es:[bx + ((pum - 1)*2)] ;/  lookup pu-table.
     mov  es,ax               ;/ -->es
```

```
;deliver msg directly to circular buffer of dest. PU...
     mov  si,es:pcircin    ;/
     cmp  si,OFFSET PTOP        ;/
     ja   msg2       ;/
     mov  si,OFFSET PBOTTOM     ;/
msg2: sub si,4        ;/
     mov  ax,datawordm
     cli                ;prevent a task-switch.
     mov  es:[si],ax        ;/ msg0,msg1
mov es:[si+2],BYTE PTR (nodem + ((termm - 1) * 32)) ;msg2
mov es:[si+3],BYTE PTR ((pum +(asyncm*64)) OR 00111111b) ;msg3
     mov  es:pcircin,si    ;update leading-edge of buffer.
     sti

;need to set flag in extmsgwtg. ie, msg to node1 must set bit1
;but only if it is sync msg...
     IF   asyncm EQ 0
       mov  cx,nodem        ;dest. node.
       mov  ax,1            ;/
       shl  ax,cl           ;convert to a flag.
       or   es:extmsgwtg,ax ;must leave existing flags alone.
       xor  cx,cx     ;small-C needs inline asm exit with cx=0.
     ENDIF
   ENDIF
ENDM
;note that TERM is stored one-less. EX:TERM 1 is stored as 00.

NORMALEXIT MACRO               ;use this one for normal operation.
     jmp  FAR PTR nodereturn
ENDM
```

POSTMESSAGE is a beautiful piece of code. It is used in application nodes whenever you want to post a message. You can see examples of this later in this file. I have taken the approach of using INCLUDEs to insert the application code of the nodes into this file, rather than using LINK to combine the files, so you can see the structure of the application nodes by browsing ahead in this file.

NORMALEXIT is placed at the end of each application node, to cause a return to the OS.

```
REGSSTRUC STRUC         ;template for task block.
sax  DW   0
sbx  DW   0
scx  DW   0
sdx  DW   0
```

```
sbp    DW   0
ssi    DW   0
sdi    DW   0
ssp    DW   0
sss    DW   0
sip    DW   0
scs    DW   0
sds    DW   0
ses    DW   0
sflags DW 0
REGSSTRUC ENDS


initTASKS MACRO
;note dataISR is current data segment when run this macro.
;initialise PU-table.... (only 2 PUs)
      mov   ax,SEG dataPU1
      mov   dsPU,ax
      mov   ax,SEG dataPU2
      mov   dsPU+2,ax
;initialise task-table.... (only 2 tasks here)
      mov   ax,SEG dataPU1   ;in DOS system initialise task table
      mov   dstasks,ax       ;/ at runtime.
      mov   ax,SEG dataPU2   ;/ In ROM embedded system, maybe
      mov   dstasks+2,ax     ;/ hardcode data seg. addresses.
      mov   ax,SEG codePU1
      mov   cstasks,ax
      mov   ax,SEG codePU2
      mov   cstasks+2,ax
;initialise task-blocks...
;firstly for PU1...
      mov   ax,SEG dataPU1
      mov   es,ax
      mov   es:regs.sds,ax
      mov   es:regs.sss,ax
      mov   bx,OFFSET stackPU + STACKSIZE - 2
      mov   es:regs.ssp,bx
      mov   es:regs.scs,cs          ;start running inside TERSE.
      mov   es:regs.sip,OFFSET start1 ;/
      ;also, save codePU1 in PU1 data seg., for easy access...
      mov   ax,SEG codePU1   ;(current-pu cs is also saved in
 mov es:csthispu,ax ;dataISR seg.,in cstask, & all in cstasks)
      mov   es:pcircin,OFFSET PBOTTOM ;initialise circ.buff
      mov   es:pcircout,OFFSET PBOTTOM ;    /
;same for PU2...
      mov   ax,SEG dataPU2
      mov   es,ax
      mov   es:regs.sds,ax
      mov   es:regs.sss,ax
      mov   bx,OFFSET stackPU + STACKSIZE - 2
```

```
        mov   es:regs.ssp,bx
        mov   es:regs.scs,cs          ;start running inside TERSE.
        mov   es:regs.sip,OFFSET start1   ;/
        ;also, save codePU2 in PU2 data seg., for easy access...
        mov   ax,SEG codePU2   ;(current-pu cs is also saved in
  mov es:csthispu,ax ;dataISR seg.,in cstask, & all in cstasks)
        mov   es:pcircin,OFFSET PBOTTOM  ;initialise circ.buff
        mov   es:pcircout,OFFSET PBOTTOM ;   /
ENDM


;##############################################################
;########################### TERSE ############################

;..............STACK SEGMENT FOR TERSE...................
;this is the startup stack, but each virt-PU has its own.
stackDEF   SEGMENT STACK
    DB 64 DUP(?)
stackDEF   ENDS

;............DATA SEGMENT FOR TERSE TIMESLICER..............
;note that there is only one copy of TERSE, with its own data
;segment for the timeslicer interrupt-routine; dataISR.
;Each virtual processor has its own data segment also, that
;TERSE uses.
;note that all data SEGMENTs are private by default with MASM,
;and are not combined.


;.........................................................


dataISR SEGMENT  'data'     ;timeslicer data.
;timerisr uses these....
globaltime0 EQU 0    ;future finer time granularity.
globaltime1 DB 0     ;granularity = 1mSec.
globaltime2 DB 0     ;granularity = 256mSec.(1/4Sec)
globaltime3 DB 0     ;granularity = 64Sec (appr. 1minute)
timercnt    DW SPEEDUP     ;how many times int8 is speed-up.
timeslicecnt DW TIMESLICE ;#msec between context switches.
int8off     DW 0     ;timerisr old vector.
int8seg     DW 0     ;/

dstask         DW 0 ;hold ds of current virt-pu.
cstask         DW 0 ;holds cs of current virt-pu.

;PU table...
NUMPUS EQU 2 ;put ds of each pu in here.(done by initTASKS)
dsPU   DW NUMPUS DUP(0) ;/ (in order of PU #)

;task-table...
offsettasks DW 0              ;which task running.0=pu1,2=pu2
```

```
dstasks  DW  0,0 ;...as many tasks as req'd(done by initTASKS)
cstasks  DW  0,0    ;...must have same # of entries here.
NUMTASKS EQU (OFFSET cstasks - OFFSET dstasks) / 2
dataISR ENDS


;.............CODE SEGMENT FOR TERSE.......................
;TERSE itself is in its own code segment, codeTERSE, and each
;virt-PU is in its own code seg. They are not combined.

codeTERSE SEGMENT 'code'

start:                      ;inital entry point, only exec. once.
    cli                     ;don't use stackDEF. assume PU1
    mov  ax,SEG dataPU1        ;/ is running initially.
    mov  ss,ax                            ;/
    mov  sp,OFFSET (stackPU + STACKSIZE - 2)  ;/
    sti                                   ;/
    ASSUME ss:dataPU1                     ;/
    mov  ax,SEG dataISR  ;in DOSless system, use RAM address.
    mov  ds,ax         ;/
    ASSUME ds:dataISR,cs:codeTERSE,es:NOTHING
    mov  timercnt,SPEEDUP
    mov  timeslicecnt,TIMESLICE
    initTASKS ;segment values have
              ;to be loaded into task-blocks and task-table
              ;at runtime.

;hook timer for TERSE timeslicer....
;NOTE, embedded system may have another (faster) timer
;available...
          ;will use int-8, the PC 55mSec interrupt...
    mov  ax,0        ;segment 0.
    mov  es,ax       ;/
    mov  di,4*8           ;ivt entry.
    mov  ax,es:[di]       ;get original. (NOTE we do not use
    mov  int8off,ax       ;/        DOS services here,
    mov  ax,es:[di+2]     ;/        as target system
    mov  int8seg,ax       ;/        may not have DOS).
    cli
    mov  WORD PTR es:[di],OFFSET timerisr      ;new vector.
    mov  es:[di+2],cs                          ;/
    sti                   ;allow interrupts.
    nop

;now, this is neat... let's speed-up the 55mSec timer to
;1mSec...
    cli
    mov  al,36h           ;select timer0, mode 3.
    out  43h,al           ;/
```

```
      jmp  SHORT $+2         ;delay.
      jmp  SHORT $+2         ;/
      mov  ax,65532/SPEEDUP  ;1192, gives 1mSec interrupts.
      out  40h,al            ;/ (65532/55 = 1192)
      jmp  SHORT $+2         ;/ (where 55 is how many times
      jmp  SHORT $+2         ;/    we are speeding up above
      mov  al,ah             ;/    the 55mSec rate)
      out  40h,al            ;/
      sti
;*NOTE* USE THIS AT YOUR OWN RISK ON A PC. LOOK AT TIMERISR.

;assume this is PU1 running initially...
      mov  ax,SEG codePU1
      mov  cstask,ax  ;in dataISR seg., holds current task cs.
      mov  ax,SEG dataPU1
      mov  dstask,ax ;in dataISR segment, holds current task ds.
      mov  ds,ax       ;from now, access data seg. of pu1.
      jmp  start1
;note, all other tasks will commence from start1...


;..................TERSE TIMESLICER.........................

timerisr:  ;hooks int-8 on PC.
;int-8 has been speeded-up to 1mSec, so requires special
;handling here...
      push ds
      push ax
      mov  ax,SEG dataISR   ;get data segment addressability.
      mov  ds,ax            ;/
;tell the assembler what our data segment is...(nothing to do
;with runtime)
      ASSUME ds:dataISR

          add globaltime1,1;note we're not using globaltime0.
          adc WORD PTR globaltime2,0  ;/
          dec timeslicecnt
          dec  timercnt
          jz   tmr00
            mov al,20h             ;/ process the interrupt here.
            out  20h,al            ;/
            jmp  SHORT tmr01
tmr00:  mov  timercnt,SPEEDUP   ;reload.
        pushf                   ;as int8 routine has iret.
        call DWORD PTR int8off  ;call original vector.
tmr01:    cmp  timeslicecnt,0
      je   doit
      pop  ax
      pop  ds
      iret
```

Interjecting here, note above that I have incremented `globaltime1`, although the time is kept in `globaltime0` — 3, i.e., it is 32 bits. It is intended that `globaltime1` have a granularity of 1 mSec, i.e., increment every 1 mSec, and as I do not have a faster timer, have to leave `globaltime0` alone. Ideally, `globaltime0` would be incremented every 1/256 of a millisecond, carrying through to 1, 2, and 3. Systems with a timer that can be read, can use the timer-counter itself (if it is an up-counter) as `globaltime0` and set it to interrupt every 1 mSec, which will increment `globaltime1`. Thus, we don't overload the system with too-rapid interrupts.

```
;let's do a task-switch ...
doit: mov  timeslicecnt,TIMESLICE     ;reload.
      mov  ax,dstask        ;get ds of current task.
      mov  ds,ax
;tell the assembler what our data segment is...(nothing to do
;with runtime)
   ASSUME ds:dataPU1
      mov  regs.sbx,bx              ;save state of current task.
      mov  regs.scx,cx              ;/   (the order here is
      mov  regs.sdx,dx              ;/           very important!)
      mov  regs.sbp,bp              ;/
      mov  regs.ssi,si              ;/
      mov  regs.sdi,di              ;/
      mov  regs.sss,ss              ;/
      mov  regs.ses,es              ;/
      pop  regs.sax    ;saved-ax  ;/  these were pushed at entry.
      pop  regs.sds    ;saved-ds  ;/   /
      pop  regs.sip    ;return-ip ;/
      pop  regs.scs    ;return-cs ;/
      pop  regs.sflags ;return-flags  ;/
      mov  regs.ssp,sp             ;/

      mov  ax,SEG dataISR ;isr data segment addressability.
      mov  ds,ax                   ;/
;tell the assembler what our data segment is...(nothing to do
;with runtime)
   ASSUME ds:dataISR

      lea  bx,dstasks              ;get next entry in task table.
      add  offsettasks,2           ;/
      cmp  offsettasks,(NUMTASKS*2) ;/
      jb   tmr2                     ;/
      mov  offsettasks,0           ;/
tmr2: add  bx,offsettasks          ;/
```

```
        mov   ax,[bx + (NUMTASKS*2)]  ;record ds/cs for new task.
        mov   cstask,ax                ;/
        mov   ax,[bx]                   ;/
        mov   dstask,ax                 ;/

        mov   ds,ax          ;get data addressability new task.
;tell the assembler what our data segment is...(nothing to do
;with runtime)
    ASSUME ds:dataPU1
        mov   bx,regs.sbx              ;get state of next task.
        mov   cx,regs.scx              ;/
        mov   dx,regs.sdx              ;/
        mov   bp,regs.sbp              ;/
        mov   si,regs.ssi              ;/
        mov   di,regs.sdi              ;/
        mov   sp,regs.ssp              ;/
        mov   ss,regs.sss              ;/
        mov   es,regs.ses              ;/
        push regs.sflags              ;get iret return.
        push regs.scs                  ;/
        push regs.sip                  ;/
        push regs.sax
        mov   ax,regs.sds
        mov   ds,ax
        pop   ax
        iret


;...................................................................
.
;*****MAIN LOOP*******
;tell the assembler what our data segment is...(nothing to do
;with runtime)
    ASSUME ds:dataPU1
start1:                        ;main program entry point.



;...................................................................
nodereturn LABEL FAR      ;<<<<<<<< Nodes return to here <<<<<
    mov sp,OFFSET (stackPU + STACKSIZE - 2) ;remove any junk.

start2:                 ;program entry point 2.
;*ASSUMPTION* here, that previous node hasn't changed ds!
;(you can reload it from dstask in dataISR).
    mov   dx,0       ;initially, make signature = zero.
    mov   _fSIGFAIL,FALSE    ;clr all error flags.
    mov   _fTIMEOUT,FALSE     ;/
;make sure es set correctly...
    mov   ax,csthispu   ;code seg. of current PU saved here.
    mov   es,ax        ;/ we need to get at data in code seg.
```

The next thing we are going to do is look at the message buffer and compute a signature. Then, having the signature, we can look up the scheduling table and determine the next node to execute.

However, it is appropriate to consider the structure of the message buffer first. I have used a circulating buffer, but it is most unusual, because messages are added to *both* ends of the buffer.

Figure E.1: Message buffer.

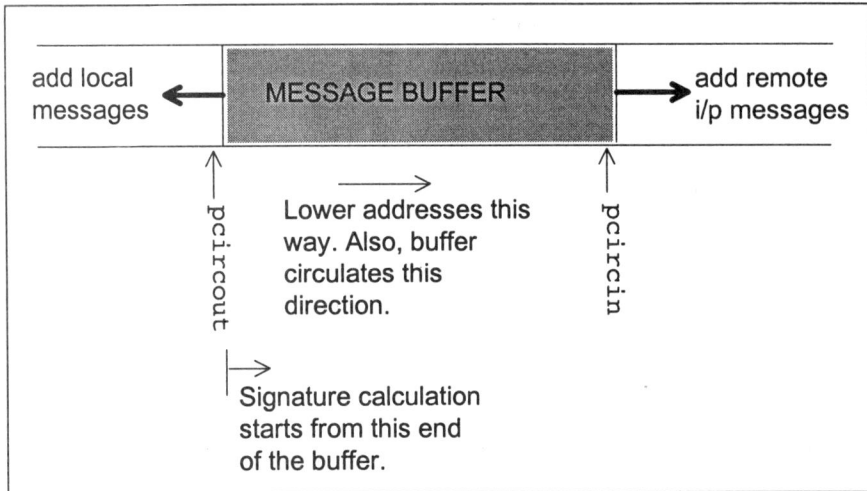

Remote input messages are those that come from a different virtual processor (which could in theory also be a different physical processor). This end always grows, to lower addresses, within the boundaries allocated for the buffer to circulate in. These messages can arrive at any time, so TERSE works on the other end of the buffer. Local messages are added at the "tail" end, and when messages are removed from the buffer, it is the tail end that shrinks.

There is one message buffer for each virtual processor.

```
;calculate the signature....
      mov  di,pcircin ;leading-edge. remote i/p msgs added here.
;check limits...
cal:  cmp  di,pcircout
      je   ca9         ;finished
      cmp  di,OFFSET PBOTTOM
      jb   ca2
      mov  di,OFFSET PTOP
      jmp  cal         ;need to test for finished again.
```

```
ca2:
;search through buffer...
      mov   al,[di+3]       ;msg3.
      cmp   al,0            ;is it empty slot?
      jz    ca3            ; ignore.
      test al,80h          ;is it a transform?        #40
      jnz   ca3            ; ignore.         #40
      test al,40h          ;ignore async.msg (bit6 set).
      jnz   ca3            ;/
      cmp   al,3Fh         ;dest.pu (=3F if remote i/p).
      je    ca3            ;/ ignore.

calcsig:
;entered with di-->msg0, dx=accumulated signature (starts =0)
      test     dh,40h
      jz calc1       ;jump if bit6 clr.(bit14 of dx)
      xor dx,0010010000010001b ;tapping points.
calc1:      xor dx,[di+2]  ;msg2,msg3.
      shl dx,1
      ;ret     ;note that lsb=0, sig is 15 bits, bits 1--15.

ca3: add  di,4         ;msg0 of next msg, going toward pcircout.
     jmp  ca1
ca9: shr  dx,1         ;make signature bits 0--14.


;came out of above with a signature in dx, now lookup node...
lookup:
      xor   cx,cx
      mov   cl,es:NUMENTRIESVAR ;this is in codePUx.
      mov   si,OFFSET signatures
      push  ds                  ;save.
      push  es
      pop   ds                  ;lodsw reads ds:si.
look1:    lodsw                 ;start at beginning of array.
      xor   ax,dx               ;compare signatures.
      jz    sigfnd              ;signature found.
      loop  look1
      pop   ds                  ;restore.
;signature not found...
      mov   destnode,0
      mov   _fSIGFAIL,TRUE      ;... go to node0.
      jmp   SHORT gonode
;.......................
sigfnd: pop   ds                ;restore.
      dec si                    ;want si-->found sig.
      dec si                    ;/
;are we in a context where we need to check any ext.i/p
;arrivals?...
```

```
        xor   bx,bx
        mov   bl,es:NUMENTRIESVAR
        shl   bx,1              ;    * 4
        shl   bx,1              ;/
        mov   ax,es:[si+bx]     ;get extmsg entry from sig.tabl
        mov   extmsgsaved,ax    ;save it.
        or    ax,ax             ;test if ax==0.
        jnz   ext1
;we are going to ignore all possible external i/ps...lookup
;nodenum...
        xor   bx,bx
        mov   bl,es:NUMENTRIESVAR
        shl   bx,1              ; * 2
        mov   ax,es:[si+bx]           ;get node.
;JUST IN CASE you set the WX flag in nodenum, it is not
;appropriate...
        and   ax,07FFFh  ;"mistake proofing" (refer Figure 37)
        mov   destnode,ax
;.....................
gonode:
        jmp   getmsgs          ;extract all msgs for this node.
retgetmsgs:                    ;...returns here.
go4:
  mov di,OFFSET nodeptr ;jump table is in code seg.,current pu
        mov   bx,destnode      ;
        shl   bx,1      ;each entry in jump table 2 bytes.
        mov   cx,csthispu      ;it was in es, but got overwritten.
        mov   es,cx            ;/
        mov   ax,es:[di+bx]    ;get entry in jump table.
        mov   ipnxtnode,ax ;form far address,  csthispu:ipnxtnode
        jmp DWORD PTR ipnxtnode ;jump to next node to execute.>>>


;........................................................................
;extmsg entry in lookup table was non-0, so look for rem.i/p
;arrivals...
ext1: and   ax,extmsgwtg       ;compare with actual arrivals.
      jz    wtg1               ;no appropriate ext.msgs arrived.
ext2:
        mov   bx,ax      ;load destnode, clr bit in extmsgwtg.
        neg   ax         ;/ my clever code to extract 1 flag!
        and   ax,bx      ;/  /         ("rightmost" flag)
        ;ax has the bit I need to clr in extmsgwtg...
        xor   extmsgwtg,ax     ;/  /
        xor   bx,bx            ;/ now load destnode.
ext3: inc   bx               ;/  /
        shr   ax,1            ;/  /
        jnc   ext3           ;/  /
        dec   bx             ;/  /
        mov   destnode,bx    ;/  /
```

```
;Note, flag of lowest-numbered node has highest priority
;always, as the above code extracts the rightmost set flag in
;extmsgwtg.
        jmp  gonode
```

WX is the WAIT flag, i.e., Wait on eXternal, which is bit 15 in a nodenum entry. Look at the following code. If WX is set, wait for an in-scope remote i/p to arrive; the other bits 0—14 of nodenum specify the timeout. If bits 0—14 = zero, wait forever. To perform the timeout, a snapshot is taken of `globaltime`, i.e., the time at start of timeout, and this forms a reference to compute the timeout.

To obtain a very wide range of timeouts, I have used bits 13 and 14 of nodenum as a granularity field. This is explained further in comments at the end of the source file. I have arranged the granularities as 1 mSec, 1/4 Sec and 1 Min.

```
;.....................
wtg1:  ;some ext.i/ps are in-scope, but none have arrived...
        xor  bx,bx
        mov  ax,csthispu       ;it was in es, but got overwritten.
        mov  es,ax       ;/
        mov  bl,es:NUMENTRIESVAR
        shl  bx,1        ;* 2
        mov  ax,es:[si+bx]     ;get corresponding nodenum entry.
        mov  nodenumsaved,ax      ;save it.
;If WX flag in nodenum =0,don't wait for rem.i/ps to arrive...
        test ax,8000h            ;bit15 set if WX.
        jz   gonode
;.......
wtg2:
;we have to wait, but bits0--14 of nodenum are a timeout...
        mov  ax,SEG dataISR
        mov  es,ax
        mov  bl,es:globaltime0         ;snapshot of globaltime.
        mov  bh,es:globaltime1         ;/ (we need this for calc
        mov  WORD PTR localref0,bx     ;/      the timeout).
        mov  bx,WORD PTR es:globaltime2 ;/
        mov  WORD PTR localref2,bx     ;/
;......
wtg3: ;calc if we have timed out...
        ;granularity of timeout can be adjusted....
        ;let's use bits 14&13 as granularity field.
    mov  cx,nodenumsaved ;nodenum entry was saved this variable.
        and  cx,1FFFh    ;mask off bits13-15.(15 is WAIT flag)
        ;if nodenum timeout ==0, wait forever...
        jz   wtg4
```

```
       and  ch,01100000b
       cmp  ch,0
       jne  wtg3b               ;finest granularity ().
         mov  bl,es:globaltime0   ;this one not implemented.<<<<<
         mov  bh,es:globaltime1
         sub  bx,WORD PTR localref0
         jmp  SHORT wtg3e
wtg3b: cmp  ch,00100000b         ;2nd finest gran (1mSec).
       jne wtg3c
         mov  bx,WORD PTR es:globaltime1 ;(timeout range 1mSec --
         sub  bx,WORD PTR localref1       ;          8191mSec)
         jmp  SHORT wtg3e
wtg3c:     cmp ch,01000000b
       jne wtg3d
         mov  bx,WORD PTR es:globaltime2 ;(256mSec, about 1/4sec)
         sub  bx,WORD PTR localref2    ;(range 1/4sec -- 2048sec)
         jmp  SHORT wtg3e
wtg3d:
 mov bl,es:globaltime3;coarsestgranularity(65.5sec,about 1min)
         sub  bl,localref3            ;(range 1min -- 256min)
         xor  bh,bh
wtg3e:     cmp  ax,bx
       jbe  wtg4                ;check arrival rem.i/p...again.
;waiting on ext.i/p, have timed out...
       mov  _fTIMEOUT,TRUE
       jmp  go4          ;re-execute previous node!!!! <<<<
                         ;(i.e. don't update destnode)
       ;<<<THIS IS DIFFERENT FROM FIGURE 37 IN TEXT 1ST ED.<<<<<
```

The above code is an important deviation. You could change it so that
execution goes to node 0, the error-handler; however, I found reentry to the
previous node to be a pragmatic distribution of error-handling. You may
need to ensure that the previous node checks _fTIMEOUT flag on entry.
Most often, this timeout situation arises in a tightly-coupled situation, when
a node has posted a message to another processor and is awaiting a response
before the local system can continue. For example, in the elevator control
system, an elevator can send a request to the Supervisor processor, and must
have a response before continuing. If the elevator-node is reentered with
_fTIMEOUT set, it knows the Supervisor has failed to do its duty, and will
respond accordingly.

```
;....
wtg4:       ;check if any in-scope rem. i/ps have arrived...
;NOTE again, we deviate slightly from Figure 37 in text
;as have repeated some code here rather than branching
;back... (this does not change the algorithm however)
```

```
      mov   ax,extmsgsaved   ;previously saved extmsg entry.
      and   ax,extmsgwtg     ;compare with actual arrivals.
      jz    wtg3             ;no appropriate ext.msgs arrived.
      ;yes, a rem.i/p has arrived!!...
      jmp   ext2             ;translate rem.i/p --> dest.node.

;*****END MAIN LOOP*****
;.......................................................
```

getmsgs:
```
;extract msgs for destnode, into msgterm"n" variables..
;removes any transforms encountered --they occupy one complete
;slot.
;places async msgs on stack, count into msgterm"n" variable.

;can't be sure what es = on entry...
      mov   ax,csthispu
      mov   es,ax
      mov   dl,es:THISPUVAR  ;number of current pu.
            ;... be careful dx not overwritten below.

;make sure es set correctly...
      push ds          ;ds and es are used by stos/movs
      pop  es          ;/            instructions.

;clear the delivery variables...
      lea di,termvars
      mov cx,NUMTERMS
      xor ax,ax
      rep stosb

      mov di,pcircin ;leading-edge. remote i/p msgs added here.
      mov si,di      ;(we search the other way, toward pcircout)
      add si,4       ;next msg. (which is going to higher addrs)
get1:
;check limits...
      cmp   di,pcircout
      jne   get1a
get1x:     jmp   retgetmsgs          ;finished>>>>>>>>>
get1a:     cmp   di,OFFSET PBOTTOM
      jb    get1b
      mov   di,OFFSET PTOP
      mov   si,OFFSET PTOP+4
      jmp   SHORT get1 ;get1c
get1b:     cmp   si,OFFSET PBOTTOM
      jb    get1c
      mov   si,OFFSET PTOP
get1c:
```

```
        mov  al,[di+3]          ;msg3.
        cmp  al,0               ;is it empty slot?
        jz   get3               ;  remove.
        test al,80h             ;is it a transform?
        jnz  get3               ;  remove.
        and  al,3Fh
          cmp  al,3Fh           ;must also deliver remote i/p msgs.
           je  get1d            ;/
        cmp  al,dl              ;THISPUVAR      ;check dest. pu.
        jne  get2               ;wrong pu.
get1d:     mov  al,[di+2]          ;msg2
        and  al,1Fh
        cmp  al,BYTE PTR destnode
        jne  get2               ;wrong node.

;success, so deliver msg...
        xor  ax,ax
        mov  al,[di+2]          ;get msg2
        mov  cl,5
        shr  al,cl       ;terminal 1--8 (stored 0--7)
        shl  ax,1        ;each pointer in termvars is 2 bytes.
        lea  bx,termvars
        add  bx,ax       ;pointer to msgterm"n".
        mov  ax,[di]            ;get msg0 and msg1.
          mov cl,[di+3]          ;get msg3.
          test cl,40h            ;bit6=1 if async msg.
          jz  del0
          inc WORD PTR [bx]     ;incr count.
          push ax               ;deliver async msg to stack.
          jmp  SHORT del10
del0:mov  [bx],ax              ;deliver sync msg.
del10:

;see if this is only msg left in buffer...
get3:mov  ax,di
        add  ax,4
        cmp  ax,pcircout
        jne  get3p
get3q:     mov  pcircout,di       ;remove it.
        jmp  SHORT get1x             ;get out.
get3p:     cmp  ax,OFFSET PBOTTOM
        jne  get3s
        cmp  pcircout,OFFSET PTOP
        je   SHORT get3q

;moves all of msgs along, to fill gap...
get3s:     push si
        push di
get3a:
```

```
        cmp  si,pcircout     ;<<? if so, there is no next msg.
        je   get3c           ;/
        cmp  si,OFFSET PBOTTOM
        jb   get3b
        mov  si,OFFSET PTOP
        jmp  SHORT get3a
get3b: ;  cmp  si,pcircout     ;if so, there is no next msg.
       ;  jae  get3c
        cmp  di,OFFSET PBOTTOM
        jb   get3d
        mov  di,OFFSET PTOP
get3d:    mov  cx,4         ;move next msg into empty slot.
        rep  movsb           ;/
        jmp  get3a
get3c:    mov  pcircout,di      ;tail msg dropped off.

;       sub  di,4         ;** fix occassional hanging problem.**
;       cmp  di,pcircin   ;/   ...have removed last msg,
;       jne  get3m        ;/      so get out.
;       mov  pcircout,di  ;/
;       jmp  get1x        ;/

get3m:    pop  di
        pop  si
        jmp  get1

get2: add  di,4
      add  si,4
      jmp  get1

  ;   ret <<<<CANNOT HAVE A RET, AS PUSHED ASYNC MSGS ON STACK

;.................................................................
beepfreq PROC FAR ;used for testing purposes.bx=counter value.
        push ax
        mov  al,0B6h
        out  43h,al
        mov  al,bl
        out  42h,al
        mov  al,bh
        out  42h,al
        in   al,61h
        or   al,03
        out  61h,al
        pop  ax
        ret
beepfreq ENDP
beepoff PROC FAR
        push ax
```

```
        in  al,61h
        and al,0FCh
        out 61h,al
        pop ax
        ret
beepoff ENDP
;..............................................................

codeTERSE ENDS
;..............................................................

;###########################################################
;################## VIRTUAL PROCESSORS BELOW ###############

;####################### PROCESSOR 1 #######################

;..........DATA SEGMENT FOR PROCESSOR 1..............
;below is the data required by TERSE, for this processor.
;we instantiate this for each processor.

dataPU1 SEGMENT  'data'

;we need somewhere to save register state when suspending this
;task...
;ds,es,ax,bx,cx,dx,bp,si,di,ip,cs,sp,ss,es,flags...
regs REGSSTRUC  <>
ipnxtnode DW 0  ;used by TERSE to form a far jump address.
csthispu DW 0    ;/loaded by initTASKS,easy access to cs of
                 ; thispu

_fSIGFAIL   DB 0  ;error flags.(I hate using a whole byte for
_fTIMEOUT   DB 0 ;one flag! ...but convenient for C interface)

localref0   DB  0     ;snapshot of globaltime.
localref1   DB  0     ;/   (used for local timeout)
localref2   DB  0     ;/
localref3   DB  0     ;/

PTOP LABEL   NEAR    ;start of circular buffer, for i/p msgs.
circbuf        DB  CIRCBUFSIZE DUP(0)
PBOTTOM LABEL NEAR          ;one past end of circ. buffer.
;... each msg is 4 bytes, so 32 msgs will fit in buffer.
pcircin    DW  0    ;ptr to top circ.buff.
pcircout   DW  0    ;ptr to end circ.buff.

transform2nd DW  0    ;saved transform. msg0,msg1
transform    DW 0    ;/           msg2,msg3
extranode    DB  0
destnode     DW  0
```

```
nodenumsaved DW 0
extmsgwtg    DW 0
extmsgsaved  DW 0


NUMTERMS     EQU 8
termvars     LABEL NEAR    ;msgs delivered here.
_msgterm1    DW  0         ;(if an async msg, only a count
_msgterm2    DW  0         ; here, msgs pushed on stack)
_msgterm3    DW  0
_msgterm4    DW  0
_msgterm5    DW  0
_msgterm6    DW  0
_msgterm7    DW  0
_msgterm8    DW  0

stackPU   DB   STACKSIZE DUP(?)        ;stack.


;...................................................................

;***PUT STATIC APPLICATION VARIABLES FOR PU1 IN HERE***<<<<<<<
beeper DW 0
togglebpr DB 0
;note: any data in small-C declared extern can be defined
;here, but must have leading underscore...
_x      DW 0


;...................................................................
dataPU1 ENDS

;................CODE FOR PROCESSOR 1..................
codePU1 SEGMENT  'code'
     ASSUME cs:codePU1,ds:dataPU1


THISPU     = 1
NUMENTRIES = 5
THISPUVAR      DB THISPU     ;range is 1 - 61(stored as 1 -- 61).
NUMENTRIESVAR DB NUMENTRIES ;number of entries in sig.table.
nodeptr DW node0
          ;...1st node in table is error-handler(always node-0)
          DW node1         ;this must be in ascending order
          DW node2         ;of node number.
          DW node3         ;
          DW node4
;....***KEEP GOING HERE, AS MANY NODES AS YOU'VE GOT***....

          ORG (2*64) + 2          ;fixed offset for sig.table.
;.........***FILL IN SIGNATURE TABLE***.............
WX      EQU 8000h                        ;bit15. used in nodenum.
signatures DW 0FFFFh,0,307h,322h,34Ch
```

```
nodenum    DW 0,     1, 2,    3,    4      ;*(comments end file)
extmsg     DW 0,     0, 0,    0,    0
;. . . . . . . . . . . . . . . . . . . . . . . . . . . . . . . . . . . . . . . . . . . . .
```

What follows is the application code for processor 1 (PU1). Each node can be written in assembly language or in Small-C. In the latter case, the C code is compiled separately, which generates assembly source, with .MAC extension. These can then be INCLUDEd into this file. I have not shown the C source files in this appendix; they are on the disk, along with instructions on how to compile them.

The GOOFEE Diagrammer can easily be used as a management tool for writing the nodes. Double-clicking on a node brings up an editor, with a unique filename generated.

```
;. . . . . . . . . . . . . . . . . . . . . . . . . . . . . . . . . . . . . . . . . . . . .
node0:                  ;node-0 is the error-handler

       NORMALEXIT

;. . . . . . . . . . . . . . . . . . . . . . . . . . . . . . . . . . . . . . . . . . . . .
node1:
;Presume that this is the first node, when signature =0.

POSTMESSAGE THISPU,2,1,SYNC,1234h ;pu1,n2,ter1,sync,data=1234h
POSTMESSAGE THISPU,3,1,SYNC,5678h ;pu1,n3,ter1,sync,data=5678h

       .IF togglebpr==FALSE
         mov beeper,1200    ;about 830Hz
         mov togglebpr,TRUE
       .ELSE
         mov beeper,300     ;about 3.3KHz.
         mov togglebpr,FALSE
       .ENDIF
POSTMESSAGE 2,4,4,SYNC,beeper ;remote o/p msg.,sync/pu2/n4/t4.
                   ;... synchronous message to processor-2

       NORMALEXIT
;. . . . . . . . . . . . . . . . . . . . . . . . . . . . . . . . . . . . . . . . . . . . .
node3 PROC
;***EXAMPLE C CODING OF NODE***
;By placing this node in PROC...ENDP, code labels become
;invisible outside.
;... but, must use MASM v6.1, not 5.1.
;Here is our code to be replaced by C...
;      mov ax,_msgterm1              ;sync msg in terminal1.
;POSTMESSAGE THISPU,4,1,SYNC,3344h   ;sync to node4/term1.
```

```
;     NORMALEXIT

;OK, here is our C code...
INCLUDE n003.mac      ;could create from GOOFEE Diagrammer.
                      ;... look on disk for source file n003.c.
node3 ENDP
;.........................................................
node2:
     mov  ax,_msgterm1                ;sync msg in terminal1.
POSTMESSAGE THISPU,4,3,ASYNC,8899h    ;async to node4/term3.
POSTMESSAGE THISPU,4,2,SYNC,2244h     ;sync to node4/term2.
     NORMALEXIT
;.........................................................
node4:
     mov  ax,_msgterm1    ;sync msg from node3.
     mov  bx,_msgterm2    ;sync msg from node2.
     cmp  _msgterm3,0     ;count of async msgs from node2.
     je   p1n4b     ; note an async coming from pu2/n1 also.
        mov cx,_msgterm3
p1n4a:      pop ax     ;get async msg off stack
          ;....do something with it.
        loop p1n4a        ;get them all off stack.
p1n4b:

     mov. cx,20 ;5  ;10           ;big delay.
zzz2:mov bx,cx      ; / we are posting variable beeper
     mov cx,-1      ; / to pu2, and want to do it slowly
zzz1:nop            ; /
     loop zzz1      ; / (beeper is posted from n1)
     mov cx,bx      ; /
     loop zzz2      ; /

     NORMALEXIT
;...............
codePU1 ENDS

;###################### PROCESSOR 2 #######################

;.........DATA SEGMENT FOR PROCESSOR 2..............
;we don't redefine all the variables that TERSE uses, just
;allocate a block of memory...
dataPU2 SEGMENT  'data'
     DB 02CFh DUP(0)     ;actually, its 2C7h.

;.........................................................
;***PUT APPLICATION VARIABLES for PU2 IN HERE***<<<<<<<<<<<<<
_z   DW 0

dataPU2 ENDS
```

```
;.......................................................
;...............CODE FOR PROCESSOR 2...................
codePU2 SEGMENT  'code'
      ASSUME cs:codePU2,ds:dataPU2

THISPU    = 2
NUMENTRIES = 5
      DB THISPU  ;THISPUVAR # of this pu.
      DB NUMENTRIES   ;NUMENTRIESVAR. # entries in sig.table.
                  ;nodeptr
      DW pu2node0 ;1st node in table is error-handler
                  ; (always node-0).
      DW pu2node1           ;this must be in ascending order
      DW pu2node2           ;of node number.
      DW pu2node3           ;
      DW pu2node4
;....***KEEP GOING HERE, AS MANY NODES AS YOU'VE GOT***....

      ORG (2*64) + 2           ;fixed offset for sig.table.
;.........***FILL IN SIGNATURE TABLE***..............
 DW 0FFFFh,0,607h,622h,64Ch       ;signatures
 DW 0,  1,  2,   3,  WX+0 ;nodenum--do NOT put 4 in last entry!
 DW 0,  0,  0,   0,  10h ;extmsg --set bit4,last entry, as sync
                  ; msg from pu1/n1 to pu2/n4/t4.
               ;WX -- wait is set, as cannot go any further
               ;until the remote i/p arrives (bit15=1).
               ;nodenum=0 means wait forever for rem.i/p.
;.......................................................


;.......................................................
pu2node0:           ;node-0 is the error-handler

      NORMALEXIT

;.......................................................
pu2node1:
;Presume that this is the first node, when signature =0.

POSTMESSAGE THISPU,2,1,SYNC,1234h ;pu,n2,term1,sync,data=1234h
POSTMESSAGE THISPU,3,1,SYNC,5678h ;pu,n3,term1,sync,data=5678h
POSTMESSAGE 1,4,3,ASYNC,1111h  ;remote o/p msg.,pu1/n4/t3/async

      NORMALEXIT
;.......................................................
pu2node3 PROC
;    mov  ax,_msgterm1     ;sync msg in terminal1.
;POSTMESSAGE THISPU,4,1,SYNC,3344h   ;sync to node4/term1.
;    NORMALEXIT
```

```
;same as node3 in pu1, so....

INCLUDE n007.mac     ;small-C equivalent.

pu2node3 ENDP
;........................................................
pu2node2:
     mov  ax,_msgterm1     ;sync msg in terminal1.
POSTMESSAGE THISPU,4,3,ASYNC,8899h   ;async to node4/term3.
POSTMESSAGE THISPU,4,2,SYNC,2244h    ;sync to node4/term2.
     NORMALEXIT
;........................................................
pu2node4:
     mov  ax,_msgterm1     ;sync msg from node3.
     mov  bx,_msgterm2     ;sync msg from node2.

     cmp  _msgterm3,0      ;count of async msgs from node2.
     je   p2n4b
       mov cx,_msgterm3
xtract1: pop  ax           ;get async msg off stack
         ;....do something with it.
       loop xtract1
p2n4b:

     mov  bx,_msgterm4     ;remote i/p sync msg from pu1/n1.
     call beepfreq         ;uses bx as timer count.


     NORMALEXIT
;..............
codePU2 ENDS

;%%%%%%%%%%%%%%%%%%%%%%%%%%%%%%%%%%%%%%%%%%%%%%%%%%%%%%%%%%%
     END    start

;........................................................

;Circular buffer: |_____|
;        PTOP = > |      |  limit
;                 |      |
;                 |_____|
;        pcircin >|      | pcircin isthe head of the circ.buff.
;                 |      |
;                 |_____|
;        pcircout >|      |pcircout isthetail(1 below,actually).
;                 |_____|
;      PBOTTOM = > |      | one past limit.
;
;VERY IMPORTANT: increasing addresses downwards.
```

```
;a message consists of 4 bytes, msg3,msg2,msg1,msg0, where
;msg3 is the msb and is at the highest address.

;ALL msgs go onto the same buffer. Remote i/p msgs add onto
;pcircin end of buffer. Local msgs add onto pcircout end of
;buffer.
;When getmsgs() extracts msgs from the buffer, msgs are moved
;up to fill the holes, contracting from the pcircout end.

;TIMEOUT
;*******
;"nodenum" entry in sig. table has timeouts.If bit15 set (WAIT
;bit) then bits 0--14 are timeout. Bits13--14 are granularity.
;localref0--3 is a snapshot of globaltime when timeout
;commences.
;BITS14,13 GLOBALTIME BYTES   TIME GRANULARITY
;00        1,0               ...globaltime0 always=0...
;01        2,1               1msec
;10        3,2               1*256mSec       appr. 1/4sec
;11        3                 1*256*256mSec   appr. 1min

;The timeout value in nodenum is in bits 0--12, so max value
;8191. so, 1msec-granularity has a timeout range of 1msec --
;8.191sec.
;
;NOTE if bits 0--12 ==0, then timeout is forever!!.


;%%%%%%%%%%%%%%%%%%%%%%%%%%%%%%%%%%%%%%%%%%%%%%%%%%%%%%%%%%%%%%
COPYRIGHT & LIABILITY NOTICE
****************************
```

Summary notes

I have a problem with CodeView (CV) 4.01 (DOS version, supplied with MASM 6.1), as it hooks interrupt 8, before I do. Because I have speeded up the timer 55 times, CV behaves a little oddly — it scrolls windows like crazy!

I recommend you mess around with this code on a PC that doesn't have your company accounts!

CodeView calls the application's interrupt 8 at a very slow rate.... I guess the idea behind this is you can observe any effect visually, but I wish Microsoft would document how CV handles interrupt 8.

Unfortunately, I wrote most of TERSE86 to assemble with both TASM 3.1 *and* MASM 6.1, but eventually I could not resist using the superior features of MASM. So, this program is written for MASM v6.1. TASM v3.1, isn't suitable because it doesn't have the nifty .IF/.ELSEIF/.ELSE/.ENDIF directives. I don't know about the latest TASM — maybe someone can enlighten me.

Also, MASM 6.1 has nice C-like rules for label scope.

So, what does the example application listed above, actually do? Find out; TERS8631.EXE is supplied on the disk and can be run from DOS, bearing in mind my warning. You should be able to figure out how it achieves the beeping pattern by examining the above code; this will be a simple learning exercise.

The file TERS8631.MAK is for use with Microsoft Programmer's Workbench (PWB), and it has the debug option turned on; hence, the .EXE file is far bigger than necessary. You can examine the file in CodeView, and you will see that TERSE code itself is only 1052 bytes, while the data segment required by TERSE for each virtual processor is 712 bytes.

The latter figure is somewhat arbitrary, because it depends on how big the various buffers are to be. I chose the circular buffer to be 128 bytes (CIRCBUFSIZE) (holds 32 messages) and the stack to be 512 bytes (STACKSIZE). The nature of TERSE is that applications do not nest functions very deeply, so particularly in a non-DOS embedded application, the stack size can be reduced markedly.

With an RTOS this compact, yet as powerful as others several times larger, you can put together a very cheap three-chip set of '188 processor, RAM, and ROM, for those cost-sensitive applications.

F

GOOFEE Diagrammer user's manual

The GOOFEE Diagrammer software is bundled with this book. It allows you to use the GOOFEE notation to construct anything from an FSM to an object-oriented design and has various tools to assist with the coding process.

Please look at the file MANUAL.TXT on the disk for notes on the latest release.

User interface

The Flow Diagrammer has an unusual interface. For example:

There are no scrollbars. To maximise working space, and to scroll, hold down the left mouse button, not over an object, and shift the mouse pointer to a window boundary — everything will scroll. Note, though, that while scrolling, it doesn't matter if objects pass under the mouse button.

The arrow keys also scroll the diagram.

Clicking on an object, to highlight it, works differently. There are no resize knobs, and normal objects cannot be resized: Composite-nodes and Super-nodes can.

You will find that to highlight a Composite- or Super-node, you have to click on its *boundary*, not anywhere inside it.

A highlighted object can be operated on in various ways. For example, pressing the delete key will erase it.

The concept is that of an "infinite" flat screen that you can scroll around in and zoom in and out as required. As per the GOOFEE 2-dimensional decomposition, a node can expand, via a Joining-bar, to a class that contains a sub-diagram within it.

You can experiment with this. To create a Composite-node class, select Composite-node from the Object menu and move the object to where you want its top-left to be. If you then just click the left button, the object will be deposited there, but if you hold down the left button and move the mouse pointer, you can drag the Composite-node to whatever size you want.

Try selecting other objects from the Object menu, and deposit them inside the Composite-node. You will then find that the Composite-node "owns" them, and if you drag the Composite-node, the sub-diagram inside it will drag also.

Also, if you assign the Composite-node to a particular processor, all nodes inside the "parent" node will also be assigned to the same processor.

Mouse buttons

Double-click

Double-click on any wire, Joining-bar, or node, including Super- and Composite-nodes, to pop up a user-specified editor. In the case of nodes, filenames are auto-generated.

For enlarged Composite- and Super-nodes, you have to double-click on the boundary, and for wires, on the "knee".

Right button

Press the right mouse button over any object to pop up a local dialog box. The location is context sensitive and will be different for each type of object. For wires and Joining-bars, the middle knee-point must be pointed to, and for enlarged Composite or Super-nodes, point to the boundary.

The right button has a useful purpose if clicked over a vacant area — it causes the screen to redraw. This can be handy if there is any "scrap" left behind, which can sometimes happen when objects are dragged or resized.

Left button

The left button is to highlight or drag objects. It also places objects. When placing nodes or resources, after selecting from the menu, move to where you want it, then click once to place it. For enlarged Composite-nodes, Super-nodes, or to place wires and Joining-bars, press the button at the starting point and drag to place the other end.

When in-place, all wires and Joining-bars can be dragged from their middle knee-point and can be highlighted at their middle knee-point.

Keyboard

Delete key

The delete key deletes highlighted objects.

Shift

Hold the shift key down when dragging a Composite- or Super-node to resize it.

Control

When dragging nodes, normally the middles (knees) of attached wires remain in-place. However, if the control key is held down, the wire-middles will move with the dragged object. This is the default behaviour of Composite and Super-node class/objects *without* the control key held down.

Arrow keys

Arrow keys scroll the diagram — see Printing section.

Terminals

One major concept of GOOFEE is that nodes connected by Joining-bars inherit the terminals, or points, at which external wires can connect. If you create two nodes and put a Joining-bar between them, then from a third node you draw a wire to one of the first two, you will see a little dot appear on the other clone in the same relative place on the boundary. This enables you to place a wire accurately on the other node, if another wire is to be placed.

If you create an enlarged Composite- or Super-node class, you will find the terminals propogating onto the big node as enlarged ellipses.

Figure F.1: Inheritance of terminals.

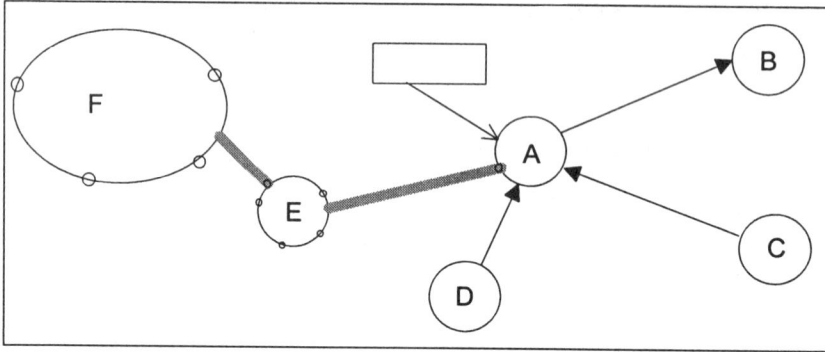

Figure F.1 shows Super-node F with terminals that are inherited across clones E and A.

Inheritance direction

I decided to introduce "direction of inheritance" into Joining-bars, which is something that I wanted to avoid. However, it is useful. When you create a chain of clones linked by Joining-bars, make sure that you create all Joining-bars going in the same direction. The expected structure is that an enlarged Composite- or Super-node would be the class, from which one or more Joining-bars can emanate, to clones or objects. Therefore, the class will always be the starting-end of a Joining-bar, and this is shown visually — the destination-end has a tiny circle, as shown in Figure F.1.

If you connect Joining-bars incorrectly, there will be visual warnings. For example, if you connect a destination-end to an enlarged Composite- or Super-node, the propogated terminals won't be enlarged. Also, if in a chain of clones one Joining-bar is the wrong way around, the terminals won't propogate across it.

If you accidentally connect Joining-bars in a loop, the program will hang — that is, from node A to node B, then chained such that a Joining-bar comes back to node A. A future version of the program will detect this and just flash a message.

Iterative-nodes

Any node can be an Iterative-node simply by highlighting it and selecting "... add a ring" from the Objects menu. Wires can terminate at any ring and can even be repositioned across rings (see below).

Wire repositioning

If you have placed a wire, you may find that its placement is not quite right. It is easy to drag the knee of a wire just by pointing to it and dragging, but you can also adjust the ends.

Snap-to positioning

When you place wires, you will see that the ends snap to the boundary, even on Iterative-nodes. Experiment with Iterative-nodes to be clear on what boundary the wire will snap to.

The Control menu has a sub-menu selection, "Snap to ...", that allows you to snap a wire-end to the same relative end coordinates as any other wire in the diagram. You must highlight a wire first.

The purpose of Control/Snap-to is more fully described in the section on automatic terminal numbering and snapping, below.

Manual positioning

You can manually reposition either wire-end. Just highlight a wire by clicking on its knee, then move the pointer close to the end to be adjusted. Drag the end as required, then release the left mouse button.

One interesting thing you will observe is that if the wire is attached to a node that is in turn a clone of another node, the terminal placement, or place on the node where the wire joins, appears as little terminals on the other clones (see Figure F.1) and will automatically track the wire-end as you adjust it. If you connect an expanded Composite- or Super-node as a class to your clone-node, the ellipse, or terminal, is expanded also.

Automatic terminal numbering and auto-snap

When a new wire is placed, its terminal number is automatically assigned. For a standalone node, that is, a node without a Joining-bar, the GOOFEE Diagrammer examines all existing wires attached to that node and assigns the lowest free number. Terminal numbers start from 1; however, each of the following is numbered independently:

- dataflow (sync or async) input
- dataflow (sync or async) output
- I/O input
- I/O output

Figure F.2: Terminal numbering, standalone node.

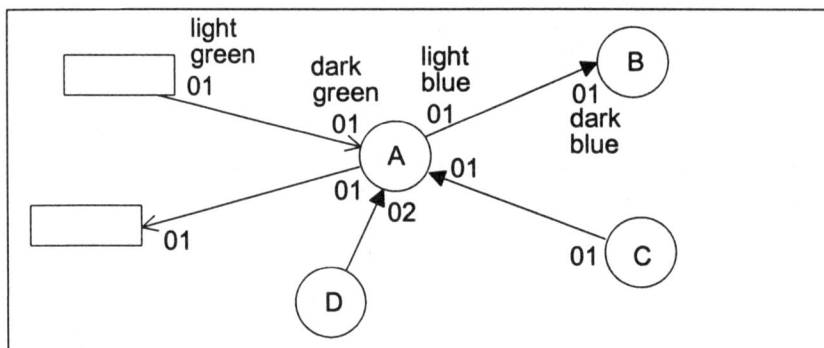

Figure F.2 illustrates this. Everything connected to node A is assigned terminal 01, except for the wire from node D. The reason is, the wire from node D is a second dataflow input.

They are distinguished on the diagram by color coding.

The automatic terminal numbering is very sophisticated and works over a chain of clones. For example, in Figure F.3, if the extra nodes E and F are added onto the previous diagram, the wire from F to E is automatically assigned terminal number 02 at input to node E. The GOOFEE Diagrammer examines all clones to determine if the new wire is being attached to an existing terminal.

Figure F.3: Auto terminal numbering of clones.

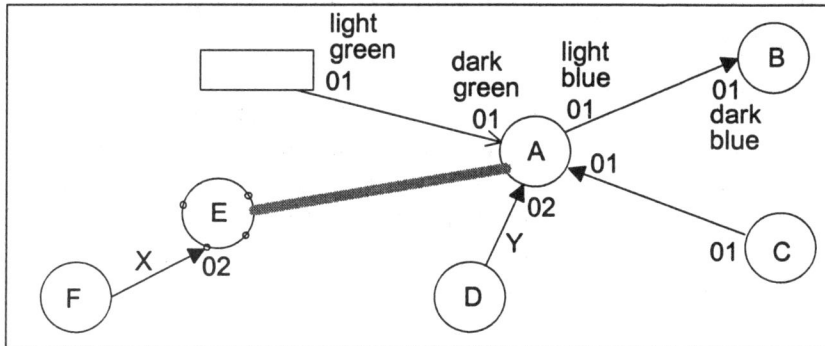

Note that node E has inherited terminals from the clone (node A), and these are shown as little "blobs" on its boundary. Furthermore, the wire from node F (wire X) will automatically snap to the existing terminal, in case it is a little off.

The snap-to action is the same as the action that can be manually selected via the "Control/Snap-to ..." menu (see *Snap-to positioning* section). In fact, if you highlight wire X, then select "Control/Snap-to ...", a dialog window will show you what each end of wire X snapped to when it was first placed — you are at liberty to manually alter this allegiance.

There is another feature that I implemented, with some trepidation — automatic renumbering of terminals. For example, if a wire attached to node E has terminal number 02 before wire X is created, when wire X is placed, the software will determine that wire X *must* be assigned to terminal 02, by virtue of it being attached to the existing terminal inherited from another clone.

Therefore, the previous wire will be reallocated a terminal number — the lowest free value.

You are at liberty to manually alter any terminal numbers by clicking the right mouse button on the knee of a wire.

The placing of wire X at the pre-existing terminal inherited from node A causes it to be assigned terminal 02, and wire X snaps to the terminal. However, how far away from the terminal does wire X have to be when first placed for the software to think it is not on the pre-existing terminal?

If wire X is placed on any free region of the boundary of node E, a new terminal is created, which will, incidentally, propogate over the chain of clones, creating a new terminal on node A. To answer the above question, the software doubles the radius of the terminal to find any wire being placed near it. At normal zoom, the terminals look like points, but zoom in, and you will see that they are ellipses. Imagine an ellipse double the size, and that is the capture zone.

Collision detection

If you drag expanded Composite- or Super-nodes around, you don't want them running into each other. A collision avoidance system prevents this.

This is something that you can experiment with. Create an expanded Composite-node, then create another expanded Composite-node inside it, then create a third Composite-node outside, somewhere else on the screen. Now try moving them around. You will find that the "child" node, the one inside another, can't get out, nor can the third one get in. In fact, when a collision occurs, the node won't go any further, and you have to release the mouse button, then re-drag the node away.

Comments

Comments can be placed anywhere. In the "Objects" menu, select "Attach a comment". This is actually a wire, and you simply move the arrow to the place on the boundary of any node where you want to attach the comment and click the left mouse button. Then you can drag the end, which has a tiny circle, to wherever you want it to be.

Clicking the right mouse button on the tiny circle pops up a dialog box that enables you to input the text. With the current version, it can only be one line, up to 49 characters.

When you drag the node that the comment is attached to, the default behaviour is that for normal nodes the comment won't move. However, if attached to a Composite- or Super-node, expanded or not, the comment will track the node if it is dragged.

And, of course, a comment inside a Composite- or Super-node will move when the parent moves.

Printing

Yes, you can print. Notice that the "Control" menu has a "Go to origin" item — this takes the screen back to 0/0 coordinates at the top-left corner, regardless of whether you are zoomed in or out. You may find it convenient to do this first, before printing, so that there is a consistent starting point.

When you select "Print" from the "File" menu, a single page is printed, at the same zoom factor, with the top-left point of the window corresponding to the top-left point on the paper. Therefore, you will see more diagram on the paper, because the window won't show the full page unless you have a large monitor.

After printing a page, you have the option of jumping in any direction, using the arrow keys, and printing again. To jump exactly one page, hold the Control key down and hit an arrow key. Then, select "Print" again.

Note that you must hold down the Control key, because just pushing an arrow key causes the diagram to scroll one window, not one page.

You can print any part of the diagram, at any zoom-factor — just remember that it is the top-left on window and paper that match.

So far, printing has been tested on a very limited range of printers — most development testing was done on a Laserjet IIIP.

Clipboard

There is no Cut or Paste, only Copy (refer to *FAQ* section below).

The "File/Copy" menu selection will copy the current client window to the clipboard as a TIF bitmap.

Frequently asked questions (FAQs)

The FAQ section will grow with time. You will have questions that relate to the mind-shift, or paradigm-shift, required with GOOFEE diagrams.

Q

Why doesn't the GOOFEE Diagrammer have Cut and Paste?

A

Why should it? With GOOFEE, you don't have to cut and paste.

If you want to move a portion of a diagram, draw a Composite-node around it, and drag it wherever you want it.

If you want to duplicate a portion of a diagram, again, draw a Composite-node around it, draw another Compsite-node in the new location, and draw a Joining-bar, of the appropriate type, between them.

By not using cut and paste, you will be forced to use the above technique, which means that you are forced to document, inherently in the diagram, every bit of code reuse.

Q

Some Software Engineering methodologies have techniques for grouping parts of the design into "domains", which is particularly suitable for larger projects.

A

That is precisely what the Composite-node does.   You can put Composite-nodes around anything, and everything inside is automatically assigned to the "processor number" of the outer Composite-node. What meaning you give to "processor number" is up to you. In a distributed system, it would perhaps be appropriate for outer Composite-nodes to represent each processor, but in a single-processor system, you may attach other meanings to this parameter.

Index

SOFTWARE REGISTRATION

NAME: ....

ADDRESS: ....

....

....

....

....

PHONE: ....

FAX: ....

EMAIL: ....

GOOFEE Diagrammer version #: ....

COMMENTS:

Please let us know how you would like the software to be enhanced.

Cut along line

POST TO:

GOOFEE Systems Pty Ltd

22 Regatta Drive, Edgewater

WA 6027

Australia

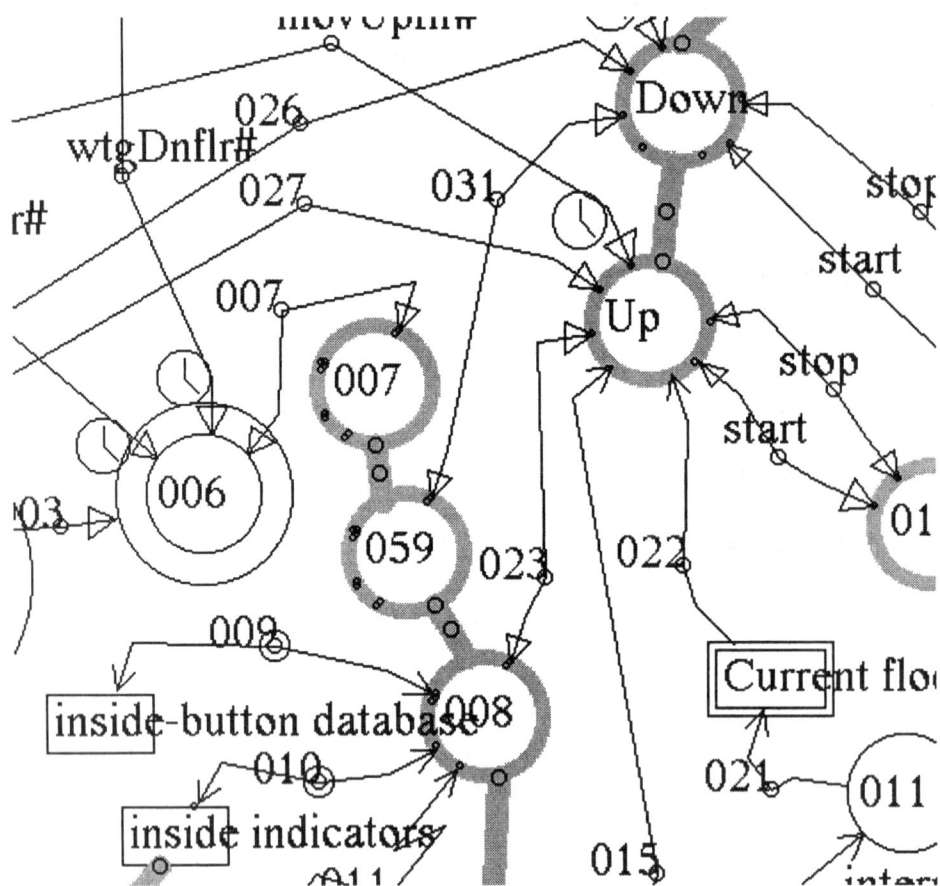

OFFICE USE ONLY